PLANT BASED
BASED
COOKBOOK

British Edition
Project Editor: Kathryn Meeker
Senior Designer: Glenda Fisher
Angliciser: Nikki Sims
Managing Editor: Stephanie Farrow
Managing Art Editor: Christine Keilty
Senior Producer: Tony Phipps
Senior Producer: Stephanie McConnell
Publisher: Mary-Clare Jerram
Art Director: Maxine Pedliham

American Edition
Publisher: Mike Sanders
Associate Publisher: Billy Fields
Executive Acquisitions Editor: Lori Cates Hand
Production Editor: Jana M. Stefanciosa
Compositor: Ayanna Lacey
Proofreader: Laura Caddell
Indexer: Heather McNeil

Cover and Book Designer: XAB Design
Photographer: Kevin Bertolacci
Food Stylist: Laura Kinsey Dolph

First published in Great Britain, 2016 by
Dorling Kindersley Limited
80 Strand, London, WC2R 0RL

Copyright © 2016 Dorling Kindersley Limited
A Penguin Random House Company
15 16 17 18   10 9 8 7 6 5 4 3 2 1
001–284172–Feb/2016

A CIP catalogue record for this book is available from the British Library.
ISBN: 978-0-2412-3003-9

Note: This publication contains the opinions and ideas of its author(s). It is intended to provide helpful and informative material on the subject matter covered. It is sold with the understanding that the author(s) and publisher are not engaged in rendering professional services in the book. If the reader requires personal assistance or advice, a competent professional should be consulted. The author(s) and publisher specifically disclaim any responsibility for any liability, loss, or risk, personal or otherwise, which is incurred as a consequence, directly or indirectly, of the use and application of any of the contents of this book.

Printed and bound in China

A WORLD OF IDEAS:
SEE ALL THERE IS TO KNOW

www.dk.com

PLANT
BASED
COOKBOOK

GOOD FOR YOUR HEART, YOUR HEALTH, AND YOUR LIFE

Contents

9   **Beginning a Plant-Based Diet**
10   What Is a Plant-Based Diet?
12   Transition Strategies
14   Filling Your Plant-Based Larder
16   Plant-Based Cooking Techniques
21   Basic Seitan
22   Meal Plans

25   **Basics**
26   Caramelized Onions
28   Simple Vegetable Stock
29   Pie Pastry
29   Nut Milk
30   Fresh Pasta Dough

33   **Sauces, Dressings, Dips, and Spreads**
34   Hummus
36   Smoky Baba Ghanoush
37   Tzatziki
39   Cashew Ricotta
39   Pimento Cheese
40   *Nuts and Seeds*
42   Truffled Mushroom Pâté
44   Béchamel Sauce
44   Tomato Sauce
45   Mushroom Gravy
45   Vinaigrette
46   *UNREFINED OILS*
47   Summer Pesto
47   Romesco Sauce
49   Pico de Gallo
49   Guacamole

51   **Breakfasts**
53   Nutty Granola
54   Breakfast Burritos
55   Wholewheat Banana Pecan Pancakes
56   Strawberry Muffins
58   *Dairy Substitutes*
60   Mushroom, Spinach, and Shallot Quiche
62   Breakfast Sausage Patties
63   *AVOCADOS*

65   **Sandwiches, Burgers, and Wraps**
66   *Bánh Mì* Portobello Burgers
68   Crispy Aubergine Subs
69   Oyster Mushroom Po'boys
70   Muffuletta

72   Falafel Burgers
73   *Pan Bagnat*
74   Korean Barbecue Sliders

77   **Soups and Stews**
79   Grandma's Chicken-y Noodle Soup
80   Ginger Kale Soup
82   *MUSHROOMS*
83   Mushroom Barley Soup
85   Curried Cauliflower Coconut Soup
86   Smoky White Bean and Tomato Soup
87   Classic Vegetable Soup
88   Tomato Rice Soup
90   Mushroom and Cabbage Borscht
91   Split-Pea Soup
93   Creamy Sweetcorn Chowder
94   *Beans and Legumes*
96   Tom Yum Soup
98   Miso Udon Bowl
99   *GINGER*
101 Meaty Mushroom Stew
102 Gumbo
103 Minestrone
104 *Giambotta* (Italian Summer Vegetable Stew)
106 Lentil and Vegetable Dhal
107 Green Curry Vegetable Stew
109 Hearty Chilli
110 Black-Eyed Pea Stew
111 Jerusalem Artichoke Soup
112 *Posole*

115 **Salads**
116 Wilted Spinach Salad
116 Celeriac Remoulade
117 *GREENS*
119 Roasted Beetroot Salad
120 Roasted Tomato and White Bean Salad
121 Picnic Potato Salad
122 *Insalata Rinforzo* (Neapolitan Christmas Salad)
124 Warm Potato Salad with Grainy Mustard Vinaigrette
125 Warm Lentil, Barley, and Sweet Potato Salad
126 Herbed Tabbouleh

129 **Vegetables**
131 *Imam Bayildi* (Turkish Stuffed Aubergine)
132 Red Cabbage with Apples and Pecans

134 Stir-Fried Chinese Cress with Fermented Black Beans
135 Roasted Tomatoes
136 Herbed Courgettes
138 Sautéed Broccoli
138 Southern-Style Braised Greens
139 *CRUCIFEROUS VEGETABLES*
141 Spinach and Rice-Stuffed Tomatoes
142 Fried Green Tomatoes
143 Stuffed Artichokes
144 Almond and Breadcrumb Stuffed Piquillo Peppers
146 *Vegetables*
148 Roasted Corn with Poblano-Coriander Butter
150 Sautéed Mushroom Medley
151 Sesame Ginger Broccoli
152 Braised Brussels Sprouts with Chestnuts
154 Stuffed Mushrooms
155 Minted Peas and Baby Potatoes
157 Sesame Asparagus
158 *Latkes*
158 Roasted Root Vegetable Medley
159 *SWEET POTATOES*
160 Southern Sweet Potatoes with Pecan Streusel

163 **Casseroles and One-Pot Meals**
165 Winter Vegetable Pot Pie
166 *Bisteeya* (Moroccan Filo Pie)
167 Savoury Stuffed Cabbage
168 Vegetable Enchiladas with Roasted Tomato Sauce
170 Mushroom Lasagne
171 Summer Squash and Onion Bake
173 Aubergine and Roasted Tomato Polenta Lasagne
174 *Tamale* Casserole
175 Mixed Vegetable Cottage Pie
176 Cassoulet
178 Butternut Squash Tagine

181 **Seeds, Grains, and Pastas**
182 Crispy Quinoa Cakes
183 *QUINOA*
184 Quinoa Vegetable Salad
186 Risotto Milanese
187 Moroccan Couscous
188 *Arancini* (Risotto Balls)
190 Farro Risotto with Roasted Fennel and Mushrooms
192 *Grains*
194 Creamy Pasta with Swiss Chard and Tomatoes

196 Wholewheat Pasta *e Ceci* (Pasta with Chickpeas)
197 Swiss Chard Ravioli
199 One-Pan Pasta Primavera
200 Sesame Noodles

203 **Tofu, Tempeh, and Seitan**
204 Tofu Summer Rolls
206 Sesame Tofu
206 Grilled Tofu Caprese
207 *ALLIUMS*
208 Tofu and Veggie Stir-Fry
210 Hearty Seitan Roast
212 Tempeh Milanese
213 Seitan and Dumplings
214 Seitan Satay
216 *Meat Substitutes*
217 Maple-Glazed Tofu
217 Tempeh Bacon
219 Seitan Gyros

221 **Breads, Pizzas, and Savory Treats**
222 Easy Slow-Rise Oatmeal Bread
224 Pizza Dough
225 Herbed Mushroom and Leek Tart
227 *Pissaladière* (Provençal Onion Tart)

229 **Desserts**
230 Pumpkin Pudding Pie
231 Apple Crumble Pie
233 Prairie Berry Pie
234 Blueberry Peach Cobbler
234 Nutty Berry Streusel Bars
235 *BERRIES*
236 Banana Chocolate-Chip Oat Cookies
238 Cherry Cheesecake Squares
239 Triple-Ginger Treacle Cookies
240 Pineapple Cornmeal Upside-Down Cake
242 Fudgy Oaty Thumbprints
243 Pumpkin Gingerbread Cupcakes with Cinnamon Frosting
245 Parsnip Cupcakes with Soured Cream Icing
246 *Baking Substitutions*
248 Green Apple Sorbet
249 Chunky Apple Sauce
250 Winter Fruit Compôte
251 Cranberry Poached Pears

252 **Index**

Introduction

Colourful vegetables, sweet fruit, hearty whole grains, nutritional nuts and seeds, protein-rich beans and legumes — these are just a few of the wholesome whole foods you'll enjoy on a plant-based diet.

The benefits of a plant-based diet are as plentiful and varied as the food you'll eat, and it's no coincidence that prominent physician agree. Dr Dean Ornish, President and founder of the not-for-profit Preventive Medicine Research Institute as well as Clinical Professor of Medicine at the University of California, and Dr. Kim Williams, distinguished cardiologist, Professor of Medicine, and President-elect of the American College of Cardiology, along with many other clinicians, cite a plant-based diet as the key to reversing heart disease and the ageing process, lowering cholesterol, and promoting overall good health and longevity.

Plant-Based Cookbook was designed to empower you to embrace a diet full of fresh and healthy plant-based foods. In these 200 recipes (including breakfasts, sauces,

salad dressings, dips, sandwiches, soups, one-pot meals, casseroles, satisfying meat substitutes, breads, pastas, and more) you'll find inspiration from many cultures and cuisines, as well as new and familiar flavours that will help you to incorporate plant-based meals into your everyday life. And, of course, there are plenty of desserts, too! In addition, you'll find new culinary techniques, tips for making recipes in advance, and instructions for freezing dishes when applicable.

I encourage you to take these recipes and make them your own. I've used all plant-based "dairy" ingredients in my versions (such as plant-based mayonnaise), but they can all be swapped out for the traditional dairy versions if you prefer. Experiment, have fun, and enjoy the journey to a happier, healthier you.

Making the Transition

Transitioning to a more plant-based diet in a way that's comfortable for you is important, and this book offers strategies to help you make these positive changes. If you aren't looking to completely give up animal-based foods, try making small changes and use this book to help you gradually replace more and more of the meat, dairy, and eggs in your favourite recipes with plant ingredients. Try plant-based milk in your morning coffee. Cook a few extra vegetable dishes each week, and enjoy them with smaller portions of familiar foods. Prepare some of the tempting recipes in this book – especially those marked with the "transition" icon. And try to eat a big salad, every day.

Just One Hour

It takes less than an hour to prepare a healthy, from-scratch, plant-based meal that leaves you feeling sated, energized, and simply fantastic. To help you get a healthy meal on the table quickly, look for the "under 30 minutes" icon on recipes throughout the book.

Other Dietary Considerations

In addition to the "transition" and "under 30 minutes" icons, the recipes are also flagged for a few other dietary considerations. Here's what to look for:

Gluten free   Soy free

Nut free   Good source of protein

A Note About the Recipes

I use a gas hob and oven, and that's what I used when I wrote the recipes in this book. Your kitchen appliances may be faster or slower, hotter or cooler than mine. Each recipe in this book was extensively tested, so if the recipe instructions say to heat food at medium–high heat, and you feel like it might burn at that temperature on your own hob, adjust the heat accordingly. An inexpensive oven thermometer can tell you if your oven runs true to temperature. Every stove has its own personality and quirks, so learn to trust your instincts.

Beginning a Plant-Based Diet

Transitioning to a plant-based diet might seem intimidating, but it needn't be. Begin by making small changes; explore transition strategies, cooking techniques, and meal plans; and stock your larder with good foods, and you're off to a healthy start.

What is a Plant-Based Diet?

A plant-based diet focuses on foods that come from plants – vegetables, fruits, whole grains, nuts, seeds, beans, and legumes – while avoiding those that come from animal sources, including meat, dairy, eggs, and food ingredients derived from animal sources, such as honey and gelatin.

Healthy and unhealthy choices still abound in the world of plant-based foods, though. It's entirely possible to make unhealthy choices when eating a plant-based diet. Whole foods in their natural state are a much better choice than a processed meal from a supermarket freezer or fast-food restaurant, so always choose wisely and be mindful.

Why Choose Plants?

People choose to transition to a plant-based diet for many reasons – to improve health, increase energy, treat and prevent disease, or lose weight, to name just a few. The following list may provide you with the inspiration you need to go "plant-based".

A plant-based diet is healthy. Many cardiologists recommend the plant-based diet for its ability to prevent and even reverse heart disease. The plant-based diet has also been repeatedly linked to cancer prevention, weight loss, maintaining healthy intestinal flora, and treating diseases, such as Parkinson's and multiple sclerosis, eye diseases, diabetes, and a host of other ailments.

A plant-based diet is beautiful. Who wouldn't want healthier skin, lustrous hair, a fit and trim body, and a whole lot more energy? Switching to a healthy, plant-based diet that relies on fresh, whole foods leaves you both looking and feeling fantastic.

A plant-based diet is youthful. A 2013 study by the Preventive Medicine Research Institute and the University of California, San Francisco, cited the plant-based diet as a key factor in reversing the ageing process. Study participants who adopted a plant-based diet (and exercised regularly) showed a 10 per cent lengthening of telomeres (the protective ends of DNA strands), which results in longer cell life. In contrast, the participants who continued on an animal-based diet shortened their telomeres by 3 per cent. According to Dr Dean Ornish, who led this groundbreaking study, "Shortened telomeres have been shown to play a role in heart disease, colon cancer, stroke, dementia, and premature death".

A plant-based diet is sustainable. According to the United Nations' 2005 Millennium Ecosystem Assessment, agriculture, particularly meat and dairy products, accounts for 70 per cent of global freshwater consumption, 38 per cent of total land use, and 19 per cent of the world's greenhouse gas emissions. Livestock farming is linked to antibiotic resistance, water pollution, and a host of other environmental catastrophes.

A plant-based diet is clean. In addition to antibiotic usage, the meat industry is rife with disease. Increasingly, we see food recalls due to contamination of meat, resulting in outbreaks of illness from potentially deadly food-borne bacteria.

What Do You Eat?

It's easy to eat a plant-based diet. Simply choose a wide variety of fresh, colourful fruits and vegetables, including plenty of dark, leafy greens. Add protein from sources such as beans, legumes, and meat substitutes, and fill in with healthy fats from nuts, seeds, and avocados.

PLANT-BASED FOOD GROUP	EXAMPLES	WHAT IT PROVIDES
FRUITS AND VEGETABLES	Apples, aubergine, avocados, bananas, berries, broccoli, Brussels sprouts, cauliflower, citrus fruits, courgette, kale, pears, root vegetables, spinach, tomatoes, winter squash	A broad spectrum of vital nutrients, fibre, protein, antioxidants, micronutrients, healthy carbohydrates, calcium, magnesium, potassium, iron, beta-carotene, vitamin B complex, vitamin C, vitamin A, and vitamin K
BEANS AND LEGUMES	Cannellini beans, chickpeas, flageolet beans, kidney beans, lentils, peas, soya beans	Protein, fibre, antioxidants, vitamins, low-glycaemic healthy carbohydrates, B vitamins, calcium, potassium, folate
WHOLE GRAINS	Amaranth, brown rice, cornmeal, couscous, farro, millet, quinoa (it's actually a seed), wheat grains, wholemeal flour	Fibre, protein, healthy carbohydrates (whole grains), B vitamins, antioxidants, iron, magnesium
NUTS AND SEEDS	Almonds, Brazil nuts, cashews, chia seeds, flax seeds, pecans, pumpkin seeds, sunflower seeds, walnuts	Healthy fats, fibre, protein, magnesium, zinc, calcium, phosphorus
MEAT SUBSTITUTES	Organic tofu, seitan, tempeh	Protein, familiar flavours, and meat-like textures

Transition Strategies

With a little planning, you'll find transitioning to more of a plant-based diet is easy. Soon you'll find that you get all the nutrients you need from plant sources without relying on processed, refined foods – and without feeling like you're missing out.

Start with Small Changes

For many, the transition to a more plant-based diet is gradual. Observing a "meatless Monday" is a great way to start. Begin with one plant-based meal a day ,then move on to two meals a day. Try to replace the worst offenders in your diet, such as bacon and cheese, and instead have a fresh vegetable dish or two with every meal.

Eat Your Veggies

The additional fibre in a plant-based diet can be a shock to the system for those accustomed to unhealthy processed foods; large quantities of meat; and few, if any, fresh vegetables, fruits, and whole grains. A gradual increase in your fibre intake can be beneficial if you're prone to digestive disturbance.

Try eating a big, raw salad every day. Increase the amount of beans, legumes, fruits, and vegetables you eat, while decreasing (or eliminating) meat, dairy, and eggs.

Vegetable Enchiladas with Roasted Tomato Sauce
Tomatoes, onions, courgettes, corn, black beans, and peppers meld with plant-based cheese in this zesty comfort dish.

Have a Plan

If you're new to the plant-based lifestyle, you'll want to do some meal planning. Planning your meals, and maybe doing a little cooking on your day off, can eliminate the urge to backslide into unhealthy eating. You'll be less likely to give in and order that pepperoni pizza if you've already shopped for healthy ingredients or have a veggie casserole in the freezer ready to pop into the oven when you're hungry but don't have a lot of time to cook.

Seek Inspiration

Websites, magazines, blogs, cookbooks – inspiration is everywhere for those who seek it. Don't be afraid to try new things. The worst that can happen is you won't like a dish or meal.

I find that the foods and techniques I've come to love the most are those I resisted making because I didn't think I had enough time, or assumed I wouldn't like the end result. Try something new a few times a week, add the dishes you love to your repertoire, and forget the rest.

Hearty Chilli

Imam Bayildi

Go Faux!

Miss the meat? A whole world of meat substitutes is out there, waiting for you to sample, from Tofurky to "veggie" pepperoni. I don't advocate eating these processed foods every day, but they do help satisfy cravings for familiar foods. And who doesn't want a little soy chorizo or a grilled veggie dog every once in a while?

Explore New Frontiers

The plant-based diet is a great opportunity to boldly go where you've not gone before. Whether you visit a vegetarian Indian restaurant or gather your friends to create a Middle Eastern meze, you'll find that many cuisines throughout the world rely on very little (or even no) meat, with vegetables and whole grains forming the bulk of the meal.

The "peasant cuisine" of the Italian countryside my grandmother favoured included vegetables grown in the garden, a salad at every meal, plenty of fresh bread, hearty soups, and stews spooned over hot and satisfying polenta. You'll find recipes throughout this book that rely on that tradition as well as ones that explore cuisines you might not be familiar with. Be daring, and jump on in!

Move at Your Own Pace

Finally, adopting more of a plant-based diet is all about the journey, and each of us experiences that journey differently. Open your mind and heart, and commit to seeking health and happiness through your diet.

Challenges will present themselves – when you're travelling, when you're a guest in someone else's home, or when you're just plain tired and hungry and tempted by the familiar. If you fall off the plant-based wagon, just dust yourself off and start again the next day.

Any change for the better is a good thing. Give yourself a break, and do the best you can.

Filling Your Plant-Based Larder

When stocking your plant-based larder, focus on healthy, whole foods in their natural, unprocessed state. In addition, try some of the speciality ingredients that can get you hooked on cooking from scratch.

Vegetables

Choose a wide array of fresh and frozen vegetables such as salad greens; leafy greens, such as spring greens or kale; mushrooms; cruciferous vegetables, such as cauliflower and cabbage; and aromatics, such as onions, carrots, and celery. Frozen vegetables can be a nutritious alternative to fresh, and in-season vegetables from a local farm are more economical and flavourful. I stock my freezer with broccoli, peas, greens, and sweetcorn from a farmers' market.

Fruits

Fresh fruits, such as bananas, berries, apples, and pears, are great to eat just as they are or to use in baked dishes. Frozen fruits are fantastic in smoothies and pies; keep a stock of peeled, ripe bananas in the freezer for baking emergencies.

Beans and Legumes

Choose a variety of dried and canned beans and legumes to provide an inexpensive, easy-to-cook protein source. I keep lentils, chickpeas, black beans, kidney beans, and cannellini beans in my larder. Many recipes in this book call for canned beans because that's what most busy cooks rely on to get dinner on the table. Don't be afraid to cook dry beans from scratch though – it's easy and economical.

Grains

Keep a variety of grains and grain-like seeds to hand, such as brown rice, basmati rice, cornmeal, wholemeal flour, plain flour, wholewheat and semolina pasta, rolled oats, barley, millet, farro, couscous, rice noodles, and quinoa. If you follow a gluten-free diet, almond flour, gluten-free flour mixes, and oat flour are wonderful additions to your larder.

Oils and Vinegars

Start with a good extra-virgin olive oil and a neutral-flavoured oil, such as grapeseed. Coconut oil is great in curries and baked goods. Nut oils add flavour to baked goods and salad dressings, and toasted sesame oil brings a smoky, nutty flavour. Refrigerate oils you don't use every day. Apple cider vinegar, red wine vinegar, and balsamic vinegar provide plenty of versatility. Rice vinegar is fabulous in Asian recipes, while umeboshi plum vinegar brings a unique salty, sour, pungent flavour to dishes.

Nuts and Seeds

Stash raw almonds and cashews in the larder for baking, making "cheese" fillings and nut milks, and plain old snacking. Walnuts and pecans make everything more delicious, especially when toasted first. Chia and flax seeds are essential to the plant-based baking larder and can be added to salads, fruit dishes, breads, and porridge. Roasted, salted pumpkin seeds are nice, too. Store nuts and seeds in tightly sealed glass jars, and freeze seldom-used ingredients.

Soy Products

No plant-based larder is complete without tofu, tempeh, edamame, and miso. Tofu absorbs the flavour of what it's cooked with, making it ideal in curries and stews. Tempeh, a fermented soy product, has a umami flavour and meaty texture, perfect for grilling, sandwiches, and casseroles. Edamame are whole soya beans and are good in soups, stews, and salads in the same way you'd use beans. Miso is an essential ingredient when building umami flavour.

Condiments

Stock a variety of home-made and shop-bought condiments to add to recipes or enjoy on cooked foods. Ketchup, hot sauce, wholegrain Dijon mustard, and plant-based mayonnaise are essentials.

Try these spices, herbs, and seasonings to complement your plant-based diet: black pepper; cayenne; cumin; dried dill, oregano, and thyme; fresh basil, chervil, coriander, dill, parsley, and tarragon; herbes de Provence; Himalayan pink salt; nutritional yeast; sea salt (regular and smoked); smoked paprika; turmeric; and more!

Plant-Based Cooking Techniques

Plant-based cooking is easy once you master some basic techniques and equip yourself with helpful supplies: a 2-litre (3½-pint) or more saucepan with a tight-fitting lid; a steamer basket; an assortment of mixing bowls; spoons and spatulas; some heavy, rimmed baking sheets; and a large, heavy frying pan. A food processor is a nice extra that helps to cut down on prep time.

Steaming Vegetables

Steaming is a simple way to cook vegetables with maximum flavour and nutrition retention. To steam, bring 7.5–10cm (3–4in) of water to the boil in a saucepan fitted with a steamer basket over a medium–high heat. Add the vegetables, cover with the lid, and cook until the vegetables are tender. The table on the right lists steaming times for several vegetables.

Steaming peas
Mangetout require only 2 or 3 minutes of steaming to come out perfectly tender and crisp. Oversteaming makes them dull and soggy.

Vegetable	Steam Time
Asparagus	3 or 4 minutes
Broccoli	4 or 5 minutes
Brussels sprouts	10 minutes
Carrots	4 or 5 minutes
Cauliflower	6 minutes
Green beans	5 minutes
Hardy greens (kale, spring greens, cabbages)	7 to 9 minutes
Peas	2 or 3 minutes

Roasting Vegetables

Roasting brings out deep flavours from root vegetables, Brussels sprouts, asparagus, broccoli, and squash. To roast, preheat the oven to 200°C (400°F/Gas 6). Cut vegetables into uniform pieces and place in a baking tray lined with baking parchment. Toss with just enough olive oil to coat; season with salt, black pepper, and dried herbs (if desired); and roast, stirring once or twice, until tender and caramelized.

Tender vegetables, such as asparagus, will roast to perfection in less than 10 minutes, while squash and potatoes need more time – up to 45 minutes. Try roasting broccoli, cauliflower, courgettes, swede, sweet potatoes, turnips, mushrooms, small onions, and even green beans!

Roasted vegetables
Add flavour, nutrition, and a pop of colour to any meal with a selection of roasted vegetables.

Ice bath

The ice bath is an essential step in blanching. It halts the cooking process, sets colour, and loosens a vegetable's or fruit's skin.

Vegetable	Blanch Time
Artichoke	7 minutes
Asparagus	2 minutes
Beans (green, runner)	2 minutes
Beans (borlotti, broad)	2 to 4 minutes
Broccoli	2 or 3 minutes
Brussels sprouts	3 minutes
Carrots	2 minutes
Cauliflower	2 or 3 minutes
Spring greens/kale	3 minutes

Blanching Vegetables

When you want vegetables to remain crunchy and fresh and preserve their bright-green colour, or if you're preparing to freeze in-season produce, you'll want to do some blanching. To blanch, bring a large pan of salted water to the boil over a medium–high heat. Prepare an ice bath by filling a bowl with cold water and ice. Cut vegetables into uniform pieces, and drop into boiling water (see the table on the right for recommended times). Using a slotted spoon, remove the vegetables from the hot water, transfer to the ice bath, and drain in a colander or on kitchen paper.

Sautéed greens
Get your daily serving of greens sautéed with a little olive oil and garlic – it is quick and delicious.

Sautéing Vegetables

A quick sauté lets you cook vegetables with aromatics, such as onions, garlic, and herbs, for fresh, fantastic flavour. To sauté, heat a small amount of fat, such as olive oil, over a medium–high heat in a heavy frying pan. Add onions, and cook for 1 or 2 minutes, stir in garlic, and cook for a further minute. Add vegetables to the pan, and cook, stirring frequently, just until vegetables are tender. Mushrooms, tender courgettes or patty pan, broccoli, spinach, and peas are all excellent candidates for the frying pan.

Aromatic vegetables
Add the building blocks of flavour to soups, stews, and sauces using aromatics, such as celery, onions, and carrot.

Cooking Rice

With the exception of Arborio rice for risottos, rinse rice before cooking it. Measure the rice, place in a large bowl, cover with cold water, and swish around with your hands to release the rice's starch and any soil. Drain and repeat three times. Place the rice in a pot with a tight-fitting lid, add the recommended amount of water, and set over a medium–high heat. Bring to a full, rolling boil, stir once, and cover. Reduce the heat to its lowest setting and cook for the time noted on the rice packet. Remove from the heat and let stand, covered, for 5–10 minutes before fluffing with a fork and serving.

Rice and water
Add rice and cold, fresh water at the same time – don't boil the water first.

Hold it
You can hold cooked rice, covered and with a clean kitchen towel under the lid, for up to 20 minutes. Fluff with a fork, just before serving.

Cooking Pasta

Cook pasta in several litres of boiling water, seasoned with about 1 teaspoon of salt. Pasta needs plenty of water, and plenty of space to expand while cooking, so use your largest pot. Bring water to a full, rolling boil over a medium–high heat, add salt, add pasta, and cook according to the packet instructions. Pasta is best when cooked "al dente", or "firm to the tooth". Drain pasta, and toss with sauce. Do not rinse pasta, unless you'll be chilling it for pasta salad, because the added starch in cooked pasta helps bind it with the sauce.

Choose the right pot
Be sure you use a pot that's large enough to allow the pasta to move around while it boils. Overcrowding yields gummy results.

Al dente pasta
For perfect pasta, boil it only until it's al dente, or cooked but still slightly firm to the bite.

Cooking Dried Beans

When cooking dried beans and peas, soak overnight in plenty of fresh water. Drain, rinse, and place in a heavy pot with 5cm (2in) water to cover. Bring to a boil over a high heat, reduce the heat to a simmer, add 1 teaspoon of salt, and cook for about 1 hour or until tender.

If you're cooking kidney beans, you need to take an extra step. Raw kidney beans contain a toxin called phytohaemagglutinin, which can only be removed by cooking at the boiling point for 10 minutes. After bringing the beans and water to a boil, cook for 10 minutes, skimming off the foam that rises to the top. Then cook as directed. This step, while only 10 extra minutes, is essential.

Canned beans are easy and convenient, but dried beans are less expensive and their texture is incomparable when cooked from scratch. If you don't have time for an overnight soak, try the quick-soak method: bring beans to a boil in a large pan with 5cm (2in) water to cover. Boil for 10 minutes and then soak for 1 hour. Rinse, drain, and cook as directed. And don't throw away the bean broth – it's full of flavour and nutrients and perfect for use in soups and stews.

Storing cooked beans
You can refrigerate beans in their cooking liquid for up to 5 days or freeze for up to 3 months.

Perfect protein
Lentils are the perfect plant-based protein – nutritious, delicious, versatile, quick-cooking, and affordable.

Cooking Lentils

Lentils do not require a soak and cook very quickly – as little as 20 minutes for red lentils and a little longer for other varieties. I like to cook lentils with a little onion and garlic to pre-season them for recipes. Heat 1 tablespoon of olive oil in a medium saucepan over a medium–high heat. Chop a small onion and a few cloves of garlic, add them to the pan, and sauté for 3 to 5 minutes. Add 450g (1lb) lentils with water or broth to cover by 5cm (2in). Bring to the boil, reduce the heat to medium–low, and cook, partially covered, until tender. Divide into 480ml (16fl oz) portions plus cooking liquid, refrigerate for up to 5 days, or freeze for up to 3 months.

If you have issues digesting beans, soaking them removes most of the phytic acid and enzyme inhibitors that cause digestive distress. Adding a strip of kombu (a type of seaweed) to the cooking water further increases the beans' digestibility.

Cooking with Tofu

Tofu is endlessly versatile. It's neutral in flavour so it takes on the flavour of whatever it's cooked with. Drain tofu before using it in recipes by placing the block on a cutting board that's wrapped in a clean tea towel. Set a heavy plate on top of the tofu and add a heavy tin on top of that. Let the tofu drain for 30 minutes, pat it dry, and proceed with your recipe. Tofu can be sliced, cubed for stews and curries, crumbled for an eggless scramble, or blended into cake batters in place of eggs.

Tofu

Cooking with Tempeh

For best flavour and texture, marinate and/or steam tempeh. To steam, cut it into strips or slices. Place it in a baking dish, cover with a marinade or vegetable stock, cover tightly, and bake until the tempeh is puffed up. This tenderizes and flavours the tempeh.

Cooking with Seitan

Seitan is a seasoned loaf made from vital wheat gluten that can be used to simulate the texture and flavours of beef or chicken. Try it grilled or seared in a cast-iron pan for use in sandwiches.

A quick trip to the produce aisle of a well-stocked supermarket yields a variety of meat substitutes – hot dogs, sausages, veggie bacon, and pepperoni. The freezer section stocks "veggie crumbles" that can fill in for minced beef, veggie burgers, and more. Try to limit meat substitutes to home-made or store-bought seitan, tempeh, or tofu.

Hearty Seitan Roast
Brown and then bake loaves of Basic Seitan with sauces and vegetables for a hearty main dish with a meat-like texture.

Basic Seitan (T)

You can find seitan in the chilled section of supermarkets or small grocers, or you can pick up some vital wheat gluten and make some! Bell's seasoning is a mix of rosemary, oregano, sage, ginger, and marjoram.

MAKES 2 LOAVES **PREP** 10 MINS **COOK** 30 MINS

1 In a food processor fitted with a metal blade, blend 360ml (12fl oz) vegetable stock; ½ small onion, roughly chopped; 1 garlic clove, roughly chopped; tamari; apple cider vinegar; Bell's seasoning; baking powder; and sweet paprika until smooth.

2 In a medium bowl, whisk together the vital wheat gluten, chickpea flour, nutritional yeast, sea salt, and black pepper. Pour in the wet ingredients, and stir with a silicone spatula until the liquid is incorporated and a rough dough is formed.

3 Cut the dough into halves, and use your hands to quickly knead into logs approximately 15cm (6in) long if the seitan will be served sliced, such as in roasts, steaks, or kebabs; or break seitan apart into rough chunks for stews or skewered items, such as satay. Set aside and allow to rest for 5 minutes.

4 Meanwhile, chop the remaining 1½ onions into rough wedges. Place in a large saucepan with a lid along with the remaining vegetable stock, bay leaf, remaining garlic, and porcini mushrooms (if using). Set over a medium–high heat, bring to the boil, reduce the heat to medium, and gently add the seitan loaves. Cover and cook over the lowest heat for 45 minutes without lifting the lid.

5 Uncover, remove the bay leaf, and cool completely in the broth before storing. Seitan will keep in the fridge, stored in its cooking broth, for up to 3 days, or can be frozen for up to 3 months. Defrost completely in the fridge overnight before using.

INGREDIENTS

1.2 litres (2 pints) vegetable stock

2 small yellow onions

2 cloves garlic

1 tbsp plus 1 tsp reduced-sodium tamari

1 tbsp apple cider vinegar

1 tsp Bell's seasoning blend

1 tsp baking powder

½ tsp sweet paprika

1¾ cups vital wheat gluten

4 tbsp chickpea flour

4 tbsp nutritional yeast

½ tsp fine sea salt

½ tsp freshly ground black pepper

1 bay leaf

2 small pieces dried porcini mushroom (optional)

Seitan prepared in this manner can be marinated with any flavour you like. Grill or sear marinated seitan in a cast-iron frying pan for the best flavour.

Meal Plans

Here's a sample one-week meal plan, including many recipes from this book. Add a snack or two every day – such as nuts, seeds, and fresh fruit or vegetables dipped in a delicious dressing or spread (such as Tzatziki, Smoky Baba Ghanoush, or Romesco Sauce) – and you're set.

When creating meal plans, think about your time, tastes, and the nutritional value of the foods you're eating. Also, do as much cooking and prep work ahead of time as you can – a little work on your day off makes the rest of your week easier. Chop onions, celery, and carrots ahead; keep in zip-lock plastic freezer bags or containers in measured portions; and use straight from the freezer – no need to thaw. Make a batch of granola when you've got time, and store it in an airtight jar for easy grab-and-go snacks. Prepare pizza dough up to 2 days ahead and keep in the fridge. Double up recipes, for example the Vinaigrette dressing, and refrigerate for up to 5 days, shake, and pour

	MONDAY	TUESDAY	WEDNESDAY
BREAKFAST	Nutty Granola* with fresh berries and plant-based yogurt	Breakfast Burritos, fresh melon with a squeeze of lime	Oatmeal, fresh blueberries
LUNCH	Roasted Beetroot Salad*, a hearty soup, 1 apple or pear	Herbed Tabbouleh*, Hummus*, wholemeal pitta, 1 banana	Classic Vegetable Soup*, cheese toastie on wholemeal bread (make using Pimento Cheese)* and sliced tomato, diced watermelon
DINNER	Stir-Fried Chinese Cress with Fermented Black Beans, Tom Yum Soup*, Seitan Satay*	Giambotta* over hot cooked polenta, green salad with Vinaigrette*, Sautéed Purple-sprouting Broccoli (blanch the broccoli in advance, add white beans for extra protein)	Oyster Mushroom Po'boys, Gumbo*, green salad with Vinaigrette*

Nutty Granola

*Can be cooked in advance.

**Roasted
Beetroot Salad**

over weekday salads. Whenever possible, double up a soup or casserole recipe and freeze some in individual- or family-sized portions. Before long, you'll have a freezer chock full of meals ready to defrost whenever you're pushed for time.

THURSDAY	FRIDAY	SATURDAY	SUNDAY
Fruit-based breakfast smoothie, wholemeal English muffin with peanut butter and apple slices	Nutty Granola* with non-dairy milk and sliced banana	Wholemeal Banana Pecan Pancakes, fresh berries	*Brunch:* Strawberry Muffins; Mushroom, Spinach, and Shallot Quiche*; Breakfast Sausage Patties
Sesame Noodles*, Sesame Asparagus*, sliced kiwi and strawberries	*Pan Bagnat* (prep ingredients ahead, and assemble sandwiches in the morning), 1 apple or pear	Miso Udon Bowl*	Tofu Summer Rolls*, miso soup
Lentil and Vegetable Dhal*, Naan, Sesame Tofu Cutlets	*Pissaladière* (or home-made pizza; make the dough and caramelized onions up to 2 days in advance), a hearty soup, green salad with Vinaigrette*	Tempeh Milanese*, Sautéed Mushroom Medley*, Summer Squash and Onion Bake*, freshly baked cookies	*Bisteeya*, Moroccan Couscous, Butternut Squash Tagine*, Chunky Apple Sauce

Grandma's Chicken-y Noodle Soup

Basics

Start with the simple things. Home-made ingredients, such as stock, pastry, and nut milk, are the building blocks of a perfect plant-based meal.

Caramelized Onions

When onions are cooked slowly in just a little bit of fat, their sugars caramelize, yielding a sweet, savoury, dark brown mass of super-delicious flavour.

SERVES 4 PREP 5 MINS COOK 45 MINS

1   Cut the onions in half and peel them. Trim the ends, and cut into 3mm (1/8in) slices.

2   Heat the extra-virgin olive oil in a 30cm (12in) frying pan over a medium–high heat. Add the onions, stir, and reduce the heat to low. Next, stir in the salt and black pepper.

3   Cook, stirring every 10 minutes or so, for about 45 minutes or until the onions are softened and a dark golden brown. The onions should cook very slowly, browning gently and barely sizzling in the pan. Adjust the heat as needed.

4   Use immediately, or refrigerate in a sealed container for up to 5 days.

INGREDIENTS

2 large yellow onions

1 tbsp extra-virgin olive oil

¼ tsp sea salt

¼ tsp freshly ground black pepper

Resist the urge to stir the onions frequently, or you'll fry them before their sugars are released. If you plan to double the recipe, use a larger pan. The onions must be in contact with the surface of the pan for caramelization to occur.

Simple Vegetable Stock Ⓣ

This light and flavourful vegetable stock blends well with all manner of other ingredients, making it the perfect base for any soup or sauce.

MAKES 4 LITRES (7 PINTS) **PREP** 15 MINS **COOK** 2 HOURS

1 In a large stockpot or deep-sided large pan, combine the leeks, onions, carrots, celery, button mushrooms, bay leaf, flat-leaf parsley, thyme, peppercorns, and tamari. Cover with filtered water.

2 Set the pan over a high heat, bring to the boil, cover, reduce the heat to a gentle simmer, and cook for 2 hours.

3 Cool completely; strain and discard the vegetables, herbs, and spices; and pour the stock into glass jars or BPA-free containers for storage. Stock will keep in the fridge for up to 7 days or in the freezer for up to 3 months.

For *Golden Chicken-y Stock*, sauté the leeks, carrots, and celery in 2 tablespoons of extra-virgin olive oil for 10 minutes or until golden, and add 70g (2½oz) sliced chestnut mushrooms and a good pinch of saffron to the pan along with raw, unpeeled onions when you add water. For *Mushroom Stock*, follow the instructions for Golden Chicken-y Stock and double the chestnut mushrooms. Cook the vegetables in extra-virgin olive oil for 5 minutes longer (15 minutes total) to achieve a deeper level of caramelization, substitute 25g (scant 1oz) dried porcini mushrooms for the saffron, and proceed as directed. For *Kombu Stock*, omit the parsley, thyme, and bay leaf; replace all the mushrooms with 175g (6oz) sliced shiitake mushrooms and 25g (scant 1oz) dried shiitake mushrooms; and add 2 (10cm; 4in) pieces of dried kombu to the pan.

INGREDIENTS

2 large leeks, halved lengthways, washed, and cut into 2.5cm (1in) chunks

2 large yellow onions, root end trimmed and cut into 2.5cm (1in) chunks

4 carrots, scrubbed and cut into 2.5cm (1in) chunks

8 large sticks celery, cut into 2.5cm (1in) chunks

140g (5oz) button mushrooms, sliced

1 bay leaf

30g (1oz) fresh flat-leaf parsley leaves and stems

3 sprigs thyme

1 tsp whole black peppercorns

2 tbsp tamari or soy sauce

4 litres (7 pints) filtered water

Pie Pastry (T)

This easy pastry comes together quickly in the food processor. it yields a flaky, tender pie crust and works equally well for both sweet and savoury recipes.

MAKES 2 CRUSTS FOR A DEEP-DISH PIE   PREP 10 MINS, PLUS 30 MINS RESTING TIME   COOK NONE

1   In a food processor fitted with a metal blade, pulse the flour and salt several times to combine.

2   Add half of the shortening cubes, pulse 5 or 6 times, and process for 5 seconds. Add remaining shortening and pulse until the shortening resembles small, pea-sized pieces.

3   Transfer the flour mixture to a large bowl. Pour a few tablespoons of iced water over the flour mix, and quickly toss with a large kitchen fork to combine. Continue adding the water and tossing until the mixture just comes together and then use the heel of your hand to press the dough against the sides of the bowl to form a moist, cohesive ball.

4   Separate the dough into two equal pieces, wrap in cling film, and use your hands to flatten each piece into a 12cm (5in) disc.

5   Chill the dough for 30 minutes and proceed as directed in your recipe.

INGREDIENTS

375g (13oz) unbleached plain flour

1½ tsp sea salt

12 tbsp non-hydrogenated organic shortening, partially frozen, cut into small cubes

120–150ml (4–5fl oz) iced water

Removing the dough to a bowl before adding the water ensures a tender crust. If you don't have a food processor, you can use a pastry blender tool to combine the flour, salt, and shortening.

Nut Milk (T)

Once you've tasted home-made nut milk, you'll never go back to shop-bought.

SERVES 4   PREP 5 MINS PLUS OVERNIGHT SOAKING TIME   COOK NONE

1   Soak almonds in cold water overnight.

2   Discard the soaking water, rinse the nuts well, and drain.

3   In a high-speed blender, process the nuts along with the filtered water, Medjool dates, vanilla extract, and cinnamon until smooth.

4   Using a nut milk bag or muslin bag, strain the solids from the milk.

5   Refrigerate the milk in a clean glass jar for up to 4 days. Shake well before using.

INGREDIENTS

140g (5oz) raw almonds, hazelnuts, or cashews

960ml (1 pint 10fl oz) filtered water

2 or 3 pitted Medjool dates

1 tsp vanilla extract

½ tsp ground cinnamon

For *Chocolate Nut Milk*, add 25g (scant 1oz) raw cacao and 1 tablespoon agave nectar to the blender with the other ingredients.

Fresh Pasta Dough (T)

You can easily make your own eggless fresh pasta dough for long shapes, such as hand-cut tagliatelle or fettuccine, or filled pasta, such as ravioli. For added flavour and a pretty golden colour, try saffron or tomato paste – or both. Use a pasta machine to roll the dough if you have one, but a rolling pin also works well if you don't.

SERVES 4   PREP 30 MINS   COOK 3 MINS

1   In a small bowl, whisk the extra-virgin olive oil into the warm water. Then, whisk in the tomato purée and/or saffron (if using).

2   In a large bowl, stir together the flour and salt. Mound the flour mixture on a wooden board or clean kitchen worktop, and make a well in the centre. Pour the olive oil–water mixture into the well.

3   Using a fork, slowly whisk the flour mixture into the olive oil mixture, a little at a time, until nearly all has been incorporated. Knead by hand for about 5 minutes, sprinkling your work surface with flour as you work. If the dough seems dry, add more water, a few drops at a time. When you've finished kneading, you should end up with a pliable ball of dough that's firm, yet springy when pressed.

4   Wrap the ball of dough in cling film, and rest at room temperature for 20 minutes. Meanwhile, prepare the pasta rolling machine or dust a rolling pin and work surface with flour.

5   Using your fingers, press the dough into a rectangle. Follow the instructions that came with your pasta machine, rolling the dough until it's thin but no longer opaque. Or use a rolling pin to roll the dough into a large rectangle, turning it a quarter-turn clockwise with each roll and flipping it over several times. Dust the board with flour frequently to prevent sticking.

6   Cut the pasta sheets into your desired shape, or fill, and cook in boiling, well-salted water for about 3 minutes or until tender. Serve immediately with your favourite sauce.

To make tagliatelle or other long pasta shapes, cut the rolled pasta dough into thirds lengthways, and quickly roll up each piece from the short side, making a flat roll. Use a sharp knife to cut the dough: 5mm (¼in) for tagliatelle, 1.5mm (¹⁄₁₆in) for fettuccine, or 3mm (⅛in) for linguine. It's important to cut or fill the pasta the moment it's been rolled, or it will dry out. Once you've mastered cutting pasta, search out one of the helpful tutorials online for creating filled pasta shapes. Experiment with different fillings: finely chopped and sautéed vegetables, puréed squash or beans, or nut cheeses, such as Cashew Ricotta.

INGREDIENTS

2 tbsp extra-virgin olive oil

240ml (8fl oz) warm water

1 tsp tomato purée and/or a pinch of saffron crushed in a mortar and pestle (optional)

450g (1lb) plain flour, plus more for kneading

½ tsp sea salt

Sauces, Dressings, Dips, and Spreads

Dress a salad with style, top your plant-based creations with a satisfying sauce or gravy, or serve an array of delicious spreads and dips that will wow your dinner guests.

Hummus

Rich, creamy, nutritious hummus is redolent with the flavours of garlic, lemon, and tahini – a paste made from sesame seeds.

SERVES 4 OR 5   PREP 10 MINS PLUS OVERNIGHT SOAKING TIME   COOK 1½ HOURS

1   Soak chickpeas in water overnight.

2   Discard the soaking water, rinse the chickpeas well, and drain.

3   Place the chickpeas in a large saucepan. Add enough water to cover by 2.5cm (1in), and bring to the boil. Reduce the heat to low so that the chickpeas bubble at a gentle simmer, and cook for 30 minutes.

4   Add salt, and cook for a further hour or until the chickpeas are soft and tender to the bite.

5   Drain the chickpeas, reserving 180ml (6fl oz) of the cooking liquid.

6   Place the warm chickpeas in a food processor fitted with a metal blade. Add lemon juice, garlic, and tahini, and pulse to combine. With the machine running, slowly drizzle in 120ml (4fl oz) extra-virgin olive oil, followed by the reserved cooking liquid.

7   Spread the hummus in a shallow bowl, and make a well in the centre. Pour the remaining extra-virgin olive oil into the well, and sprinkle sumac over the top to garnish. Serve immediately with warm pitta bread, or refrigerate in a sealed container for up to 5 days.

INGREDIENTS

400g (14oz) dried chickpeas

2 tsp sea salt

Juice of 1½ lemons (¼ cup)

2 cloves garlic, smashed and chopped

4 tbsp tahini

150ml (5fl oz) extra-virgin olive oil

1 tsp ground sumac

The secret to really great, creamy hummus is to use dried chickpeas and make the hummus while they're still warm. If you're in a hurry, you can make a passable hummus with canned chickpeas. For *Quick and Easy Hummus*, substitute 2 x 400g (14oz) cans of chickpeas, rinsed and drained, for the cooked chickpeas in this recipe. Take the time to make it from scratch just once, though, and you might agree that sometimes the long way is the best way! If sumac is unavailable, search for online sources or substitute a squeeze of fresh lemon juice to imitate the tart, authentic flavour of ground sumac.

Smoky Baba Ghanoush Ⓣ

The secret to excellent baba ghanoush is getting the aubergine charred on the outside, with the flesh on the inside collapsed upon itself. After the aubergine pulp is drained, it's mixed with tahini, garlic, lemon juice, and herbs for that signature creamy, smoky flavour – no meze platter is complete without it.

SERVES 8   PREP 15 MINS   COOK 30 MINS PLUS 1 HOUR DRAINING TIME

1   Preheat the oven to 230°C (450°F/Gas 8), or prepare a grill for direct, high heat.

2   Place the aubergines directly on the oven or grill rack, and cook, turning once if grilling, for about 30 minutes or until the skin is charred and the flesh has begun to collapse into a soft mass. If cooking in the oven, place a baking sheet lined with foil on the rack below to catch any drips.

3   Using a spatula, gently transfer the aubergines to a cutting board, cut in half, remove the seeds, and scoop the flesh from the charred skin into a fine-mesh sieve. Set over a large bowl, and drain for 1 hour. Discard liquid.

4   Place the drained aubergine pulp in a food processor fitted with a metal blade. Add the lemon juice, olive oil, tahini, garlic, and salt, and process. You may choose to keep a chunky consistency by pulsing several times or run the machine for 1 or 2 minutes for a smooth and creamy consistency.

5   Spoon the baba ghanoush into a shallow bowl and serve immediately, or refrigerate in a sealed container for up to 5 days.

INGREDIENTS

2 large, firm aubergines

Juice of 1–1½ lemons (4 tbsp)

4 tbsp extra-virgin olive oil

3 tbsp tahini

2 cloves garlic, smashed and chopped

1 tsp sea salt

It's important to take the time to thoroughly cook the aubergines. Undercooked aubergine is bitter and tough to chew. Thoroughly draining the aubergine flesh is another essential step. If you're in a hurry, gently press the flesh as it drains to facilitate the removal of the bitter liquid. For a pretty and traditional garnish, sprinkle pomegranate seeds over the dish just before serving.

Tzatziki

Cool, creamy yogurt combines with cucumber, garlic, and dill in this classic Greek sauce or dip. Use it alongside raw or grilled vegetables or as a dip for warm pitta.

SERVES 5   PREP 10 MINS PLUS 4 HOURS DRAINING AND CHILLING TIME   **COOK** NONE

1   Place the grated cucumber in a fine-mesh sieve, sprinkle with salt, toss, and set the sieve over a bowl to drain for 30 minutes. Press the cucumber gently, and discard the liquid.

2   In a medium bowl, gently combine the drained cucumber, yogurt, lemon juice, extra-virgin olive oil, dill, flat-leaf parsley, and garlic.

3   Refrigerate for 3½ hours to chill and blend flavours before serving. Tzatziki will keep in the fridge for 3 days in a tightly sealed container.

INGREDIENTS

2 cucumbers, halved, seeded, and grated

1 tsp sea salt

480ml (16fl oz) unflavoured plant-based yogurt, such as coconut milk or soya

Juice of 1 lemon (3 tbsp)

2 tbsp extra-virgin olive oil

4 tbsp finely chopped fresh dill

2 tbsp finely chopped fresh flat-leaf parsley

2 cloves garlic, minced

Garlic

For *Extra Garlicky Tzatziki,* increase the garlic to 4 cloves. For *Fresh Mint Tzatziki,* add 2 tablespoons along with the dill and parsley.

Cashew Ricotta

Spread this nutty "cheese" on crackers or use it as a filling for ravioli or lasagna. You'll love its light, airy texture of ricotta with a mild, cheesy flavour that's even better when heated.

SERVES 8 PREP 10 MINS PLUS OVERNIGHT SOAKING TIME COOK NONE

1 Soak the cashews in water overnight.

2 Discard the soaking water, rinse the cashews well, and drain.

3 In a food processor fitted with a metal blade, process the cashews along with the extra-virgin olive oil, warm water, lemon juice, nutritional yeast, parsley, chives, miso, marjoram, salt, and black pepper until smooth, scraping down the bowl several times with a spatula.

4 Use immediately or store in the fridge for up to 5 days.

INGREDIENTS

280g (9½oz) raw cashews
4tbsp extra-virgin olive oil
4 tbsp warm water
Juice of 1½ lemons (3 tbsp)
2 tbsp nutritional yeast
1 tbsp finely chopped fresh parsley
1 tbsp finely chopped chives
1 tsp white (shiro) miso
½ tsp dried marjoram
½ tsp sea salt
½ tsp freshly ground black pepper

Pimento Cheese

Pimento cheese is a cheesy, addictive, piquant spread that's fabulous on sandwiches, with crackers, or stirred into cooked pasta for a fast and flavourful macaroni cheese dish.

SERVES 14 PREP 15 MINS COOK NONE

1 In a food processor fitted with a metal blade, process the Cheddar-style cheese, cream cheese, mayonnaise, onion, drained peppers, garlic, hot sauce, sweet paprika, and cayenne until smooth.

2 Spoon the pimento cheese into a serving bowl and chill for 1 hour.

3 Serve immediately or refrigerate for up to 3 days.

For a thicker spread perfect for pan-style cheese toasties, look for almond-based Cheddar-style cheese, which is firmer than the tapioca-based products, and reduce the mayonnaise to 4 tbsp. Spread the sourdough or your favourite bread with a little plant-based butter on one side of each slice, and fill with a generous amount of Pimento Cheese. Heat a small frying pan over a medium heat, and toast your sandwich on both sides, turning once, until golden brown.

INGREDIENTS

225g (8oz) plant-based Cheddar-style cheese, preferably almond-based, shredded
225g (8oz) plant-based cream cheese
8 tbsp plant-based mayonnaise
¼ large onion (or sweet onion), finely minced
115g (4oz) jarred peppers, drained
1 clove garlic, finely chopped
½ tsp Louisiana hot sauce
½ tsp sweet paprika
¼ tsp cayenne

Nuts and Seeds

Many nuts and seeds are a good source of plant-based protein. Enjoy them as a snack, a main dish ingredient, or as butters and pastes. (Tahini, for example, is a paste made from sesame seeds.) Choose a wide variety for the best dietary value. Some nuts and seeds are better sources of protein, while others offer a wide array of vitamins and minerals.

    Purchase nuts and seeds as raw or toasted, and once opened, store them in a tightly sealed glass jar. Store at room temperature for up to 1 month, or freeze for up to 6 months. Discard rancid nuts and seeds.

Almonds

	ALMONDS	BRAZIL NUTS	CASHEWS	CHESTNUTS	CHIA SEEDS	FLAX SEEDS	HAZELNUTS
USES	Soak for nut milks and cheeses. Use raw or toasted in sweet and savoury recipes.	Use in salads, granola, pancakes, and baked goods.	Soak for nut milks and cheeses. Use raw or toasted in sweet and savoury recipes.	Cut an X in the shell, and roast until the chestnut opens. Use in desserts, sauté with vegetables, or purée for ravioli filling or in biscuits.	Soak in warm water as an egg replacer. Sprinkle whole seeds on porridge, add to granola, or use in salads.	Grind and soak in warm water as an egg replacer. Add whole seeds or ground meal to pancakes, porridge, biscuits, or desserts, or sprinkle onto salads.	Soak for nut milks and cheeses. Toast and add to salads, such as pear and spinach. Use in baked goods, pesto, granola, and pasta dishes.
GOOD SOURCE OF ...	Protein, fibre, calcium, iron, vitamin B$_2$, manganese, magnesium, vitamin E, and potassium.	Protein, fibre, calcium, iron, magnesium, potassium, phosphorus, copper, and selenium.	Iron, magnesium, phosphorus, copper, manganese, and potassium.	Fibre, vitamin C, copper, and manganese.	Calcium, fibre, phosphorus, and manganese.	Protein, fibre, calcium, iron, magnesium, copper, phosphorus, vitamin B$_1$, and manganese.	Protein, fibre, calcium, iron, vitamins C and E, copper, and manganese.

Brazil nuts

Flax seeds

Pumpkin seeds

Macadamia nuts

Pistachios

Pecans

MACADAMIA NUTS	PECANS	PINE NUTS	PISTACHIOS	PUMPKIN SEEDS	SESAME SEEDS	SUNFLOWER SEEDS	WALNUTS
Use in baked goods, sprinkled onto salads, or in granola or porridge.	Toast and add to baked goods, salads, porridge, granola, or sautéed vegetable dishes.	Toast and use for flavour and texture in pasta dishes, pesto, vegetable dishes, salads, and baked goods.	Add to pasta dishes, salads, dips, granola, and baked goods.	Toast and add to pesto, casseroles, pasta dishes, salads, dips, porridge, granola, and baked goods.	Use raw or toasted as a garnish for noodle dishes, stir-fries, and salads, or try in desserts. Use tahini (sesame seed paste) in dips and dressings.	Add to pesto, pasta dishes, sautéed vegetables, granola, or porridge.	Toast and use in desserts, pancakes, porridge, salads, pesto, and granola.
Protein, fibre, calcium, iron, vitamin B_1, and manganese.	Protein, fibre, iron, calcium, and manganese.	Protein, iron, and manganese.	Protein, fibre, calcium, iron, vitamin B_6, copper, manganese, and potassium.	Protein, magnesium, zinc, and potassium.	Calcium, iron, magnesium, phosphorus, copper, manganese, and potassium.	Protein, iron, vitamins B_6 and E, magnesium, phosphorus, copper, manganese, selenium, and potassium.	Protein, calcium, iron, copper, and manganese.

Hazelnuts

Sesame seeds

Truffled Mushroom Pâté (T)

This silky pâté with the umami flavours of mushrooms and truffles is an easy-to-make, elegant appetizer. Toss leftovers (if you have any) with hot, cooked pasta for a super-easy, creamy pasta dish the day after.

SERVES 12 **PREP** 15 MINS **COOK** 10 MINS, PLUS SOAKING AND CHILLING TIME

1 Soak the cashews in cold water for at least 4 hours.

2 Discard the soaking water, rinse the nuts well, and set aside.

3 Place the porcini mushrooms in a small bowl. Pour boiling water over them and soak for about 5 minutes or until the mushrooms are softened. Lift them from the soaking water, agitating gently to release any soil. Reserve the soaking liquid. Chop the mushrooms, and set aside.

4 Heat the olive oil in a large frying pan over a medium–high heat. Add shallots and garlic, and cook, stirring continuously, for 2 minutes.

5 Add the porcini mushrooms, chestnut mushrooms, button mushrooms, and rosemary, and cook, stirring occasionally, for about 10 minutes or until the mushrooms begin to brown, adjusting the heat as necessary to keep the mushrooms at a brisk sizzle but without burning.

6 Deglaze the pan with the white wine, and cook for a further minute. Season with salt and black pepper, and remove from the heat.

7 In a food processor fitted with a metal blade, combine the cashews, mushrooms, miso, tamari, lemon juice, chives, and truffle oil.

8 Strain the porcini liquid, leaving the last 1 or 2 teaspoons to eliminate any grit. Pour into the food processor, and whizz until completely smooth. Taste the pâté and season with additional salt and black pepper, if desired.

9 Pack the pâté into a large ramekin or a terrine mould and chill completely before serving with crackers or toasted French bread slices.

INGREDIENTS

140g (5oz) raw cashews

25g (scant 1oz) dried porcini mushrooms

120ml (4fl oz) boiling water

2 tbsp extra-virgin olive oil

2 shallots, finely chopped

2 cloves garlic, minced

225g (8oz) chestnut mushrooms, sliced

225g (8oz) white button mushrooms, sliced

1 tsp chopped fresh rosemary, or ½ tsp dried

4 tbsp dry white wine

½ tsp sea salt, or to taste

¼ tsp freshly ground black pepper, or to taste

1 tbsp white (shiro) miso

1 tbsp reduced-sodium tamari

Juice of ½ medium lemon (1 tbsp)

1 tbsp finely chopped fresh chives

1 tsp truffle oil, or to taste

Truffle oil has a very strong flavor. If you haven't had it before, you might want to begin with ½ teaspoon and add more to taste. For a milder truffle essence, omit the truffle oil and replace the sea salt with truffle salt.

Béchamel Sauce (T) (UNDER 30)

Smooth béchamel is the perfect choice when a creamy sauce is desired. A hint of onion, clove, and nutmeg adds just a bit of spice to this delicious and versatile sauce.

MAKES 480ML (16FL OZ) PREP 5 MINS COOK 10–15 MINS

1 Heat the grapeseed oil in a small saucepan over a medium–high heat. Add the flour all at once and stir vigorously with a whisk.

2 When the flour mixture is golden and begins to smell nutty (but before it browns, about 2 minutes), add the non-dairy milk, continuing to whisk vigorously to prevent lumps.

3 Add the clove-studded onion and bay leaf, reduce the heat to low, and cook, stirring frequently, for about 10 minutes or until the sauce thickens.

4 Remove from the heat, and stir in salt, black pepper, and nutmeg. Taste and adjust seasonings.

5 Strain the sauce through a fine-mesh sieve to remove any solids, and use immediately.

INGREDIENTS

4 tbsp grapeseed oil

3 tbsp plain flour

600ml (1 pint) unflavoured non-dairy milk, preferably soya or rice

¼ small onion, studded with 1 whole clove

1 bay leaf

¼ tsp sea salt

Pinch freshly ground black pepper

Pinch freshly grated nutmeg

Tomato Sauce (UNDER 30)

This simple, fresh-tasting tomato sauce comes together in minutes. Use the best-quality canned tomatoes you can find for this quick and easy sauce that's perfect with pasta or as a base for soup.

MAKES 840ML (1½ PINTS) PREP 5 MINS COOK 15 MINS

1 Heat the olive oil in a large saucepan over a medium–high heat. When the oil is shimmering (but before it begins to smoke), add the garlic and salt. Cook, stirring, for 30 seconds, to allow the garlic to release its fragrance without browning.

2 Add the plum tomatoes with their juice and the white wine to the pan, and cook for 5 minutes.

3 Using a potato masher or a large fork, crush the tomatoes. Reduce the heat to medium and cook, stirring occasionally, for a further 10 minutes.

4 Stir in the basil and black pepper, and remove from the heat.

5 Use immediately, or pour into freezer-safe containers with 2.5cm (1in) headspace and freeze for up to 3 months.

INGREDIENTS

2 tbsp extra-virgin olive oil

2 cloves garlic, peeled, smashed, and finely chopped

½ tsp sea salt

2 (400g; 14oz) cans peeled plum tomatoes, with juice

4 tbsp dry white wine

4 leaves fresh basil, torn

¼ tsp freshly ground black pepper

Mushroom Gravy Ⓣ

This rich, brown, flavourful gravy never disappoints. Using a deep, wondrous mushroom stock (see page 28) and taking time to cook the roux without burning it are the secrets to this great gravy.

MAKES 960ML (1¾ PINTS) **PREP** 10 MINS **COOK** 25 MINS

1 Heat 3 tablespoons of the grapeseed oil in a medium frying pan over a medium–high heat, until it shimmers (but before it begins to smoke). Add the shallots and cook, stirring occasionally, for about 5 minutes or until softened.

2 Add the garlic, both lots of mushrooms, and cook, stirring often, for 10 minutes or until the mushrooms have released their liquid.

3 Add the mushroom stock and tamari, reduce the heat to medium, and cook, stirring occasionally, while you make the roux.

4 In a small pan over a medium heat, heat the remaining 2 tablespoons grapeseed oil. Whisk in the flour and cook, stirring frequently, for about 10 minutes or until the mixture is a rich brown colour.

5 Whisk the roux into the mushroom mixture, and cook for a further 5–10 minutes or until the gravy is as thick as you like it. Stir in bourbon (if using) and black pepper, and serve immediately. This gravy will keep in a tightly sealed container in the fridge for 3 days.

INGREDIENTS

5 tbsp grapeseed oil

2 medium shallots, finely chopped (½ cup)

1 clove garlic, smashed and finely chopped

225g (8oz) chestnut mushrooms, thinly sliced

225g (8oz) shiitake mushrooms, thinly sliced

960ml (1¾ pints) *Mushroom Stock*

1 tbsp low-sodium tamari or soy sauce

3 tbsp plain flour

1 tbsp bourbon (optional)

½ tsp freshly ground black pepper

Vinaigrette (UNDER 30)

Whisk together this simple, easily varied vinaigrette dressing in minutes to give your salads and steamed veggies a flavour-packed punch.

MAKES 240ML (8FL OZ) **PREP** 10 MINS **COOK** NONE

1 In a small bowl, whisk together the shallot, herbs, apple cider vinegar, salt, and Dijon mustard.

2 Slowly whisk in the extra-virgin olive oil, a few drops at a time, until the dressing is smooth and all the oil has been incorporated.

3 Whisk in the black pepper and use immediately, or refrigerate in a tightly sealed jar for up to 3 days.

Flat-leaf parsley

INGREDIENTS

1 medium shallot, finely minced

2 tbsp minced fresh herbs, such as chives, tarragon, or parsley

120ml (4fl oz) apple cider vinegar

½ tsp sea salt

1 tbsp Dijon mustard

120ml (4fl oz) extra-virgin olive oil

½ tsp freshly ground black pepper

UNREFINED OILS

You need some fat in your diet to keep your joints and skin healthy. Fat also provides flavour as well as that delicious, "fatty" mouthfeel to food, which makes some dishes more satisfying. Use minimally processed unrefined oils – such as extra-virgin olive oil; unrefined grapeseed or sunflower oil; and virgin, cold-pressed coconut oil – and in moderation. **Benefits** Lower cholesterol; control blood sugar levels; and aid digestive health. **Uses** Opt for oil that hasn't been exposed to direct sunlight if you can, and use in dressings, for frying, and in baked goods. **Recipes** *Arancini*, Butternut Squash Tagine, *Imam Bayildi*, Summer Pesto, Vinaigrette.

Summer Pesto (T) (UNDER 30)

Nothing evokes warm summer days like the smell and taste of fresh basil pesto. For the best flavour, make your pesto early in the season, when the basil is sweet and hasn't yet flowered.

MAKES 480ML (16FL OZ)   **PREP** 15 MINS   **COOK** NONE

1 In a food processor fitted with a metal blade, pulse the basil, pine nuts, almonds, nutritional yeast, and garlic until combined.

2 With the machine running, drizzle in the lemon juice, followed by the extra-virgin olive oil. Using a spatula, scrape down the sides of the bowl once or twice during this process.

3 Add the salt and black pepper, and pulse a few more times to combine.

4 Use immediately or freeze for up to 6 months.

INGREDIENTS

50g (1¾oz) fresh basil leaves

65g (2oz) pine nuts, toasted

2 tbsp blanched sliced almonds, toasted

2 tbsp nutritional yeast

1 clove garlic, smashed and chopped

Juice of 1 medium lemon (2 tbsp)

120ml (4fl oz) extra-virgin olive oil

½ tsp sea salt

¼ tsp freshly ground black pepper

Romesco Sauce (UNDER 30)

This savoury Spanish sauce combines sweet roasted bell peppers, toasted almonds, bread fried in olive oil, and flavourful spices.

MAKES 360ML (12FL OZ)   **PREP** 25 MINS   **COOK** 5 MINS

1 Heat 2 tablespoons of the extra-virgin olive oil in a small frying pan over a medium–high heat for 1 minute, or until it shimmers (but before it begins to smoke). Add the bread and fry, turning once, for 1 minute per side, or until golden on both sides.

2 In a food processor fitted with a metal blade, pulse the bread, almonds, and garlic 5 or 6 times to combine.

3 Add the plum tomatoes, red pepper, sherry vinegar, flat-leaf parsley, crushed chillies, sweet paprika, salt, and black pepper, and pulse several more times.

4 With the machine running, slowly drizzle in the remaining extra-virgin olive oil, and process until well combined.

5 Use immediately or refrigerate in a sealed container for up to 3 days.

INGREDIENTS

6 tbsp extra-virgin olive oil

1 2.5cm (1in)-thick slice country bread

50g (1¾oz) sliced almonds, toasted and cooled

1 clove garlic, crushed and chopped

4 ripe plum tomatoes, cored and roughly chopped

1 red pepper, roasted, peeled, and cooled slightly

2 tbsp sherry vinegar

1 tbsp chopped fresh flat-leaf parsley

1 tsp crushed chillies

1 tsp sweet paprika

½ tsp sea salt

¼ tsp freshly ground black pepper

Pico de Gallo

Fresh salsa is easy to make and it complements so many foods. Spoon it over tacos, breakfast butties, or casseroles – or just enjoy it with crispy tortilla chips.

MAKES 600ML (1 PINT) PREP 15 MINS COOK NONE

1 In a medium bowl of iced water, soak the chopped red onion for 10 minutes.

2 Over an open gas flame using tongs, or under a grill set to high, char the chilli pepper on all sides. When the skin is evenly charred, place the chilli in a small bowl, cover with cling film and set aside for 2 minutes. Use kitchen paper to rub the skin off the softened chilli, and then core, seed, and finely chop it.

3 Core the tomatoes, cut in half, and gently squeeze out the seeds and pulp. Chop the remaining flesh as finely as possible, and place in another bowl.

4 Drain the onion in a colander, pat dry with kitchen paper, and add to the tomatoes. Stir in the chopped chilli, coriander, lime juice, and salt.

5 Serve immediately or refrigerate leftovers for up to 48 hours.

INGREDIENTS

½ small red onion, finely chopped (¼ cup)

1 mild green chilli

2 large tomatoes

4 tbsp finely chopped fresh coriander

Juice of 1½ limes (2 tbsp)

½ tsp sea salt, or to taste

Guacamole

Creamy guacamole is a party essential, but it's not just for dipping. Try it on sandwiches or salads or spooned onto enchiladas, nachos, and tacos. The key to an excellent guacamole is perfectly ripe Hass avocados. A ripe avocado has a dark skin and the flesh yields when pressed gently.

MAKES 720ML (1 PINT 4FL OZ) PREP 10 MINS COOK NONE

1 In a medium bowl, and using a fork, mash the Hass avocado flesh to a chunky consistency.

2 Stir in the lime juice, plum tomato, red onion, coriander, jalapeño chilli, cumin, and salt. Taste and add more salt if necessary.

3 Serve immediately.

INGREDIENTS

4 ripe Hass avocados, pitted and peeled

Juice of 2 limes (4 tbsp)

1 ripe plum tomato, cored, deseeded, and finely chopped

½ small red onion, finely minced

4 tbsp finely chopped fresh coriander

1 jalapeño chilli, deseeded and finely minced

½ tsp ground cumin

½ tsp sea salt, or to taste

Breakfasts

Give your body the nutrition it needs by starting every day with a healthy breakfast. Savour a leisurely weekend brunch or dash out the door with a pot of granola.

Nutty Granola (T) (UNDER 30)

Making your own granola is so easy and you can even personalise it, adding the exact ingredients you want. Enjoy it as cold breakfast cereal, layer it with yogurt and sliced fruit for a pud, or just have some as a nutritious on-the-go snack.

SERVES 10 **PREP** 5 MINS **COOK** 20–25 MINS

1 Preheat the oven to 150°C (300°F/Gas 2).

2 In a large bowl, combine the rolled oats, brown sugar, cinnamon, and salt.

3 In a small bowl, whisk together the grapeseed oil and maple syrup, and pour over the oat mixture. Using a large spatula, fold the ingredients together until everything is well mixed.

4 Spread the granola on a large baking sheet, and bake for 20–25 minutes, stirring twice during baking, until the granola is toasted and golden brown.

5 Transfer to a clean bowl; stir in the pecans, raisins, and pumpkin seeds; and allow to cool completely. Store in a tightly sealed glass jar for up to 1 week.

INGREDIENTS

320g (11oz) rolled oats

2 tbsp brown sugar

1 tsp ground cinnamon

½ tsp sea salt

120ml (4fl oz) grapeseed oil

120ml (4fl oz) maple syrup

75g (2½oz) chopped pecans, walnuts, or your favourite nut

85g (3oz) raisins

4 tbsp pumpkin seeds

You can easily customize this recipe. For *Nutty Chocolate Granola,* add some chocolate chips. For *Coconutty Granola,* add some flaked coconut. Change the nuts or seeds as you like, use as many different kinds of dried fruit as you like, include some candied ginger. Try cardamom or ground nutmeg instead of, or in addition to, the cinnamon.

Breakfast Burritos ⓣ (UNDER 30)

For a fantastic on-the-go breakfast, cook some onions, mushrooms, and black beans with traditional sausage seasonings of sage and black pepper; load up on the toppings; roll; and go!

MAKES 2 **PREP** 10 MINS **COOK** 10 MINS

1 Heat the olive oil in a medium sauté pan over medium-high heat. Add the onion and mushrooms, and cook for 2 or 3 minutes, stirring once or twice.

2 Add sage, salt, and black pepper, and cook for 2 more minutes.

3 Stir in the black beans and cook, turning a few times and pressing to break up the beans and brown them a little, for about 5 minutes. Remove from the heat, and set aside.

4 Lay each tortilla on a plate, and spoon half of the mushroom filling down the centre of each, and divide the tomato, avocado, and salsa between each burrito. Roll the burritos by folding two sides in first and then folding one long side inwards.

INGREDIENTS

2 tbsp olive oil

½ small red onion, thinly sliced

140g (5oz) button mushrooms, sliced

1 tsp crumbled dried sage

½ tsp sea salt

½ tsp freshly ground black pepper

1 cup cooked black beans

2 (25cm; 10in) wholewheat tortillas

1 large tomato, diced

1 Hass avocado, halved, seeded, and sliced

4 tbsp prepared salsa

Button mushrooms

For a *Breakfast Scramble*, toss 125g (4½oz) of crumbled silken tofu and 1 tablespoon of nutritional yeast with the black beans. Or add plant-based soured cream, chopped coriander, or chopped fresh fruits or veggies to your burrito.

Wholewheat Banana Pecan Pancakes (T) (UNDER 30)

Buckwheat flour, white wholemeal flour, flax meal, and toasted pecans offer a super protein boost in the morning, with the sweet flavour of bananas and warm spices.

MAKES 12 **PREP** 15 MINS **COOK** 10 MINS

1 Warm 60ml (2fl oz) of soya milk in a small pan over a medium–high heat.

2 Place the flax meal in a bowl, add the warmed milk, stir well, and set aside.

3 In a small bowl, whisk the apple cider vinegar into the remaining soya milk, and set aside to thicken and curdle.

4 In another small bowl, mash the banana with the brown sugar, maple syrup, and vanilla extract. Whisk in the flax mixture, followed by the curdled soya milk, and blend well.

5 Heat a cast-iron griddle or frying pan over a medium heat until a drop of water sizzles and evaporates immediately.

6 Meanwhile, in a medium bowl, whisk together the white wholemeal flour, buckwheat flour, baking powder, salt, cinnamon, and nutmeg. Stir in the wet ingredients until just combined, and quickly fold in the chopped pecans. Stir in more soya milk, as needed, to make a thick batter; you want it to be the consistency of a heavy cake mixture.

7 Lightly oil or butter the griddle, and drop 3 tablespoon-size scoops of batter into the pan, spreading with a small spatula if necessary. Cook for 2 minutes without disturbing or until bubbles form on the surface of the pancakes, carefully flip over the pancakes, and cook for a further 1½ minutes. Grease the pan a little between each batch, as these pancakes like to stick otherwise.

8 Serve hot with mixed fruit (if using) and more maple syrup (if using).

INGREDIENTS

300ml (10fl oz) soya milk or coconut milk beverage, plus extra if needed

1 tbsp flax meal (ground flax seeds)

1 tsp apple cider vinegar

1 large ripe banana, peeled and mashed well

1 tbsp brown sugar

1 tbsp maple syrup, plus more for serving (optional)

1 tsp vanilla extract

120g (4oz) white wholemeal flour or wholemeal flour

45g (1½oz) buckwheat flour

2 tsp baking powder

½ tsp sea salt

½ tsp ground cinnamon

¼ tsp ground nutmeg

75g (2½oz) pecans, toasted and finely chopped

150g (5½oz) fresh mixed raspberries, blueberries, and/or strawberries (optional)

The success of this recipe depends on using a non-dairy milk that will curdle. Choose a soya or coconut milk beverage, as both will thicken and sour nicely when the apple cider vinegar is introduced.

Strawberry Muffins Ⓣ

These tender, biscuit-like muffins are kissed with a little lemon and studded with pieces of strawberry. For best results, skip the paper cases and bake these muffins directly in the tin.

MAKES 12 **PREP** 15 MINS **COOK** 22–25 MINS

1   Preheat the oven to 180°C (350°F/Gas 4). Lightly coat the holes of a 12-hole muffin tin with non-stick baking spray.

2   In a medium bowl, whisk together the flour, sugar, bicarbonate of soda, baking powder, salt, and nutmeg.

3   In a small bowl, whisk the egg replacer with warm water until well blended. Whisk in the vanilla-flavoured non-dairy yogurt, grapeseed oil, non-dairy milk, lemon zest, and lemon juice.

4   Quickly stir the wet ingredients into the flour mixture until the ingredients are just combined, taking care not to overmix. Fold in the strawberries.

5   Using an ice-cream scoop or a large spoon, evenly divide the muffin batter between the muffin holes. The batter will be thick, a bit like biscuit dough.

6   Bake on the bottom shelf for 22–25 minutes or until the muffins spring back when lightly pressed in the centre. Cool in the tin for 5 minutes before turning out on a wire rack to cool. Serve warm or at room temperature.

INGREDIENTS

225g (8oz) plain flour

115g (4oz) sugar

½ tsp bicarbonate of soda

½ tsp baking powder

¼ tsp sea salt

¼ tsp ground nutmeg

3 tsp egg replacer

4 tbsp warm water

120ml (4fl oz) vanilla flavoured non-dairy yogurt

4 tbsp grapeseed oil

2 tbsp non-dairy milk

1 tsp lemon zest

1 tsp freshly squeezed lemon juice

200g (7oz) fresh or frozen strawberries, roughly chopped

For *Blueberry Muffins*, replace nutmeg with ¼ teaspoon ground cinnamon and strawberries with 200g (7oz) of fresh or frozen blueberries. If desired, combine 1 tablespoon of raw sugar with ¼ teaspoon of ground cinnamon, and sprinkle the tops of the muffins before baking for a crunchy topping.

Dairy Substitutes

Replacing dairy in your recipes is easy. A plethora of plant-based milks are available, such as soya, hemp, oat, almond, rice, and coconut. If you need a "milk" to curdle in a baking recipe, go with soya, hemp, or coconut. If you need the most neutral flavour possible, such as when making a sauce, rice milk is a good choice. When a rich, indulgent result is desired, try coconut milk coffee creamer. And don't overlook plant-based cheeses; there are some wonderful options out there.

Almonds

	ALMOND CHEESE	ALMOND MILK	CASHEW RICOTTA	COCONUT MILK BEVERAGE	COCONUT MILK CREAMER	HEMP MILK
WHAT IT IS	Made from ground almonds or almond milk; it has a neutral, mozzarella-like flavour.	Made from ground almonds; it has a creamy texture and neutral, slightly sweet flavour.	Made from cashew milk; it has a creamy texture and nutty, savoury flavour.	Made from grated coconut meat; it has a sweet, creamy taste.	Made with coconut milk, sweeteners (such as maple syrup or stevia), and flavourings (such as vanilla); it's sweet and creamy.	Made from a ble of ground hemp seeds and water; has a nutty, fairly neutral flavour.
USES	Melting and in cheese sauces, sandwiches, lasagna, and pasta dishes.	Drinking, cooking, and baking.	Hors d'oeuvres and lasagna.	Drinking, cooking, and baking (curdles when acid is added).	Rich and creamy desserts. Use in desserts when a creamy consistency is needed.	Drinking, cookin, and baking (curd when acid is add
GOOD SOURCE OF …	Protein and calcium.	Vitamins A and D and calcium. (See label for fortified products.)	Iron, magnesium, phosphorus, copper, manganese, and potassium.	Vitamins A and B_{12} and calcium.	High in calories and low in nutrients – use sparingly.	Protein and iron. label for fortified products.)

Cashews

Coconut

Brazil nuts

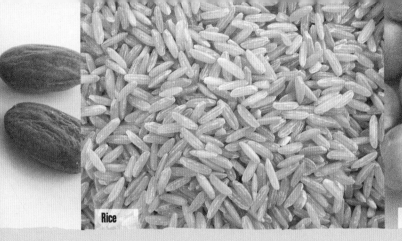

Rice

Soya beans

NUT MiLK	OAT MiLK	RiCE MiLK	SOYA MiLK	TAPiOCA CHEESE
Made from ground nuts, such as Brazil nuts, hazelnuts, pecans, or macadamias; flavour varies by the nut used.	Made with oats, water, and flavourings; it has a slightly sweet and nutty flavour.	Made from unsweetened brown rice; it has a neutral flavour and works well in savoury recipes.	Made from ground dried soya beans and water; it has a slightly sweet flavour and is also available in vanilla and chocolate flavours.	A mozzarella-style cheese made from cassava root starch; it has a tangy flavour and melts well.
Drinking, cooking, and baking.	Drinking, cooking, and baking.	Drinking and cooking when a neutral flavour is desired.	Drinking, cooking, and baking (curdles when acid is added).	Melting and in cheese sauces and sandwiches.
Varies by nut.	Protein, iron, fibre, phosphorus, and selenium. (See label for fortified products.)	Not a significant source of nutrients unless fortified – use sparingly. (See label for fortified products.)	Protein, iron, magnesium, and selenium. (See label for fortified products.)	Not a significant source of nutrients – use sparingly. (See label for fortified products.)

Hazelnuts

Oats

Mushroom, Spinach, and Shallot Quiche

Using chickpea flour gives this quiche a smooth texture and pleasant flavour that makes an excellent base for traditional quiche ingredients. This tasty version is chock full of sweet, lightly caramelized shallots, sautéed mushrooms, and spinach.

SERVES 8   **PREP** 15 MINS   **COOK** 60 MINS

1   Preheat the oven to 180°C (350°F/Gas 4).

2   Roll out Pie Pastry to a 28cm (11in) circle and transfer to a deep 23cm (9in) pie dish or tin. Fold the edges of dough inwards and crimp using your thumb and two fingers to pinch the dough all around. Refrigerate until ready to fill.

3   Heat 2 tablespoons of the extra-virgin olive oil in a large frying pan over a medium heat. Add the shallots and cook, stirring once, for 4 minutes or until they begin to brown.

4   Add the button mushrooms and cook, stirring frequently, for about 5 minutes or until the mushrooms are golden.

5   Add the spinach, ½ teaspoon salt, and the pepper, and stir till wilted. Set aside.

6   In a medium saucepan over a medium heat, bring the water and vegetable stock to the boil. Meanwhile, in a small bowl, whisk together the chickpea flour, nutritional yeast, turmeric, and sweet paprika.

7   Add the remaining extra-virgin olive oil to the boiling stock mixture and pour in the chickpea flour a little at a time, whisking vigorously to eliminate any lumps. Continue whisking for 2 minutes, or until the mixture thickens, and whisk in the remaining salt along with the butter and chives. Next, stir in the mushroom mixture.

8   Pour this mixture into the prepared pastry case and bake for 40 minutes or until the filling is set. Cool for 20 minutes before slicing. Serve warm or cold.

INGREDIENTS

1 batch *Pie Pastry* for a deep 23cm (9in) pie dish or tart tin

4 tbsp extra-virgin olive oil

4 shallots, thinly sliced

175g (6oz) white button mushrooms, thinly sliced

140g (5oz) baby spinach

1 tsp sea salt

¼ tsp freshly ground black pepper

360ml (12fl oz) water

240ml (8fl oz) vegetable stock

90g (3oz) chickpea flour

2 tbsp nutritional yeast

½ tsp turmeric

Pinch sweet paprika

1 tbsp plant-based butter

2 tbsp finely chopped fresh chives

For a *"Cheesy" Breakfast Quiche*, simply add 50g (1¾oz) of your favourite grated plant-based cheese.

Breakfast Sausage Patties (T) (UNDER 30)

Salty, tasty, and perfectly spiced, this plant-based sausage is packed with protein. Make a big batch and freeze them for any rushed weekday mornings.

SERVES 2 PREP 10 MINS COOK 4 MINS

1   In a small bowl, whisk together the flax meal and warm water. Set aside.

2   In a medium frying pan over a medium–high heat, heat 1 tablespoon of grapeseed oil. Add the onion and mushrooms, and cook, stirring frequently, for 10 minutes or until the onions soften and the mushrooms begin to brown.

3   Stir in the sage, thyme, marjoram, nutmeg, and cloves, and stir for 1 minute. Season with salt and black pepper, and set aside to cool slightly.

4   In a food processor fitted with a metal blade, pulse the black beans, kidney beans, quinoa, rolled oats, flour, mushroom mixture, and the flax mixture 5 or 6 times or until the mixture reaches a chunky but cohesive consistency.

5   Heat a large non-stick frying pan over a medium heat, add just enough grapeseed oil to coat the bottom of the pan (about 2 or 3 tablespoons). Using an ice-cream scoop, scoop out portions (about 4 tablespoons) of bean mixture directly into the hot pan, spacing them well apart. Use the back of a wet tablespoon to gently pat each one down into a 7.5cm (3in) patty. Cook for 2 minutes per side, turning carefully with a thin spatula (patties are somewhat delicate).

6   Serve immediately, or cool completely and freeze in an airtight container separated by layers of baking parchment. Reheat frozen sausage patties in the microwave for about 1 minute or in a 200°C (400°F/Gas 6) oven for 8–10 minutes.

INGREDIENTS

1 tbsp flax meal (ground flax seeds)

3 tbsp warm water

1 tbsp grapeseed oil, plus extra for frying

1 small onion, finely chopped

170g (6oz) chestnut mushrooms, finely chopped

2 tsp crumbled dried sage

1½ tsp dried thyme

1 tsp dried marjoram

½ tsp ground nutmeg

Pinch ground cloves

2 tsp sea salt

1 tsp freshly ground black pepper

1 (400g; 14oz) can black beans, rinsed and drained

1 (400g; 14oz) can kidney beans, rinsed and drained

185g (6½oz) cooked quinoa

2 tbsp rolled oats

1 tbsp gluten-free plain flour or fine cornmeal

For *Spicy Sausage Patties,* sauté 1 finely minced jalapeño chilli along with the onions and mushrooms.

AVOCADOS

This tropical fruit is a favourite in Mexican dishes. It has a smooth texture, a nutty flavour, packs a nutritional wallop, and pairs well with tomatoes, grapefruit, limes, mangoes, pineapple, sugar, and balsamic vinegar. **Benefits** High in fibre and potassium; lowers blood pressure; is anti-inflammatory; lubricates joints. **Uses** Opt for firm avocados and let them ripen at home, or choose ripe ones by pressing gently on the shoulder area and feeling for "give". Eat fresh in salads, in soups, or spread on wholegrain toast and topped with a Breakfast Sausage Patty and sliced tomato for a quick breakfast sandwich. **Recipes** Guacamole, Breakfast Burritos, and *Posole*.

Sandwiches, Burgers, and Wraps

You'll find a world of flavours in these tasty meat-free recipes — from the classic italian muffuletta, to authentic po'boys and Asian-inspired sandwiches with delicious sauces. Enjoy as lunch or with soup for supper.

Bánh Mì Portobello Burgers (T)

The humble portobello mushroom makes a delicious, all-natural substitute for hamburger patties. This savoury take on a traditional Vietnamese sandwich – *bánh mì* – is packed with flavour: a meaty mushroom "burger", crunchy pickled veggies, and spicy Sriracha "mayo" are piled on a crusty baguette.

SERVES 4 PREP 40 MINS COOK 10 MINS

1 In a small bowl, whisk together the lime juice, tamari, toasted sesame oil, garlic powder, and ginger.

2 Wipe each mushroom clean with damp kitchen paper, place mushrooms in a zip-lock plastic bag, pour in the lime juice marinade, seal the bag, and shake gently to distribute the marinade. Set aside.

3 In a medium bowl, gently toss the daikon radish and carrot.

4 In a small saucepan over a medium heat, combine the rice vinegar, water, sugar, and salt. Bring to the boil, stirring to dissolve the sugar and salt.

5 Pour the vinegar mixture over the daikon and carrot, stir, and set aside for about 30 minutes.

6 In another small bowl, whisk together the plant-based mayonnaise and the Sriracha hot sauce.

7 Preheat a grill to high or set a grill pan over a high heat on your hob. Place the mushrooms on the grill, gill side down, and cook for 3 minutes. Turn them over and cook for a further 2 minutes or until the mushrooms are juicy and tender.

8 During the last minute of mushroom cooking time, place the baguette pieces on the grill, split side down, to toast.

9 Drain the pickled vegetables in a fine-mesh sieve.

10 To assemble the sandwiches, spread one-quarter of the mayonnaise mixture on one side of each baguette and add a layer of cucumber slices. Place 1 mushroom burger on each sandwich and top with one-quarter of the drained pickled vegetables. Garnish with coriander leaves (if using), and serve immediately.

INGREDIENTS

Juice of 1 lime (2 tbsp)

2 tbsp reduced-sodium tamari or soy sauce

1 tsp toasted sesame oil

½ tsp garlic powder

½ tsp ground ginger

4 large portobello mushrooms, stems removed

1 small daikon radish, peeled and shredded

1 carrot, shredded

4 tbsp rice vinegar

4 tbsp water

1 tbsp sugar

1 tsp sea salt

2 tbsp plant-based mayonnaise

1 tsp Sriracha hot sauce

4 (10cm; 4in) pieces crusty baguette, split

½ cucumber, thinly sliced

Coriander leaves (optional)

Daikon radish, also known as Japanese horseradish, is a staple in Asian cuisine. It resembles a large, white parsnip and has a mild, radish-like flavour. Smaller varieties are terrific raw or lightly pickled, while the larger roots can be thinly sliced and baked as chips or shredded and pan-fried for a unique alternative to a potato pancake.

Crispy Aubergine Subs (T) (UNDER 30)

A crispy breadcrumb coating surrounds tender aubergine slices in these subs, layered on hearty rolls with sliced hot peppers, lettuce, tomato, sliced onion, and plenty of olive oil and red wine vinegar.

SERVES 4 **PREP** 15 MINS **COOK** 15 MINS

1 Sprinkle the salt over the aubergine slices, place these in a colander, and set aside to drain for 10 minutes. Pat the slices dry, squeezing gently to remove any bitter liquid.

2 In three separate shallow bowls, place the water; flour; and breadcrumbs, Italian herb seasoning, and garlic salt.

3 Coat the aubergine slices in the following manner: dip each slice first in the water, then in the flour, quickly dip in the water again, followed by the breadcrumbs. Dredge one last time in flour, and shake off any excess. Set aside each breaded slice, and continue until all slices are coated in this way.

4 In a large frying pan over medium–high heat, heat enough olive oil (or grapeseed oil) to come 5mm (¼in) up the side of the pan for shallow frying. When the oil shimmers, add the aubergine slices a few at a time, taking care not to crowd the pan. Fry for about 2 minutes or until golden and crispy, turn over the slices and fry the other side until golden. Set the cooked slices aside on a kitchen-paper-lined baking sheet, and repeat until all the aubergine has been fried.

5 Heat a grill to high, place the split sub rolls on a baking sheet, and toast for 2–3 minutes or until golden. Rub the toasted rolls with the cut garlic clove, and drizzle them evenly with the 2 tablespoons of olive oil.

6 To assemble the sandwiches, evenly divide the aubergine slices between the rolls. Top with the tomato, shredded lettuce, and red onion slices, again evenly distributing ingredients. Place a few hot pepper slices (if using) on each sandwich, drizzle with the red wine vinegar, and serve.

INGREDIENTS

½ tsp sea salt

1 large aubergine, sliced lengthways in 5mm (¼in) slices

120ml (4fl oz) water

60g (2oz) plain flour

60g (2oz) breadcrumbs

2 tbsp Italian herb seasoning

1 tsp garlic salt

4 15cm (6in) sub rolls, sliced horizontally

1 clove garlic, halved

2 tbsp olive oil, plus more olive oil (or grapeseed oil), for frying

2 tomatoes, sliced

140g (5oz) romaine or iceberg lettuce, shredded

½ small red onion, sliced paper thin

Hot Peppadew peppers, drained and sliced (optional)

2 tbsp red wine vinegar

For *Aubergine Parm Subs,* spoon 120ml (4fl oz) of tomato pasta sauce over the sandwiches, top each with 30g (1oz) of shredded plant-based, or regular, mozzarella cheese, and grill until melted.

Oyster Mushroom Po'boys (T) (UNDER 30)

These subs, based on the classic from Louisiana, feature oyster mushrooms breaded in polenta, quickly fried until crisp, and slathered with a savoury dressing and shredded lettuce on soft rolls. Delicious!

SERVES 4 **PREP** 15 MINS **COOK** 5 MINS

1 In a small bowl, combine the mayonnaise, ketchup, grated onion, relish, and chives. Refrigerate until ready to use (this dressing can be made up to 3 days in advance).

2 In three separate shallow bowls, place the water, flour, and polenta.

3 Coat the oyster mushrooms as follows: dip each first in the water, then in the flour, quickly dip in the water again, and then dredge thoroughly in polenta. Set aside each mushroom, and continue until all the mushrooms are coated in this way.

4 In a large frying pan over a medium heat, heat enough grapeseed oil to come 2cm (¾in) up the sides of the pan.

5 Add the breaded mushrooms to the frying pan, and fry for about 3 minutes, turning once or twice, until golden on all sides. Drain on kitchen paper, and sprinkle with Old Bay seasoning and sweet paprika.

6 Pile the mushrooms generously onto the sub rolls, drizzle each sandwich with about 1 tablespoon of dressing, top with the iceberg lettuce, and serve with lemon wedges on the side.

INGREDIENTS

4 tbsp plant-based mayonnaise

1 tbsp tomato ketchup

1 tbsp grated sweet onion

1 tbsp pickled cucumber relish

1 tsp finely chopped chives

Grapeseed oil, for frying

120ml (4fl oz) water

125g (4½oz) plain flour

150g (5½oz) fine polenta (or cornmeal)

340g (¾ lb) oyster mushrooms, pulled apart into oyster-sized chunks

1 tsp Old Bay seasoning

½ tsp sweet paprika

4 15cm (6in) soft sub rolls, sliced horizontally

140g (5oz) iceberg lettuce, shredded

Lemon wedges, to serve

Oyster mushrooms

Muffuletta (T) (30 UNDER)

Muffuletta is a classic New Orleans sandwich that features a whole round loaf of crusty bread, hollowed out and slathered in a salty, savoury olive salad of the same name. Grilled vegetables are a healthy and delicious alternative to the fatty meats that usually fill this sandwich. This recipe is a great choice for picnics because you can pack a well-wrapped muffuletta, allow the flavours to meld, and slice it just before serving.

SERVES 4   **PREP** 20 MINS   **COOK** 15 MINS

1   In a medium bowl, combine the green olives, black olives, giardiniera mix, capers, celery, carrot, garlic, oregano, and 2 tablespoons of the extra-virgin olive oil. Stir in crushed chillies and set aside.

2   Preheat a grill pan or a grill for high heat.

3   In a large dish, stir together 1 tablespoon of the extra-virgin olive oil and the balsamic vinegar. Add the mushrooms and courgettes, and toss gently to coat. Sprinkle with salt and black pepper. Transfer the vegetables to the grill pan or grill, and cook for 2 minutes per side. Set aside.

4   Cut the bread in half horizontally and use your hands to pull out most of the soft insides of bread. (Save it to make breadcrumbs!)

5   Layer the grilled mushrooms and courgettes evenly over the bread, followed by the olive salad mix. Top with the baby rocket and red onion, and drizzle with the remaining olive oil and the red wine vinegar. Press the sandwich gently to pack the layers tightly. Cut the sandwich into quarters and serve, or wrap tightly in cling film for up to 4 hours.

Giardiniera is a delicious mix of pickled vegetables that usually includes cauliflower, carrot, celery, and pepperoncini (pickled peppers) preserved in vinegar. You can find it in Italian delis or online specialist shops.

INGREDIENTS

100g (3½oz) pimento-stuffed green olives, roughly chopped

60g (2oz) pitted oil-cured black olives, roughly chopped

60g (2oz) giardiniera mix, roughly chopped

2 tbsp salt-packed capers, rinsed and drained

2 tbsp finely chopped celery

2 tbsp finely chopped carrot

2 cloves garlic, finely chopped

1 tsp dried oregano

4 tbsp extra-virgin olive oil

Pinch crushed chillies

2 tbsp balsamic vinegar

3 portobello mushrooms, cut into 5mm (¼in)-thick slices

1 large courgette, sliced lengthways in 5mm (¼in)-thick slices

½ tsp sea salt

½ tsp freshly ground black pepper

1 25cm (10in) round loaf country bread, preferably semolina

45g (1½oz) baby rocket

½ small red onion, sliced paper thin

2 tbsp red wine vinegar

Falafel Burgers (UNDER 30)

These super-tasty pitta bread sandwiches pack all the deliciously spiced flavour of traditional falafel but without the deep-fried fat.

SERVES 4   PREP 15 MINS   COOK 10 MINS

1   In a small bowl, combine the flax meal and 3 tablespoons of warm water. Set aside.

2   Heat 2 tablespoons of the extra-virgin olive oil in a small frying pan over a medium heat, until it shimmers (but before it begins to smoke). Add the onion, cumin, and coriander, and sauté, stirring constantly, for 5 minutes or until the onion softens and begins to brown.

3   Stir in the salt, black pepper, lemon zest, and 2 tablespoons of lemon juice. Remove from the heat, and stir in the coriander and flat-leaf parsley.

4   In a food processor fitted with a metal blade, process the chickpeas, breadcrumbs, and onion mixture for 1 minute or until chunky. Reserve 4 tablespoons of this mixture. Continue to process, adding the flax mixture, the remaining extra-virgin olive oil, and the reserved liquid from the chickpeas, until smooth. Pulse in the reserved chickpea mixture in 1 or 2 pulses, just to evenly distribute. Divide the mixture into 8 evenly sized burgers 7.5cm (3in) wide and about 2.5cm (1in) thick.

5   In a large non-stick frying pan over a medium–high heat, heat the grapeseed oil. Add the falafel "burgers", and cook, turning once, until both sides are golden brown and the falafels are heated through.

6   In a small bowl, whisk together the tahini, garlic, and remaining lemon juice. Add 1 or 2 tablespoons of warm water or enough to make a smooth dressing.

7   Fill each pitta with 2 falafel burgers and evenly divide the plum tomatoes, romaine lettuce, and red onion between the pittas. Drizzle each pitta with one-quarter of the tahini mixture, and serve immediately.

INGREDIENTS

1 tbsp flax meal (ground flax seeds)

4 or 5 tbsp warm water

4 tbsp extra-virgin olive oil

1 onion, finely chopped

2 tsp ground cumin

1 tsp ground coriander

½ tsp sea salt

¼ tsp freshly ground black pepper

1 tsp lemon zest

Juice of 2 lemons (4 tbsp)

4 tbsp finely chopped fresh coriander

2 tbsp finely chopped fresh flat-leaf parsley

2 (400g; 14oz) cans chickpeas, drained and rinsed, 4 tbsp liquid reserved

60g (2oz) fresh breadcrumbs (from 1 or 2 slices bread)

3 tbsp grapeseed oil

2 tbsp tahini

1 clove garlic, minced

4 pitta breads, split on one side

2 plum tomatoes, finely diced

25g (scant 1oz) romaine lettuce, thinly sliced

½ red onion, thinly sliced

For *Gluten-Free Falafel,* use fresh gluten-free breadcrumbs and serve the falafel burgers on a bed of green salad.

Pan Bagnat (T)

Chickpeas and artichoke hearts are seasoned with dulse (a seaweed flake), along with capers and vinegar, for a delicious take on this Niçoise "street food" classic. And it's good to know that the chickpea spread also makes an excellent spread for crostini!

SERVES 4 PREP 20 MINS COOK NONE

1 In a food processor fitted with a metal blade, pulse the chickpeas, artichoke hearts, reserved artichoke heart marinade, capers, red wine vinegar, and dulse flakes until a rough, chunky purée consistency is reached.

2 Divide the chickpea mixture equally between the rolls. Top with tomato slices, romaine lettuce, and red onion slices.

3 Sprinkle the olives over the vegetables, drizzle each sandwich with a tablespoon of extra-virgin olive oil, and season liberally with black pepper. Serve with plenty of napkins!

Capers

INGREDIENTS

1 (400g; 14oz) can chickpeas, rinsed and drained

1 (170g; 6oz) jar marinated grilled artichoke hearts, drained, 2 tbsp marinade reserved

1 tbsp salted capers, rinsed and drained

1 tbsp red wine vinegar

1 tsp dulse flakes

4 crusty round wholemeal rolls, sliced

2 large tomatoes, sliced

4 leaves romaine lettuce

½ small red onion, sliced paper thin

2 tbsp chopped, pitted black olives

4 tbsp extra-virgin olive oil

½ tsp freshly ground black pepper

Pan bagnat means "bathed bread," which alludes to the generous amounts of olive oil slathered on this delicious sandwich. You'll need a roll that can stand up to this kind of treatment, so look for the sturdiest country bread you can find. Pan bagnat is traditionally sold in individual paper-wrapped portions, but you can pack all the fillings into a large, round loaf in the manner of muffuletta to serve a crowd. If you have extra time, add lightly steamed French green beans to this sandwich for added nutrition and crunch.

Korean Barbecue Sliders (T)

These little sandwiches pack a lot of flavor. Tempeh is steamed, smothered in a savory Korean barbecue sauce, piled on slider buns, and topped with a crunchy salad. The prep time seems long, but most of it is spent chopping ingredients and steaming and marinating the tempeh.

SERVES 4 PREP 45 MiNS COOK 10 MiNS

1 Place the tempeh in a small frying pan, cover with water, set over a medium heat, and bring to a simmer. Cover and cook for 10 minutes. Remove the lid, drain, and cool.

2 Cut the tempeh into 2 horizontal slices, and cut each of those into 4 equal pieces, so you have 8 small "burgers". Place the tempeh slices in a shallow pan that will accommodate them in a single layer.

3 In a small pan over a high heat, combine 120ml (4fl oz) of the tamari, brown sugar, garlic, sambal oelek, ginger, 1 tablespoon of the rice vinegar, and 1 teaspoon of the sesame oil. Bring to the boil.

4 In a small bowl, combine the cornflour and cold water until smooth. Add to the sauce in the pan and cook for about 1 minute or until thickened.

5 Pour the hot barbecue sauce over the tempeh, and marinate at room temperature for 30 minutes (or for up to 24 hours in the fridge).

6 Preheat a grill to high.

7 In a medium bowl, whisk together the remaining 2 teaspoons of rice vinegar, remaining 1 teaspoon of tamari, remaining 1 teaspoon of sesame oil, toasted sesame seeds, and granulated sugar. Set aside.

8 Grill the tempeh slices, turning once, until they're hot and crispy. Place 1 tempeh slice on each bun.

9 In a small bowl, toss the romaine lettuce and radishes with the dressing. Distribute equally between the sandwiches and serve immediately.

INGREDiENTS

225g (8oz) tempeh

125ml (4fl oz) reduced-sodium tamari

55g (scant 2oz) brown sugar

3 cloves garlic, finely chopped

1 tbsp sambal oelek (chilli garlic sauce)

1 tbsp finely chopped fresh ginger

1 tbsp plus 2 tsp rice vinegar

2 tsp toasted sesame oil

1 tbsp cornflour

1 tbsp cold water

1 tsp toasted sesame seeds

1 tsp granulated sugar

8 small buns, such as wholemeal rolls or slider buns

50g (1¾oz) romaine lettuce, shredded

60g (2oz) radishes, thinly sliced

Instead of using water to cook the tempeh, you could substitute vegetable stock. Also, check the ingredients on your rolls. I like to get mine from a local bakery, which ensures that they're minimally processed and completely plant based.

Soups and Stews

Soups and stews are the perfect plant-based food: healthy, hearty, and satisfying. You won't mind eating your vegetables when you're enjoying a big bowl of deeply flavoured comforting food.

Grandma's Chicken-y Noodle Soup (T) (UNDER 30)

This soup is just the thing if you or someone you love is feeling under the weather. A gently seasoned, golden broth is accented with fresh vegetables, herbs, and pasta for a perfect, comforting bowl.

SERVES 5   PREP 10 MINS   COOK 20 MINS

1   Bring a medium pan of salted water to the boil over a high heat, add the spaghetti, and cook according to the package directions until pasta is al dente. Drain, rinse with cold water, and set aside.

2   Heat the extra-virgin olive oil in a large pan over a medium–high heat. Add the onion, reduce the heat to medium, and cook, stirring frequently, for 5–10 minutes or until the onion is golden and softened.

3   Add the carrot, celery, parsnip, garlic, and salt, and cook for 3 minutes.

4   Stir in the Golden Chicken-y Stock, nutritional yeast, tamari, and black pepper. Increase the heat to high, bring to the boil, then reduce the heat to medium, and simmer for 10 minutes.

5   Stir in the spaghetti, and cook for a further minute.

6   Stir in the flat-leaf parsley and dill, and serve immediately.

INGREDIENTS

60g (2oz) spaghetti or fettuccine, broken into small pieces

1 tbsp extra-virgin olive oil

1 onion, finely chopped

1 large carrot, cut into 5mm (¼in) dice

1 or 2 sticks celery, , cut into 5mm (¼in) dice

1 small parsnip, , cut into 5mm (¼in) dice

1 clove garlic, minced

1 tsp sea salt

960ml (1¾ pints) *Golden Chicken-y Stock* or vegetable stock

1 tsp nutritional yeast

½ tsp reduced-sodium tamari

¼ tsp freshly ground black pepper

1 tbsp finely chopped fresh flat-leaf parsley

1 tbsp finely chopped fresh dill

For *Hearty Chicken-y and Rice Soup*, add 200g (7oz) shredded or cubed seitan when you add vegetable stock and use 325g (11oz) freshly cooked rice instead of cooked pasta. Once you've added your starch, serve immediately, or it will "drink" up all the stock. If you're making this in advance, or you're planning to freeze a batch, add the pasta or rice just before serving. If you don't have time to make home-made stock, choose a low- or no-salt boxed vegetable stock over bouillons or pastes, as these are salty and frequently taste unpleasant.

Ginger Kale Soup

The flavours of this soup are perfectly pitched – just enough ginger and garlic to stand up to the hearty kale and shiitake mushrooms. This soup is light and gentle enough for anyone feeling "under the weather".

SERVES 5–10 PREP 10 MINS COOK 25 MINS

1 Heat the sesame oil in a medium saucepan over a medium–high heat. Add the ginger, garlic, and white parts of the spring onions, and stir for 1 minute.

2 Add the carrot and celery, and stir for 1 minute.

3 Add the vegetable stock, tamari, and dried shiitake mushrooms, and simmer the soup for 15 minutes.

4 Add the fresh shiitake mushrooms along with the kale, and simmer, covered, for 5 minutes.

5 Remove the dried shiitake mushrooms (compost them, or save them in the freezer for stock), and remove the pan from the heat. Add the lemon juice and a little Sriracha (if using).

6 Divide the basmati rice between 4 bowls and ladle the soup over the top. Garnish each bowl with the reserved green parts of the spring onions. Serve.

INGREDIENTS

1 tbsp sesame oil

1 (5cm; 2in) piece fresh ginger, peeled and finely chopped (2 tbsp)

3 cloves garlic, peeled and finely chopped

4 spring onions, thinly sliced, white and green parts separated

1 large carrot, peeled and thinly sliced

2 large sticks celery, thinly sliced

2 litres (3½ pints) vegetable stock

1 tsp tamari

4 dried shiitake mushrooms, rinsed well

170g (6oz) fresh shiitake mushrooms, stems removed, and thinly sliced

8 leaves kale, stemmed and sliced into thin ribbons

Juice of 1 lemon (2 tbsp)

1 tsp Sriracha, or to taste (optional)

320g (11oz) cooked basmati or jasmine rice

This soup is perfect for fighting a winter cold. Ginger is a natural anti-inflammatory and painkiller; garlic has antibiotic properties; and shiitake mushrooms are valued for their immune system support, iron, and B vitamins, and are used in Eastern medicine to cure headaches. Spring onions and kale are rich in phytonutrients and help cleanse the blood, while rice is gentle on an upset stomach.

MUSHROOMS

The chewy texture and umami flavour of mushrooms – from simple white button mushrooms, to heartier chestnuts and portobello, to delicate chanterelles, to full-flavoured wild varieties, such as hen of the woods – easily stand in for meat. **Benefits** Anti-inflammatory; promote good gut bacteria; have anticancer properties; are a good source of vitamin D. **Uses** Choose fresh mushrooms free of dried ends. Eat fresh in salads, cooked in dishes, or whole as burgers. **Recipes** Truffled Mushroom Pâté; *Bánh Mì* Portobello Burgers; Mushroom, Spinach, and Shallot Quiche; Oyster Mushroom Po' boys; Mushroom Barley Soup.

Mushroom Barley Soup

Fortifying Polish mushroom barley soup, or *krupnik,* contains fresh and dried mushrooms, pearl barley, and root vegetables. Dried *borowik* mushrooms lend an authentic flavour if you can find them; otherwise, try porcini or dried forest mix mushrooms.

SERVES 5 PREP 20 MINS COOK 70 MINS

1 Bring 240ml (8fl oz) of vegetable stock to a simmer in a small pan over a medium heat.

2 Rinse the dried mushrooms, place in a small bowl, and pour hot stock on top of them. Set aside to soften for 10 minutes.

3 When the mushrooms are softened, lift them out of the stock, gently agitating to loosen any remaining soil, and lightly squeeze them dry and finely chop. Reserve the mushroom soaking liquid.

4 Heat the grapeseed oil in a large, heavy, deep-sided pan over a medium heat. Add the onions, celery, and carrots, and cook, stirring frequently, for 10 minutes.

5 Add the chopped dried mushrooms, garlic, and button mushrooms, and cook for 5 minutes.

6 Line a fine-mesh sieve with muslin, and pour the reserved mushroom soaking liquid through this into the large pan. Add the remaining vegetable stock, increase the heat to high, and bring to the boil.

7 Stir in the pearl barley, potatoes, bay leaf, 2 tablespoons of flat-leaf parsley, salt, and black pepper. Reduce the heat to medium–low, and cook for about 45 minutes more or until the barley and vegetables are tender.

8 Remove the soup from the heat, and remove the bay leaf. Stir in the lemon juice and the remaining flat-leaf parsley, taste to see if the soup needs more salt, and serve hot. This soup will keep in the fridge for up to 5 days.

INGREDIENTS

2.2 litres (3¾ pints) vegetable stock

25g (scant 1 oz) dried borowik, porcini, or forest mix mushrooms

2 tbsp grapeseed oil

2 large onions, finely chopped

4 small sticks celery, finely chopped

2 small carrots, finely chopped

3 cloves garlic, finely chopped

350g (12oz) button mushrooms, thinly sliced

200g (7oz) pearl barley

4 yellow potatoes (such as Roosters), peeled and cut in 1cm(½in) dice

1 bay leaf

4 tbsp finely chopped fresh flat-leaf parsley

1 tsp sea salt, plus extra to taste

½ tsp freshly ground black pepper

Juice of ½ lemon (1 tbsp)

If you're making a big batch of soup for the freezer, leave out the potato (which will become mealy when thawed) and increase the barley by 100g (3½oz). The soup will keep for up to 3 months when frozen in an airtight container. Don't forget to leave 2.5cm (1in) gap at the top of the container to account for expansion when the soup freezes.

Curried Cauliflower Coconut Soup

Creamy cauliflower is accented with warm spices, coconut milk, and fresh lime juice in this soup. The sunny colour and bright flavours make it a fantastic choice to simmer on a rainy afternoon.

SERVES 8 PREP 10 MINS COOK 20 MINS

1 Heat the grapeseed oil in a medium, deep-sided pan over a medium–high heat. Add the onion, carrot, celery, garlic, and salt, and cook, stirring gently, for about 5 minutes or until the onion is softened.

2 Add the cauliflower and vegetable stock. Reduce the heat to medium–low, cover, and cook for about 10 minutes or until the cauliflower is tender.

3 Stir in the coconut milk, curry powder, and sambal oelek, and cook for a further 2 minutes.

4 Remove from the heat and stir in the lime juice.

5 Using a hand-held blender, purée the soup until smooth, or transfer in batches to a blender to purée. Serve immediately, garnished with a few whole coriander leaves.

INGREDIENTS

1 tbsp grapeseed oil

1 onion, finely chopped

1 large carrot, finely chopped

2 medium sticks celery, finely chopped

1 clove garlic, minced

1 tsp sea salt

1 head cauliflower, cut into florets

960ml (1¾ pints) vegetable stock

1 (425g; 15oz) can coconut milk

1 tsp curry powder

½ tsp sambal oelek (chilli garlic paste)

Juice of ½ lime (1 tsp)

Fresh coriander leaves

If you have Jamaican or West Indian curry power, use it in this soup. Caribbean curries contain allspice rather than cardamom like Indian curries do. The allspice gives this soup a warm, gentle curry flavour that works well with the sweet, nutty notes of cauliflower and coconut milk. Indian curry makes a soup that's sharper tasting but still very good.

Smoky White Bean and Tomato Soup

Protein-packed white beans are cooked with garlic and fragrant rosemary and enhanced with tomatoes, smoked sea salt, and aromatic vegetables in this easy-to-make soup. Soak the beans for at least 6 hours beforehand to shorten the cooking time and produce creamy, evenly cooked beans.

SERVES 6–12 PREP 10 MINS COOK 40–60 MINUTES

1 Drain the soaked beans, rinse well, and place in a large, deep-sided pan or stockpot. Cover with the vegetable stock, add the garlic, rosemary, and thyme, and bring to the boil over a high heat. Reduce the heat to a simmer, and cook, partially covered, for 30 minutes. Taste the beans for tenderness; they should be almost completely cooked but slightly al dente at this point. If not, cook for a further 10–15 minutes.

2 Place the tomato purée in a small bowl, and ladle in a little of the hot stock. Stir well, and add this tomatoey mixture, along with the smoked sea salt, sea salt, onion, celery, tomatoes with juice, 4 tablespoons of extra-virgin olive oil, crushed chillies, and black pepper. Increase the heat to high, and return to the boil. Reduce the heat to medium–low, and simmer, uncovered, for 30 minutes or until the beans are completely tender.

3 Remove from the heat, and stir in the apple cider vinegar and remaining olive oil. If desired, remove 120ml (4lf oz) of the soup to a blender, purée, return to the pan, and stir (or use a hand-held blender to purée slightly). Serve hot. This soup will keep in the fridge for several days and can be frozen for up to 3 months.

INGREDIENTS

400g (14oz) dried haricot or other small white beans, soaked 6 hours or overnight

2 litres (3½ pints) vegetable stock or filtered water

4 cloves garlic, thinly sliced

1 tbsp finely chopped fresh rosemary

1 tsp finely chopped fresh thyme or ½ tsp dried

4 tbsp tomato purée

1 tsp smoked sea salt

1 tsp sea salt

1 large onion, chopped

4 small sticks celery, cut in 5mm (¼in) dice

2 (400g; 14oz) cans diced tomatoes, with juice

6 tbsp extra-virgin olive oil

¼ tsp crushed chillies

¼ tsp freshly ground black pepper

1 tbsp apple cider vinegar

The success of this recipe relies on the flavour the beans both absorb and create as they cook. Be sure your beans are fresh and well soaked for best results. "Old" beans can take forever to cook; and canned beans won't provide the same result. However, if you must have them, reduce the stock or water to 8 cups, and combine the beans, water, tomatoes, vegetables, extra-virgin olive oil, and spices, and simmer for about 20 minutes or until vegetables are tender.

Black pepper

Classic Vegetable Soup (UNDER 30)

This simple but delicious soup comes together fast. With one spoonful of this flavourful tomato vegetable broth, chock full of chunky veggies and pasta, you'll find instant comfort.

SERVES 8   PREP 10 MINS   COOK 20 MINS

1   Bring a pan of water to the boil over a medium–high heat, add the alphabet pasta, and cook according to the packet instructions. Drain and set aside.

2   Heat the grapeseed oil in a medium, deep-sided pan or stockpot over a medium–high heat. Add the onion, celery, red pepper, garlic, and salt, and cook, stirring frequently, for about 5 minutes or until softened.

3   Add the allspice, vegetable stock, tomato-vegetable juice, and frozen mixed vegetables, and bring to a boil. Reduce the heat to medium, and cook, partially covered, for 10 minutes.

4   Stir in the cooked pasta and lemon juice, cook for 1 minute or until pasta is heated through, and serve.

INGREDIENTS

85g (3oz) pasta shells, or pasta of your choice

1 tsp grapeseed oil

1 onion, finely chopped

2 large sticks celery, finely chopped

¼ large red pepper, finely chopped

1 clove garlic, minced

1 tsp sea salt

¼ tsp ground allspice

960ml (1¾ pints) vegetable stock

480ml (16fl oz) tomato-vegetable juice

350g (12oz) frozen mixed vegetables (green beans, peas, carrots, sweetcorn)

Juice of ½ lemon (1 tbsp)

This soup is very mild in flavour, making it perfect for children, for whom complex tastes can be overwhelming and sometimes unpleasant. If you want a more grown-up version, add as many fresh vegetables as you like, use black pepper and hot sauce, or add more spices to the pan when you sauté the veggies.

Tomato Rice Soup (T) (UNDER 30)

There's nothing nicer on a cold day than a bowl of hot tomato rice soup. This gently spiced, comfort food classic tastes like it has simmered all day, but takes less than half an hour to make. Whip up a double batch and put some in the freezer for easy meals at a later date.

SERVES 8 PREP 10 MINS COOK 20 MINS

1　Heat the extra-virgin olive oil in a medium, deep-sided pan or stockpot over a medium–high heat. Add the leeks, carrot, and celery, and cook for about 5 minutes or until the leek is reduced and softened.

2　Add the garlic, salt, sweet Hungarian paprika, black pepper, smoked paprika, allspice, cloves, and bay leaf, and stir for 1 minute.

3　Add the crushed tomatoes with juice and the vegetable stock, bring to the boil, and stir in the white basmati rice. Reduce the heat to medium, cover, and cook, stirring occasionally, for 15 minutes or until the rice is tender.

4　Remove the bay leaf and stir in the white wine and hot sauce (if using). Serve immediately or freeze in an airtight container for up to 3 months.

INGREDIENTS

3 tbsp extra-virgin olive oil

2 leeks, thinly sliced

1 large carrot, finely chopped

4 sticks celery, finely chopped

2 cloves garlic, finely chopped

1 tsp sea salt

1 tsp sweet Hungarian paprika

½ tsp freshly ground black pepper

¼ tsp smoked paprika

¼ tsp ground allspice

¼ tsp ground cloves

1 bay leaf

2 (400g; 14oz) cans plum tomatoes, with juice, crushed by hand

960ml (1¾ pints) vegetable stock or filtered water

95g (3oz) white basmati rice

4 tbsp dry white wine

½ tsp hot pepper sauce (optional)

If you prefer the added fibre and nutritional value of brown rice, you can replace the white basmati rice above with 195g (7oz) of cooked brown rice, added during the last 5 minutes of cooking.

Mushroom and Cabbage Borscht

This sweet and sour Ukrainian standard is made throughout Eastern and Central Europe with many variations. It's equally good served steaming hot in cold weather as it is chilled and topped with a dollop of plant-based soured cream on a warm summer's day.

SERVES 6–12 PREP 10 MINS COOK 70 MINS

1 Preheat the oven to 200°C (400°F/Gas 6).

2 Scrub the beetroots, but do not peel them. Roast the beetroots on a baking sheet lined with baking parchment for about 30 minutes or until tender. Cool slightly, peel, and cut into 5mm (¼in) dice. (Beetroots can be roasted a day in advance.)

3 Heat the grapeseed oil in a large, deep-sided pan or stockpot over a medium–high heat. Add the onions, carrots, celery, button mushrooms, sugar, and salt. Cook, stirring frequently, for 5–10 minutes or until the onions are softened and vegetables begin to colour.

4 Stir in the black pepper and tomato purée. Add the mushroom stock and reserved beetroots. Increase the heat to high, bring to the boil, and stir in the savoy cabbage. Reduce the heat to medium–low, and cook, partially covered and stirring occasionally, for about 30 minutes or until the cabbage is tender.

5 Remove from the heat, stir in the lemon juice and fresh dill, and serve. Leftovers will keep in the fridge for 3 days and can be served hot or cold.

INGREDIENTS

4 small beetroots

1 tbsp grapeseed oil

2 onions, halved and thinly sliced

2 carrots, thinly sliced

3 large sticks celery, thinly sliced

300g (10oz) white button mushrooms, thinly sliced

1 tbsp sugar

2 tsp sea salt

¼ tsp freshly ground black pepper

2 tbsp tomato purée

2 litres (3½ pints) mushroom stock

1 small head savoy cabbage, shredded

2 tbsp freshly squeezed lemon juice, or apple cider vinegar

4 tbsp finely chopped fresh dill

When you have time to cook, make a double batch of this soup and freeze it. I love taking some soup or pasta sauce out of the freezer in the morning, knowing all I have to do when I come home from work is cook some pasta or heat up the soup, and toss together a green salad.

Split-Pea Soup Ⓣ

Smoked sea salt is the secret to creating the smoky flavour that characterizes this excellent soup. This split-pea soup is thick, but not too thick, and perfectly seasoned with a long-cooked flavour.

SERVES 6–12 PREP 15 MINS COOK 40–60 MINS

1   Pick over the split peas, removing any small stones or debris. Rinse well, and set aside.

2   Heat the extra-virgin olive oil in a large, deep-sided pan or stockpot over a medium–high heat. Add the onion, carrots, celery, garlic, smoked sea salt, sea salt, thyme, and sage. Reduce the heat to medium, and cook, stirring frequently, for 5 minutes or until the vegetables are softened.

3   Add the split peas, vegetable stock, 960ml (1¾ pints) of filtered water, cayenne, and crushed chillies, and cook, stirring frequently, for a further 30 minutes or so, or until the peas are mushy and broken down.

4   Stir in the black pepper, white wine, and lemon juice. Remove from the heat, and purée with a hand-held blender or in batches in a blender. Add more water if needed to thin to the desired consistency, and taste and add more salt or black pepper if necessary.

5   Serve hot. This pea soup will keep in the freezer in an airtight container for up to 3 months.

INGREDIENTS

675g (1½lb) split peas (green, yellow, or a mix of both)

2 tbsp extra-virgin olive oil

1 large onion, chopped

2 carrots, cut into 5mm (¼in) dice

4 sticks celery, cut into 5mm (¼in) dice

2 cloves garlic, minced

1 tsp smoked sea salt

½ tsp sea salt

½ tsp dried thyme

½ tsp crumbled dried sage

1.4 litres (2½ pints) vegetable stock

1.0–1.4 litres (1¾–2½ pints) filtered water

Pinch cayenne

Pinch crushed chillies

¼ tsp freshly ground black pepper

4 tbsp dry white wine

Juice of 1 lemon (2 tbsp)

While your soup is simmering, make some *Croutons*. Preheat the oven to 200°C (400°F/Gas 6). Cut 3 or 4 slices of rye or pumpernickel bread into 5mm (¼in) cubes. Melt 2 tablespoons of a plant-based butter and toss with the bread, a pinch of salt, and a pinch of cayenne. Spread on a baking-parchment-lined baking sheet, and bake, stirring frequently, for 10 minutes or until the croutons are brown and crispy. Store any leftovers in an airtight container for up to 1 week.

Split green peas

Creamy Sweetcorn Chowder

Almonds lend a creamy consistency to this delicious soup, which is brimming with potatoes, sweetcorn, and aromatic vegetables.

SERVES 4   PREP 10 MINS   COOK 20 MINS PLUS OVERNIGHT SOAKING TIME

1   Soak the almonds in cold water overnight.

2   Discard the soaking water, rinse the nuts well, and drain. Set aside.

3   Heat the extra-virgin olive oil in a large, deep-sided pan or stockpot over a medium heat. Add the onion, and cook, stirring frequently, for 5 minutes.

4   Add the celery, red pepper, carrot, and salt, and cook for a further 3 minutes or until the vegetables are softened and just beginning to colour.

5   Add the flour and stir for 1 minute.

6   Add the vegetable stock, stirring vigorously to combine. Bring to the boil, and reserve 240ml (8fl oz) of stock. Add the potatoes and sweetcorn.

7   In a blender, combine the almonds and the reserved vegetable stock, and blend until smooth. Stir the almond mixture into the soup, and simmer until the potatoes are tender.

8   Add the plant-based butter, lemon juice, hot sauce, and black pepper. Serve immediately.

INGREDIENTS

150g (5½oz) blanched almonds

2 tbsp extra-virgin olive oil

1 large onion, finely chopped

2 small sticks celery, finely chopped

½ red pepper, finely chopped

1 carrot, finely chopped

1 tsp sea salt

2 tbsp plain flour

1.4 litres (2½ pints) light vegetable stock

3 large potatoes (such as Roosters), peeled and cut into 5mm (¼in) dice

4 ears of sweetcorn, stripped of their corn kernels

1 tbsp plant-based butter

1 tsp freshly squeezed lemon juice

½ tsp hot sauce, such as Sriracha

¼ tsp freshly ground black pepper

For *Gluten-Free Corn Chowder,* omit the flour. When the potatoes are tender, whisk 2 tablespoons of cornflour with 2 tablespoons of cold water until smooth and then stir into the soup to thicken.

Beans and Legumes

Beans pack a lot of protein into a small package. Chickpeas are the basis of hummus, and many dried beans add nutrition to soups, stews, burgers, and more. When shopping for dried beans, avoid buying bags where you can see broken or shrivelled beans. Soak dried beans overnight, or quick-soak them by boiling for 10 minutes and soaking for 1 hour. Rinse, drain, and proceed with the recipe.

Sugar-snap peas

Fresh Beans

	FRENCH BEANS	GARDEN PEAS	BROAD BEANS	RUNNER BEANS	MANGETOUT	SUGAR-SNAP PEAS
USES	Lightly steam or blanch slender, firm, dark green beans. Alternatively, sauté or toss with vinaigrette.	Opt for unshelled fresh peas, shell them yourself, and blanch or steam for 2 or 3 minutes. Drizzle with olive oil, salt, and pepper. Add fresh herbs, such as tarragon, chives, parsley, or chervil.	Opt for unshelled beans with firm, dark green pods. Steam or blanch shelled beans for 5 minutes. Use in vegetable soups or stews, or sauté.	Steam, blanch, or stir-fry firm, crisp, brightly coloured beans. Use in salads and vegetable soups, or sauté or roast.	Choose light green, firm, smooth pods with small peas visible inside. Scrub well, and pull the string-like fibre from one end to remove. Serve raw, steamed, blanched, sautéed, or stir-fried.	Choose chubby, firm pods with a bright green colo[ur]. Scrub well, pull t[he] string-like fibre fr[om] one end to remov[e] and cut off both ends. Add to sala[ds], stir-fries, or soup[s].
GOOD SOURCE OF ...	Antioxidants, fibre, vitamins K, C, B₂, B₁, folate, and iron.	Protein, phytonutrients, antioxidants, omega-3 fats, fibre, manganese, copper, phosphorus, folate, vitamins K, B₁, B₂, B₃, B₆, iron, and potassium.	Protein, fibre, copper, manganese, folate, iron, potassium, phosphorus, and vitamins B₁ and B₆.	Antioxidants, fibre, vitamins K, C, B₂, B₁, folate, and iron.	Fibre, vitamins B₁, B₂, B₆, A, C, K, magnesium, phosphorus, potassium, fibre, folate, iron, and manganese.	Fibre, vitamins C and K, iron, magnesium, phosphorus, potassium, and antioxidants.

French beans

Peas

Black-eyed peas

Peanuts

Dried Beans and Legumes

	BLACK-EYED PEAS	CHICKPEAS	KIDNEY BEANS	LENTILS	MUNG BEANS	PEANUTS	SOYBEANS
...S	Pair with collard greens, brussel tops or kale, potatoes, smoked salt or paprika, corn, summer squash, butter or broad beans, garlic, onions, and tomatoes.	Use in hummus, salads, burgers, soups, stews, and pasta dishes.	Enjoy in chillies, soups, stews, and salads.	Lentils don't need soaking, and cook quickly. Green lentils are firm and best in soups and salads. Brown lentils are tender and good in soups, stews, and as a ground beef substitute. Red lentils are best in soups and purées.	Pair with coconut, curries, soups, stews, garlic, onions, and ginger.	Enjoy as a snack, or use in sauces or stews. Pair with strong flavours, such as ginger and garlic.	Use in burgers, soups, stews, or purées.
...ND ...RCE OF ...	Protein, fibre, vitamins A and K, B vitamins, and potassium.	Protein, fibre, copper, folate, and manganese.	Protein, vitamin , B_6, pantothenic acid, iron, magnesium, phosphorus, potassium, vitamins C, B_1, B_2, B_3, folate, copper, and manganese.	Protein, iron, phosphorus, copper, fibre, folate, and manganese.	Protein, fibre, vitamins C and B_1, folate, calcium, magnesium, phosphorus, potassium, and manganese.	Protein, fibre, vitamin B_3, manganese, iron, and calcium.	Protein, fibre, vitamins C and B_1, folate, calcium, magnesium, phosphorus, potassium, and manganese.

Chickpeas

Lentils

Tom Yum Soup

Tom yum has an addictive flavour that's tart, tangy, and spicy all at once, with the exotic notes of lemongrass, galangal (Thai ginger), Kaffir lime, and plenty of hot chillies. It's surprisingly comforting and is especially wonderful when you're suffering from a cold.

SERVES 4   PREP 15 MINS   COOK 10 MINS

1 Peel the tough outer layer from the lemongrass stalks, and smash the stalks with the flat side of your knife to tenderize. Chop finely.

2 Heat the coconut oil in a medium saucepan over a medium–high heat. Add the lemongrass, galangal, Kaffir lime leaves, hot red chilli, and sambal oelek, and stir for 1 minute.

3 Add the Golden Chicken-y Stock, button mushrooms, tofu, and tamari, and bring to the boil.

4 Reduce the heat to medium and cook for 10 minutes or until the mushrooms are tender.

5 Remove from the heat, remove and discard the lime leaves, stir in the lime juice and coriander, and serve. This soup can be made 1 day in advance. Add the lime juice and coriander just before serving.

INGREDIENTS

2 large stalks fresh lemongrass

1 tsp coconut oil or grapeseed oil

2 tbsp finely chopped galangal or ginger

3 Kaffir lime leaves, fresh or frozen, or the zest of 1 medium lime

1 small fresh hot red chilli such as Thai bird's eye chilli, thinly sliced

2 tsp sambal oelek (chilli garlic sauce)

1.2 litres (2 pints) *Golden Chicken-y Stock* or vegetable stock

175g (6oz) white button mushrooms, sliced

115g (4oz) firm silken tofu, cut into 1cm (½in) cubes

2 tbsp reduced-sodium tamari

Juice of 1½ limes (2 tbsp)

4 tbsp finely chopped fresh coriander

Tom yum is traditionally made with Thai curry paste, an ingredient that almost always contains shrimp paste or fish sauce. A quick online search yields dozens of recipes for home-made vegetarian versions of such pastes, so if you like this recipe and want to create something more authentic, you can try making your own at home. If you don't want a very spicy soup, add half of a 400g (14oz) can of full-fat coconut milk, and reduce the amount of sambal oelek to 1 teaspoon, or to taste. To reduce the heat factor more, you also can halve the fresh chilli, sauté it, and remove it before serving.

Miso Udon Bowl

Miso soup makes the base for a nourishing meal with the addition of mushrooms, tofu, tender baby spinach leaves, and hearty udon noodles.

SERVES 4   PREP 5 MINS   COOK 20 MINS

1   Cook the udon noodles in boiling water according to the packet instructions. Drain in a colander, rinse with cold water, and set aside.

2   Heat kombu stock in a small saucepan over a medium–high heat until simmering.

3   Heat the grapeseed oil in a medium pan over a medium–high heat. Add the shiitake mushrooms and sauté for 1 minute.

4   Add the ginger and garlic, and sauté for 30 seconds. Add the heated stock, bring to the boil, and then reduce the heat to a simmer. Stir in the wakame and tofu, and cook for 5 minutes.

5   Ladle 120ml (4fl oz) of soup into a small bowl, and whisk in the miso paste.

6   Stir the baby spinach and noodles into the soup, and cook for 1 minute or until the spinach has wilted. Remove from the heat and stir in the miso mixture. Serve immediately.

INGREDIENTS

225g (8oz) udon noodles

960ml (1¾ pints) kombu stock or vegetable stock

1 tsp grapeseed oil

115g (4oz) shiitake mushrooms, stemmed and thinly sliced

1 (2.5cm; 1in) piece fresh ginger, finely grated (2 tbsp)

1 clove garlic, minced

80g (3oz) wakame (seaweed)

175g (6oz) firm silken tofu, cut into 1cm (½in) cubes

2 tbsp white (shiro) miso paste

140g (5oz) baby spinach

For *Quick Miso Soup,* heat 240ml (8fl oz) of kombu or vegetable stock per serving. Ladle 120ml (4fl oz) of simmering stock into a small bowl and stir in 1 teaspoon of white miso paste per serving. If desired, add 4 tablespoons of cubed tofu per serving to the soup as it simmers.

GINGER

Ginger is an ancient root spice with hot and tangy flavour that pairs well with chillies, coconut, garlic, limes, and green onions. It can alleviate many types of pain and inflammation. **Benefits** Is an anti-inflammatory; aids digestive health; counters nausea; and increases absorption of nutrients. **Uses** Choose fresh whole roots or frozen as a paste, and use in Asian dishes, juice with fresh fruits and vegetables, or add to baked goods. **Recipes** Ginger Kale Soup, Sesame Ginger Broccoli, Lentil and Vegetable Dhal, Triple-Ginger Treacle Cookies, Pumpkin Gingerbread Cupcakes.

Meaty Mushroom Stew (T)

This mushroom stew is rich, meaty-tasting, and delicious, thanks to a mix of mushrooms, including hen of the woods varieties, which lend a chicken-y texture and incredible flavour to this cold-weather delight.

SERVES 6 PREP 15 MINS COOK 30 MINS

1 Heat 2 tablespoons of extra-virgin olive oil in a 4-litre (7-pint) large, deep-sided pan or stockpot over a medium–high heat. Add the onions and shallot, and cook, stirring frequently, for 5 minutes.

2 Add the celery, carrot, the mushrooms, and garlic, and cook, stirring frequently, for about 10 minutes or until the mushrooms begin to turn golden. Add the remaining olive oil as the mushrooms begin to stick to the pan.

3 Stir in the salt, black pepper, sweet Hungarian paprika, thyme, and dill.

4 Add the flour to the mushroom mixture and stir for 2 minutes.

5 Add 720ml (1 pint 4fl oz) of Mushroom Stock, red wine, and potato, and bring to a boil. Reduce the heat to medium and cook, stirring often, for 10 minutes or until the stew is thickened and vegetables are tender. Add additional stock if stew is too thick for your liking.

6 Remove from the heat, and stir in the flat-leaf parsley and balsamic vinegar. Taste, add more salt and black pepper if needed, and serve. The stew will keep in the fridge for up to 5 days and is even more delicious the next day.

INGREDIENTS

4 tbsp extra-virgin olive oil

2 onions, finely chopped

1 small shallot, halved and finely chopped

2 sticks celery, finely chopped

1 large carrot, finely chopped

300g (10oz) tiny white button mushrooms, halved

225g (8oz) hen of the woods mushrooms, sliced

225g (8oz) fresh chanterelle mushrooms, sliced

3 cloves garlic, finely chopped

1 tsp sea salt, plus more to taste

½ tsp freshly ground black pepper, plus more to taste

1 tbsp sweet Hungarian paprika

1 tsp dried thyme

1 tsp dried dill

2 tbsp plain flour

720–960ml (1 pint 4fl oz–1¾ pints) *Mushroom Stock*

240ml (8fl oz) dry red wine

1 large Desiree potato, peeled and diced

4 tbsp finely chopped fresh flat-leaf parsley

1 tbsp balsamic vinegar

Feel free to experiment with different kinds of mushrooms in this stew – trumpet, oyster, morels, or even just chestnut and shiitakes if you aren't on a wild mushroom budget. You also can substitute 60g (2oz) of dried chanterelles if you can't find fresh or you can use dried porcini instead.

Gumbo Ⓣ

Gumbo – or gumbo filé, to give it its true name – is an amazing Creole stew layered with flavour. Oyster mushrooms and veggie Andouille sausage swim in a fragrant, deliciously spiced, roux-thickened broth. The ingredient list seems long, but once your veggies are chopped and the spices are measured out, making this is a doddle. Take the time to make it right and everyone you feed will love you forever.

SERVES 5 PREP 25 MINS COOK 90 MINS

1 Heat the grapeseed oil in a large, deep-sided pan or stockpot over a medium heat. Whisk in the flour until well combined. Using a wooden spoon, stir the roux constantly over a medium heat until mixture is a golden, caramel brown colour.

2 Stir in the onion, celery, peppers, and cook, stirring frequently, for a further 10 minutes. Reduce the heat to medium–low if necessary to prevent burning.

3 Add half of the garlic, stir for 1 minute, and bring to a simmer.

4 Stir in the vegetable stock, bring to the boil, and reduce the heat to a gentle simmer.

5 Meanwhile, heat the extra-virgin olive oil in a wide frying pan over a medium heat. Add the sliced veggie Andouille sausage and stir for 1 minute. Using a slotted spoon, transfer the sausage to a bowl and set aside.

6 Add the oyster mushrooms and remaining garlic to the frying pan, and stir until the mushrooms are golden.

7 Add the sweet paprika, salt, Creole seasoning, oregano, thyme, black pepper, allspice, and cayenne, and stir for 1 minute.

8 Add the amber beer, increase the heat to high, and stir vigorously to deglaze the pan, releasing any browned bits stuck to the pan.

9 Stir the mushroom mixture into the large pan or stockpot along with the fire-roasted tomatoes, balsamic vinegar, vegan Worcestershire sauce, and hot sauce. Bring to the boil, reduce the heat to low or medium–low, and simmer for 1 hour, stirring occasionally and adjusting heat as necessary.

10 Stir in the reserved Andouille sausage along with the filé powder, and simmer for 5 minutes.

11 Stir in the spring onions, flat-leaf parsley, and dark rum (if using). Ladle into bowls over hot, cooked rice or serve with plenty of French bread, offering extra filé powder and hot sauce at the table.

INGREDIENTS

120ml (4fl oz) grapeseed oil

60g (2oz) plain flour

1 large onion, finely chopped

4 sticks celery, finely chopped

1 green pepper, ribs and seeds removed, and finely chopped

1 red pepper, ribs and seeds removed, and finely chopped

6 cloves garlic, chopped

1.4 litres (2½ pints) vegetable stock

4 tbsp extra-virgin olive oil

2 veggie Andouille sausages, thinly sliced

450g (1lb) oyster mushrooms, roughly chopped

1 tsp sweet paprika

1 tsp sea salt

½ tsp Creole seasoning

½ tsp dried oregano

½ tsp dried thyme

½ tsp freshly ground black pepper

¼ tsp ground allspice

Pinch cayenne

350ml (12fl oz) amber beer

1 (400g; 14oz) can diced fire-roasted tomatoes, with juice

1 tbsp balsamic vinegar

1 tbsp vegan Worcestershire sauce

1 tsp Louisiana hot sauce

2 tsp filé powder

8 tbsp thinly sliced spring onions

4 tbsp finely chopped fresh flat-leaf parsley

2 tbsp dark rum (optional)

Minestrone

A *minestre* is a soup thickened with beans, pasta, or even day-old country bread. Beans and potatoes thicken this hearty vegetable soup nicely. Minestrone makes a nourishing and comforting supper with the addition of nothing more than a loaf of good bread and a simple green salad.

SERVES 5 PREP 15 MINS COOK 60 MINS

1 Heat 2 tablespoons of extra-virgin olive oil in a large, deep-sided pan or stockpot over a medium–high heat. Add the red onion, carrots, and celery, and cook, stirring often, for 5 minutes.

2 Add 2 cloves of the garlic and stir for 1 minute more.

3 Stir in the tomato purée, mix well, and add vegetable stock. Bring to the boil.

4 Add the potato, bay leaf, and salt. Reduce the heat to a simmer and cook for 15 minutes.

5 Meanwhile, in a wide frying pan over a medium–high heat, heat the remaining 2 tablespoons of extra-virgin olive oil. Add the remaining garlic and stir for 30 seconds.

6 Add the savoy cabbage, and cook, stirring frequently, for about 10 minutes or until the cabbage is softened.

7 Add the cabbage to the large pan along with the cannellini beans, borlotti beans, tomatoes with juice, and 2 tablespoons of flat-leaf parsley, and simmer for 30 minutes.

8 Stir in the red wine vinegar and black pepper. Allow the soup to rest for 10 minutes, remove the bay leaf, stir in the remaining flat-leaf parsley. Serve.

INGREDIENTS

4 tbsp extra-virgin olive oil

1 large red onion, cut into small dice

3 carrots, cut into small dice

4 large sticks celery, cut into small dice

5 cloves garlic, minced

3 tbsp tomato purée

1.4 litres (2½ pints) vegetable stock

1 large potato, such as Desiree, peeled and cut in small dice

1 bay leaf

1 tsp sea salt, plus more to taste

½ small head savoy cabbage, thinly sliced

1 (400g; 14oz) can cannellini beans, rinsed and drained

1 (400g; 14oz) can borlotti beans, rinsed and drained

2 (400g; 14oz) cans diced tomatoes, with juice

4 tbsp finely chopped fresh flat-leaf parsley

1 tbsp red wine vinegar

½ tsp freshly ground black pepper

Feel free to vary your minestrone seasonally based on what vegetables are fresh and available. For *Minestrone with Pasta*, eliminate the potato, increase the broth by 480ml (16fl oz), and add 100g (3½oz) small pasta, such as ditalini, during the last 15 minutes of cooking. Leftover minestrone is wonderful hot or at room temperature. When my grandmother was a little girl, her father would stir the leftover vegetables and beans from a pot of minestrone into some hot polenta, cool it in a baking dish, and cut it into wedges for the children to eat for lunch.

Carrots

Giambotta (italian Summer Vegetable Stew)

My grandmother often made this summer vegetable stew with ingredients fresh from the garden, and it was amazing. Every italian American family i know has their own way of making this tomato-based stew. i like to wait for late summer to make *giambotta*, when tomatoes and peppers are sweet and courgettes and aubergines are in season.

SERVES 5 PREP 20 MINS COOK 60 MINS

1 In a colander, toss the aubergine with 1 teaspoon of the salt, and set aside to drain over a bowl. After 30 minutes, discard the liquid, rinse the aubergine, and gently squeeze excess water from the aubergine. Set aside.

2 Bring a medium pan of salted water to the boil over a high heat. Add the green beans and cook for 5 minutes. Using a slotted spoon, transfer the beans to a bowl of iced water, immediately drain, and set aside.

3 In the same pan, cook the potatoes for about 15 minutes or until tender. Remove to a chopping board to cool slightly. Meanwhile, core the plum tomatoes and score a small X in the bottom of each one.

4 When the potatoes are done, using the same pan of boiling water and adding a little more if necessary, work in batches to quickly blanch the tomatoes, about 1 minute at a time, transferring them to an iced bath immediately after. Peel the tomatoes, deseed, and cut into slices, reserving tomatoes and juice in a bowl.

5 Heat the extra-virgin olive oil in a 4-litre (7-pint) large, deep-sided pan or stockpot over a medium–high heat. Add the onions and cook for 5 minutes.

6 Add the garlic and cook for 1 minute.

7 Stir in the aubergine and cook for another 5 minutes, stirring frequently to avoid the vegetables sticking while cooking.

8 Stir in the tomatoes, red peppers, courgettes, green beans, and remaining salt, reduce the heat to medium–low, and simmer for 20 minutes.

9 Meanwhile, peel the potatoes and cut into quarters. When the vegetables are tender, stir in the potatoes and black pepper, and cook for 5 minutes. Remove from the heat and stir in the basil. Serve hot, warm, or cold.

INGREDIENTS

1 aubergine, quartered and cut in 1cm (½in) slices

2 tsp sea salt

225g (8oz) fine green beans, trimmed

3 large white potatoes, unpeeled

12 plum tomatoes

4 tbsp extra-virgin olive oil

2 large onions, halved and thinly sliced

2 cloves garlic, smashed and roughly chopped

2 red peppers, ribs and seeds removed, and thinly sliced

2 large courgettes, halved and thinly sliced

½ tsp freshly ground black pepper

4 tbsp fresh basil leaves

For *Vegetable Stew with Polenta*, leave out the potatoes and serve the stew over hot, cooked polenta.

Lentil and Vegetable Dhal

Lentil dhal gets a makeover here with the addition of cauliflower and spinach. Before you start making the dhal, whip up a quick batch of dough and make your own fresh naan – you'll have the most amazing feast ready in less than an hour.

SERVES 4 **PREP** 10 MiNS **COOK** 30 MiNS

1. Heat coconut oil in a large, deep-sided pot or stockpot over a medium-high heat. Add the onion, ginger, and garlic, and cook, stirring frequently, for 5 minutes. Reduce the heat if necessary to prevent burning.

2. Stir in the vegetable stock, red lentils, cauliflower, turmeric, coriander, cumin, cinnamon, and cayenne. Bring to the boil, reduce the heat, and simmer for 20 minutes.

3. When the lentils and cauliflower are tender, squeeze the tomato purée into a small bowl. Ladle a little bit of broth into the bowl, stir until smooth, and then stir this mixture back into the soup pan.

4. Add the spinach, salt, lime juice, and 1 tablespoon or chopped coriander, and simmer for 5 minutes.

5. Whisk the remaining chopped coriander into the yogurt, and serve dhal warm with a dollop of this coriander yogurt.

INGREDIENTS

2 tbsp coconut oil

1 large onion, finely chopped

1 tbsp finely chopped fresh ginger

2 cloves garlic, minced

1.4 litres (2½ pints) vegetable stock

200g (7oz) red lentils, picked over and rinsed

⅓ small head cauliflower, separated into florets and finely chopped

1 tbsp ground turmeric

1 tsp ground coriander

½ tsp ground cumin

¼ tsp ground cinnamon

¼ tsp cayenne

2 tbsp tomato purée

1 bunch spinach, washed well, stemmed, and thinly sliced

1 tsp sea salt

Juice of 1 lime (1 tbsp)

2 tbsp finely chopped fresh coriander

125g (4½oz) plant-based plain yogurt

Make *Naan* to serve with dhal. Before making dhal, in a large bowl, whisk together 300g (10oz) plain flour with 1 packet of fast-acting instant yeast, 2 teaspoons of salt, and 1 teaspoon of baking powder. In a medium bowl, whisk together 180ml (6fl oz) of warm water, 3 tablespoons of plain plant-based yogurt, and 2 tablespoons of melted coconut oil. Stir the wet ingredients into the dry and knead with your hands for 1 or 2 minutes to form a sticky dough. Let the dough rise at room temperature for 45 minutes or until doubled. Ten minutes before serving, heat a large cast-iron frying pan over a medium heat. Divide the dough into 6 balls and stretch into teardrop shapes about 12cm (5in) long. Dampen the dough with a little water, add to the hot pan a few at a time, and cook for about 1 minute per side. Brush the pan with ½ teaspoon grapeseed oil to keep the naan from sticking if necessary.

Green Curry Vegetable Stew

There's something special about the fragrance and flavour of green curry spices, Kaffir lime, ginger, and coconut milk; and the bounty of vegetables in this dish is so good for you. Treat yourself to a steaming bowl of this wonderful, fragrant stew as often as you can.

SERVES 3 PREP 10 MINS COOK 20 MINS

1 Heat virgin coconut oil in a large saucepan over a medium–high heat. Add the garlic, ginger, Thai green curry paste, and hot chilli, and stir for 1 minute.

2 Add the onion, shiitake mushrooms, and salt, and stir for a further 2 minutes.

3 Stir in the coconut milk, vegetable stock, Kaffir lime leaves, and carrot. Bring to the boil, reduce the heat to a simmer, and cook for 5 minutes.

4 Stir in the courgettes and simmer for 5 minutes.

5 Stir in the baby spinach, spring onion, and coriander, and cook for a further minute. Remove from the heat, and serve.

INGREDIENTS

2 tbsp virgin coconut oil

2 cloves garlic, finely chopped

1 (2.5–5cm; 1–2in) piece ginger, peeled and grated (1 or 2 tbsp)

2 tbsp Thai green curry paste

1 hot chilli, such as Serrano or bird's eye, deseeded and thinly sliced

1 onion, halved and thinly sliced

225g (8oz) shiitake mushrooms, stemmed and thinly sliced

1 tsp sea salt, plus more to taste

1 (400g; 14oz) can full-fat, best-quality Thai coconut milk

240ml (8fl oz) vegetable stock or water

2 Kaffir lime leaves, or 1 tbsp grated lime zest

115g (4oz) carrot, thinly sliced

1 large courgette, halved and thinly sliced

300g (10oz) baby spinach

50g (1¾oz) spring onions, thinly sliced

4 tbsp finely chopped fresh coriander

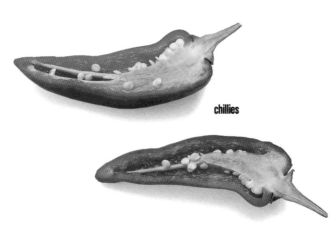

chillies

This stew is easy to vary. Use button mushrooms instead of shiitakes, or try red curry paste instead of green. Add baby pak choi, sautéed aubergine, daikon radish, or burdock root, or stir in cubed firm tofu with carrot. For a *Green Curry Dinner*, serve this stew over some hot, cooked rice or rice noodles.

Hearty Chilli (T) (UNDER 30)

I come from a family who loves chilli and making a pot on a snowy day is almost standard for us. My meat-free version of this family favourite is packed with beans, mushrooms, peppers, onions, and tomatoes, with a bit of a kick from some hot pepper sauce.

SERVES 6 PREP 10 MINS COOK 45 MINS

1 Heat the extra-virgin olive oil in a large, deep-sided pan or stockpot over a medium heat. Add the onions, and red and yellow peppers, and cook, stirring often, for 10 minutes.

2 Stir in the mushrooms, garlic, salt, chilli powder, cumin, Anaheim chilli powder, oregano, and black pepper, and cook, stirring frequently, for 10 minutes.

3 Add the tomatoes with their juice, stir, and bring to a boil. Reduce the heat to low or medium–low, and cook at a gently bubbling simmer, uncovered, for about 30 minutes or until the peppers and onions are very tender.

4 Stir in the kidney beans, black beans, and hot pepper sauce, and cook for 5 minutes. Serve in big bowls with a spoonful of plant-based soured cream (if using) and plenty of tortilla chips (if using).

INGREDIENTS

4 tbsp extra-virgin olive oil

2 large onions, diced

4 red peppers, ribs and seeds removed, and diced

2 yellow peppers, ribs and seeds removed, and diced

300g (10oz) chestnut mushrooms, thinly sliced

4 cloves garlic, finely chopped

1 tsp sea salt

2 tbsp chilli powder

1 tsp ground cumin

1 tsp Anaheim chilli powder

1 tsp dried oregano

1 tsp freshly ground black pepper

4 (400g; 14oz) cans diced tomatoes, with juice

2 (400g; 14oz) cans kidney beans, rinsed and drained

2 (400g; 14oz) cans black beans, rinsed and drained

1 tbsp habanero hot pepper sauce, plus more for serving

Plant-based soured cream (optional)

Tortilla chips (optional)

My mother adds about 4 tablespoons of tequila to her chilli during the last 5 minutes of cooking. It adds that delicious "What is that ingredient?" note. Try it, unless you're cooking for children or pregnant women.

Black-Eyed Pea Stew

What I call the "Holy Trinity" of Louisiana cooking – celery, onions, and pepper – provides the flavour base in this tomato-rich, Creole-style stew, while a little veggie Andouille sausage pumps up the protein content and spice.

SERVES 8　PREP 10 MINS　COOK 20 MINS

1　Heat the extra-virgin olive oil in a large saucepan over a medium–high heat. Add the onion, celery, and green pepper, and cook, stirring frequently and adjusting the heat as necessary, for 5 minutes.

2　Stir in the veggie Andouille sausage and cook for 2 minutes.

3　Add the garlic, Creole seasoning, salt, and black pepper, and stir for 1 minute.

4　Stir in the diced tomatoes with their juice, red wine, and black-eyed peas. Reduce the heat to medium and cook, stirring frequently, for 10 minutes.

5　When the vegetables are tender, remove from the heat; stir in the flat-leaf parsley, apple cider vinegar, and hot sauce; and serve.

The level of heat in Andouille sausage varies, so if you're sensitive to spice, you might want to reduce the Creole seasoning or hot sauce. Taste and adjust as you cook. You can serve this quick-and-easy stew over hot, cooked rice or sop it up with some good, crusty French bread. All you need is a salad dressed with a simple vinaigrette and dinner is served. This stew freezes well, so make a double batch and keep in the freezer for 3 months.

INGREDIENTS

2 tbsp extra-virgin olive oil

1 large sweet onion, finely chopped

3 sticks celery, finely chopped

1 large green pepper, ribs and seeds removed, and finely chopped

2 veggie Andouille sausages, removed from casing (if necessary) and sliced or crumbled

3 cloves garlic, finely chopped

1 tbsp Creole seasoning

1 tsp sea salt, plus more to taste

½ tsp freshly ground black pepper, plus more to taste

2 (400g; 14oz) cans diced tomatoes, with juice

240ml (8fl oz) dry red wine

2 (400g; 14oz) cans black-eyed peas, rinsed and drained

4 tbsp finely chopped fresh flat-leaf parsley

1 tbsp apple cider vinegar

1 tsp Louisiana hot pepper sauce

Jerusalem Artichoke Soup

Jerusalem artichokes combine the nutty flavour of an artichoke with the creamy consistency of a potato, making them perfect for this comforting soup.

SERVES 4 PREP 15 MINS COOK 35–45 MINS

1 Heat virgin grapeseed oil in a large, deep-sided pan or stockpot over a medium heat. Add the onions, and cook, stirring frequently, for 5–10 minutes or until soft and translucent.

2 Add the garlic and cook for 30 seconds or until fragrant.

3 Stir in the Jerusalem artichokes, carrots, and salt, cover, reduce the heat to low, and cook, stirring frequently, for 10–15 minutes or until the vegetables are softened.

4 Add the vegetable stock, thyme, and saffron. Bring to the boil, reduce the heat to a simmer, and cook for 20 minutes or until the vegetables are soft.

5 Cool briefly and purée until smooth using a hand-held blender or by transferring to a food processor or blender in batches if necessary.

6 Stir in the lemon juice, season to taste with more salt and black pepper, and serve in warm bowls with a drizzle of olive oil on top.

INGREDIENTS

2 tbsp virgin grapeseed oil or extra-virgin olive oil, plus more for garnish

2 onions, chopped

3 cloves garlic, finely chopped

350g (12oz) Jerusalem artichokes, peeled or scrubbed well, and coarsely chopped

1 carrot, peeled and coarsely chopped

½ tsp sea salt, plus more to taste

1.2 litres (2 pints) hot vegetable stock

1 tbsp chopped fresh thyme leaves, or 1½ tsp dried

Large pinch (about 30 strands) saffron

Juice of ½ lemon (2 tbsp)

¼ tsp freshly ground black pepper, or to taste

Jerusalem artichokes

Posole  T (UNDER 30)

This updated version of the traditionally long-simmered Mexican stew can be made in under half an hour, but it packs a huge punch of savoury chilli flavour. Hominy is a type of dried maize that you can buy dried or canned. Here we use canned hominy and quickly sautéed vegetables, which are bathed in a savoury broth of ground New Mexico chillies and spices.

SERVES 4–6   PREP 10 MINS   COOK 20 MINS

1 Heat the olive oil in a large, deep-sided pan or stockpot over a medium-high heat. Add the onion and cook, stirring frequently and adjusting heat as necessary, for 5 minutes.

2 Stir in the carrots and mushrooms, and cook for 5 minutes.

3 Add the garlic and stir for 1 minute.

4 Sprinkle the chilli powder, cumin, salt, and oregano over the vegetable mixture and stir for 30 seconds.

5 Add the vegetable stock, bring to a simmer, and cook for 5 minutes.

6 Add the hominy and courgette, bring to the boil, reduce the heat to medium–low, and cook for 10 minutes.

7 Remove from the heat, stir in the lime juice and coriander and serve.

INGREDIENTS

3 tbsp olive oil

1 large onion, finely chopped

2 carrots, cut into 5mm (¼in) rounds

225g (8oz) chestnut mushrooms, thinly sliced

2 cloves garlic, finely chopped

3 tbsp dried ground New Mexico chilli powder

1 tsp ground cumin

1 tsp sea salt

½ tsp dried oregano

960ml (1¾ pints) vegetable stock

425g (15oz) canned hominy, rinsed and drained

1 courgette, trimmed, quartered lengthways, and cut into 1cm (½in) chunks

Juice of 1 lime (1 tbsp)

2 tbsp finely chopped fresh coriander

Posole is traditionally served for special occasions. Putting little bowls on the table with different garnishes and letting guests sort out their own bowls is a fun way to make this party dish really festive. Try thinly sliced radishes, jalapeños, spring onions, shredded cabbage or romaine lettuce, sliced avocado, lime wedges, plant-based soured cream, hot sauce, and tortilla chips or tostadas.

Salads

Delight in the unexpected flavours and textures of the salads in this section. Choose a hearty main-dish salad or something lighter to get things started.

Wilted Spinach Salad

Baby spinach is quickly wilted in a flavourful dressing of shiitake mushrooms accented with walnuts, Dijon mustard, and tangy apple cider vinegar.

SERVES 3 PREP 5 MINS COOK 10 MINS

1   Heat the sesame oil in a medium frying pan over a medium–high heat. Add the shiitake mushrooms and stir for 2 minutes.

2   Add the walnuts and garlic, and stir for 2 minutes. Adjust the heat as needed.

3   Add the onion, salt, mustard, and apple cider vinegar, and bring to the boil. Remove from the heat.

4   Slowly stir in the extra-virgin olive oil. Add the baby spinach, toss with hot dressing until wilted, season with black pepper, and serve.

For a *Dinner Salad*, choose a hearty green, such as baby kale, then add some cooked quinoa, with steamed vegetables or chopped, raw veggies, and a can of rinsed and drained beans. Serve with Romesco Sauce.

INGREDIENTS

1 tbsp sesame oil

115g (4oz) shiitake mushrooms, stemmed and thinly sliced

110g (3½oz) walnuts, finely chopped

1 clove garlic, finely chopped

1 small red onion, halved and thinly sliced

½ tsp sea salt

1 tbsp wholegrain Dijon mustard

4 tbsp apple cider vinegar

8 tbsp extra-virgin olive oil

360g (12oz) baby spinach, washed and spun dry

½ tsp freshly ground black pepper

Celeriac Remoulade

Whether you call it celeriac or celery root, this knobbly vegetable is grated and tossed in a sauce for a quick, healthy, and delicious no-cook salad. Serve it over crisp lettuce or watercress or spread on toast.

SERVES 10 PREP 10 MINS COOK NONE

1   In a large bowl, whisk together the mayo, extra-virgin olive oil, Dijon mustard, lemon juice, cornichon pickles, grated onion, flat-leaf parsley, salt, and black pepper. Set the remoulade sauce aside.

2   Wash and peel the celeriac and quarter it. Working quickly, grate each quarter into the bowl with the remoulade sauce. Toss and serve over lettuce leaves immediately. Once made, this dish will keep in the fridge for up to 2 days.

INGREDIENTS

5 tbsp plant-based mayo

2 tbsp extra-virgin olive oil

2 tbsp Dijon mustard

Juice of 1 medium lemon (2 tbsp)

2 tbsp finely chopped cornichon pickles

1 tbsp finely grated onion

1 tbsp finely chopped fresh Italian flat-leaf parsley

½ tsp sea salt

½ tsp freshly ground black pepper

1 celeriac (about 675g; 1½lb)

Lettuce leaves or toast

GREENS

Delicious and nutrient-packed greens include kale, spinach, spring greens, and chard. Their flavours pair well with cheese, garlic, onions, potatoes, olive oil, avocados, mushrooms, lemons, nutmeg, curry, and chillies. **Benefits** Strengthen bones; are anti-inflammatory; lower cholesterol; reduce cancer risk. **Uses** Kale is in season in autumn and winter, spinach is good late spring to autumn, and chard is at its peak in early summer and early autumn. Eat fresh during these times in salads or cooked in soups and stews. **Recipes** Ginger Kale Soup; Wilted Spinach Salad; Spinach and Rice Stuffed Tomatoes; Creamy Pasta with Swiss Chard and Roasted Tomatoes; Swiss Chard Ravioli.

Roasted Beetroot Salad

Sweet beetroots combine with the bright flavours of citrus and toasty walnuts for a delicious and very fancy-looking salad that's perfect for a celebration meal or dinner party.

SERVES 4   PREP 10 MINS   COOK 30 MINS

1   Preheat the oven to 200°C (400°F/Gas 6).

2   Scrub the beetroots but do not peel. Place them in a baking dish, drizzle with 1 tablespoon of extra-virgin olive oil, and roast for 30–40 minutes or until easily pierced with a fork. Remove from the oven, and set aside to cool.

3   Reduce oven temperature to 180°C (350°F/Gas 4).

4   Spread the walnuts in a single layer on a baking sheet, and toast for 7 minutes or until golden, stirring once. Cool slightly, and chop coarsely.

5   After using a Microplane grater to remove the zest from 1 orange, segment both oranges. Using a sharp paring knife, cut about 5mm (¼in) from the top and bottom of the fruit, and carefully cut away the peel and pith. You should see the membrane that separates each segment. Place the orange flat, cut side down on a rimmed chopping board, and very carefully use your paring knife to cut along the inside of each segment, slicing as close to the membrane as possible. A neat supreme of orange will pop out. Place these supremes in a separate bowl, and repeat with the remaining segments, stopping occasionally to pour juice from the board into a bowl.

6   In the bowl with the reserved orange juice, whisk together the orange zest, shallot, lemon juice, Dijon mustard, salt, and black pepper. Slowly drizzle in the remaining extra-virgin olive oil, whisking constantly.

7   Peel the beetroots, cut into 1cm (½in) wedges, and toss with half of the vinaigrette and orange segments.

8   Arrange one-quarter of the lettuce leaves on each of 4 plates, drizzle with the remaining dressing, and evenly divide the beetroot mixture over the leaves. Sprinkle each salad with one-quarter of the walnuts, and serve.

The beetroot mixture can be prepared up to 3 days in advance. When ready to serve, toast the walnuts and plate as directed.

INGREDIENTS

4 large beetroots

5 tbsp extra-virgin olive oil

100g (3½oz) walnut halves

Zest of 1 orange (1 tbsp)

2 seedless navel oranges

1 shallot, finely minced

Juice of 1 lemon (2 tbsp)

1 tsp Dijon mustard

1 tsp sea salt

½ tsp freshly ground black pepper

200g (7oz) baby salad leaves or torn lettuce

Roasted Tomato and White Bean Salad

Plum tomatoes are roasted until they're super-sweet and then tossed with cannellini beans, red onion, and rocket for a healthy and vibrant salad.

SERVES 4   PREP 10 MINS   COOK 40 MINS

1   Preheat the oven to 180°C (350°F/Gas 4).

2   Place the plum tomato halves on a rimmed baking sheet, cut side up, and tuck 1 or 2 slices of garlic into each piece. Drizzle with 1 tablespoon of the olive oil, and season with salt and black pepper. Roast for 40 minutes, remove from the oven, and cool slightly.

3   In a medium bowl, toss the cannellini beans with the remaining olive oil and the red onion and rocket leaves.

4   Divide the salad between 4 chilled plates, spoon the roasted tomatoes and any juices remaining in the pan over the salad, and serve immediately.

INGREDIENTS

12 plum tomatoes, cored and halved lengthwise

2 cloves garlic, cut in very thin slices

3 tbsp olive oil

1 tsp sea salt

½ tsp freshly ground black pepper

1 (400g; 14oz) can cannellini beans, rinsed and drained

½ small red onion, very thinly sliced

1 bunch rocket leaves, tough stems removed, washed, spun dry, and chilled

Plum tomatoes

For *White Bean and Red Pepper Salad,* use slices of jarred roasted red peppers (drain them on kitchen paper) instead of tomatoes.

Picnic Potato Salad Ⓣ

Tender new potatoes are bathed in a sauce of mayo and herbs, as well as lots of crunchy celery and dill pickles in this hard-to-beat potato salad. And it's perfect for picnics.

SERVES 14   PREP 10 MINS   COOK 15 MINS PLUS COOLING TIME

1   In a pan with a tight-fitting lid, bring 5cm (2in) of water to the boil over a medium–high heat. Place the new potatoes in a steamer basket, set in the pan, and steam for about 10 minutes or until tender and easily pierced with a fork. Transfer to a wide colander to drain and cool for 15 minutes.

2   Meanwhile, in a large bowl, whisk together the mayo, extra-virgin olive oil, mustard, vinegar, dill, flat-leaf parsley, hot pepper sauce, salt, and black pepper until smooth and well combined. Transfer half of this dressing to a small bowl, and set aside.

3   When the potatoes are cool enough to handle, cut into halves or quarters.

4   Fold the red onion, celery, and dill pickle into the sauce in the large bowl, and gently fold in the potatoes. Refrigerate along with the reserved dressing for 1 hour or until chilled.

5   Fold in the reserved dressing and serve. This potato salad will keep in the fridge for up to 3 days.

INGREDIENTS

1.35kg (3lb) small new potatoes

175g (6oz) plant-based mayo

4 tbsp extra-virgin olive oil

2 tbsp wholegrain Dijon mustard

2 tbsp apple cider vinegar

2 tbsp finely chopped fresh dill

2 tbsp finely chopped fresh flat-leaf parsley

1 tsp hot pepper sauce

1½ tsp sea salt

½ tsp freshly ground black pepper

1 red onion, finely chopped

4 sticks celery, finely chopped

70g (2½oz) finely chopped dill pickle

Waxy potatoes make the best potato salads. Floury potatoes absorb too much dressing and fall apart, resulting in a salad with a mashed-potato consistency. I like the extra nutrition of unpeeled potatoes, but if you prefer a potato salad with peeled potatoes, substitute larger white or yellow potatoes. Steam in their skins, cool, and peel.

Insalata Rinforzo (Neapolitan Christmas Salad)

UNDER 30

This traditional Neapolitan Christmas salad features tender cauliflower that's taken to flavourful perfection with briny olives and capers and just the right amount of vinegar. *Rinforzo* means "reinforcement", as this salad is traditionally made for Christmas Eve and then replenished throughout the days of the Christmas season.

SERVES 6   PREP 10 MINS   COOK 20 MINS

1   In a pan with a tight-fitting lid, bring 2.5cm (1in) of water to the boil over a medium–high heat. Place the cauliflower in a steamer basket, set in the pan, and steam for about 6 minutes or until tender. Remove the cauliflower to a large bowl and immediately toss with the garlic and red onion.

2   Using a silicone spatula, gently stir in the roasted red peppers, olives, and capers. Drizzle with the extra-virgin olive oil, and toss gently.

3   Add the vinegar, flat-leaf parsley, and black pepper, and toss again. Taste and add more vinegar or black pepper if desired. Serve immediately, or refrigerate for up to 1 week.

INGREDIENTS

1 head cauliflower, broken into small florets

1 clove garlic, finely chopped, plus more to taste

½ small red onion, sliced paper thin

4 roasted red peppers, thinly sliced

140g (5oz) pitted black Gaeta olives

140g (5oz) pitted green Cerignola olives

4 tbsp salted capers, rinsed and drained

120ml (4fl oz) extra-virgin olive oil

4 tbsp red wine vinegar, or to taste

4 tbsp finely chopped fresh flat-leaf parsley

½ tsp freshly ground black pepper, plus more to taste

Tossing the hot cauliflower with the onion and garlic cooks and softens the garlic and onion, tempering their flavours. You can vary the amount of garlic to your liking, too. To "reinforce" the salad, steam some more cauliflower, add more olives, peppers, and whatever else you like, and drizzle with more oil and vinegar. If you can't find Gaeta or Cerignola olives, substitute any flavourful olives you like. Oil-cured black olives are another great choice.

Warm Potato Salad
with Grainy Mustard Vinaigrette (UNDER 30)

The taste of these potatoes shouts loud as they are dressed quite simply, with plenty of shallots and grainy mustard, and spooned over a bed of leafy greens.

SERVES 4   PREP 5 MINS   COOK 10 MINS

1   In a pan with a tight-fitting lid, bring 5cm (2in) of water to the boil over a medium–high heat. Place the potatoes in a steamer basket, set in the pan, and steam for about 8–10 minutes or until tender and easily pierced with a fork. Transfer the potatoes to a large bowl.

2   While the potatoes are steaming, in a small bowl, whisk together the shallots, mustard, vinegar, and salt. Slowly whisk in the extra-virgin olive oil in a thin stream, and whisk in the chopped herbs and black pepper.

3   Reserve 4 tablespoons of dressing, and toss the potatoes with the remainder of the dressing.

4   Divide the salad leaves between 4 chilled plates, spoon one-quarter of the potato salad over the leaves, and drizzle each serving with 1 tablespoon of the reserved dressing. Serve immediately.

INGREDIENTS

450g (1lb) small Anya or pink fir apple potatoes, halved lengthwise

1 shallot, halved and very thinly sliced

2 tbsp wholegrain Dijon mustard

4 tbsp sherry vinegar

1 tsp sea salt

120ml (4fl oz) extra-virgin olive oil

2 tbsp finely chopped fresh chervil

2 tbsp finely chopped fresh chives

2 tbsp finely chopped fresh flat-leaf parsley

½ tsp freshly ground black pepper

400g (14oz) baby salad leaves, baby spinach, washed, spun dry, and chilled

Shallot

For *Warm Potato Salad Supper*, add 1 (400g; 14oz) can of cannellini beans, rinsed and drained, and 300g (10oz) of halved cherry or grape tomatoes.

Warm Lentil, Barley, and Sweet Potato Salad Ⓣ

Warm lentils, barley, and roasted sweet potatoes are tossed in a pomegranate and Dijon mustard dressing, then sprinkled with bright, nutrient-packed pomegranate seeds for a delicious, filling, and nutritious "main dish" salad.

SERVES 4–5 PREP 10 MINS COOK 40 MINS

1 In a medium saucepan with a lid, combine the green lentils, pearl barley, garlic, and bay leaf. Add water to cover by 5cm (2in) and bring to the boil, reduce the heat to medium–low, and cook for 40 minutes or until tender. Drain, remove and discard the bay leaf, and cool slightly.

2 Meanwhile, preheat the oven to 200°C (400°F/Gas 6).

3 On a baking sheet lined with baking parchment, toss the sweet potato with 1 tablespoon of the oil. Roast, stirring once, for 30 minutes. Cool slightly.

4 In a small bowl, whisk together the lemon juice, shallot, pomegranate molasses, mustard, salt, and black pepper until well combined. Slowly drizzle in the remaining extra-virgin olive oil, whisking continuously.

5 In a wide serving bowl, gently fold together the lentils, barley, and sweet potatoes. Toss with three-quarters of the dressing. Sprinkle with pomegranate seeds, drizzle with the remaining dressing, and serve warm.

INGREDIENTS

100g (3½oz) Puy lentils

100g (3½oz) pearl barley

1 clove garlic, lightly smashed

1 bay leaf

1 large sweet potato, peeled and cut in 2.5cm (1in) dice

3 tbsp extra-virgin olive oil

Juice of 1 lemon (2 tbsp)

1 small shallot, finely chopped

1 tbsp pomegranate molasses

1 tbsp Dijon mustard

½ tsp sea salt

¼ tsp freshly ground black pepper

Seeds from 1 pomegranate

Pomegranate molasses is sold in Middle Eastern groceries and some large chain shops. If you can't find it locally, order a bottle online. It's a fantastic addition to aubergine stew, salad dressings, and anything that needs a sweet – but not too sweet – flavour enhancement. Everyone has their own way of seeding a fresh pomegranate. A quick internet search should yield plenty of instructional videos if you need help.

Herbed Tabbouleh

Tabbouleh is a wonderful Middle Eastern dish of bulgur wheat, tomatoes, onions, and plenty of parsley. Serve it with hummus, lentil soup, and some warm pitta for a soul-satisfying meal, or simply enjoy it for lunch with crisp spears of romaine lettuce for scooping.

SERVES 6 PREP 15 MINS COOK NONE

1   Rinse the bulgur wheat. Add to a medium bowl with 1 tablespoon of the extra-virgin olive oil, pour near-boiling water over the top, and stir. Let it stand for 15 minutes and then strain in a fine-mesh sieve, pressing gently to remove all the liquid. Fluff with a fork.

2   In a large bowl, toss the bulgur with parsley, mint, spring onions, tomatoes, cucumber, red onion, lemon juice, the remaining extra-virgin olive oil, salt, and black pepper. Cover, and set aside to allow flavours to blend for 1 hour.

3   Serve at room temperature or cold. Tabbouleh keeps in the fridge for 3 days.

INGREDIENTS

100g (3½oz) fine bulgur wheat

4 tbsp extra-virgin olive oil

240ml (8fl oz) near-boiling water

3 bunches fresh curly parsley, stems removed, finely chopped

4 tbsp finely chopped fresh mint

4 spring onions, thinly sliced

2 large tomatoes, cored, deseeded, and finely chopped

½ cucumber, peeled, deseeded, and finely chopped

½ small red onion, finely chopped

Juice of 2 lemons (4 tbsp)

1 tsp sea salt

½ tsp freshly ground black pepper

Tabbouleh is traditionally made with curly parsley. Flat-leaf parsley won't provide the same slightly chewy consistency or intensity of flavour.

Vegetables

Eating a plant-based diet means you don't have to think about what will fill the centre of your plate – vegetables! Serve several veggie dishes together for an unforgettable meal.

Imam Bayildi (Turkish Stuffed Aubergine) (T)

Wait for aubergines to be in season to try this delicious dish. The olive oil, onions, tomatoes, and garlic are the perfect complement to the "meaty" aubergine. Soak up the delicious juices with pitta bread or rice.

SERVES 6   PREP 10 MINS PLUS 1 HOUR SOAK TIME   COOK 60 MINS

1   Fill the kitchen sink or a large bowl with well-salted water. Cut a small slit in each aubergine, remove the stems (if desired), transfer them to the salt-water bath, and soak for 1 hour. Drain, squeeze gently, and pat dry.

2   Heat the extra-virgin olive oil in a wide, ovenproof frying pan or a cast-iron casserole dish with a lid over a medium heat. Add the onions and cook, stirring occasionally, for about 5–10 minutes or until golden.

3   Add the aubergines, plum tomatoes, and garlic, reduce the heat to medium–low (adjust as needed), cover, and cook, stirring onions once or twice without disturbing the aubergines, for 10 minutes.

4   Turn the aubergines and cook for 10 minutes.

5   Preheat the oven to 190°C (375°F/Gas 5).

6   Remove the pan from the heat and gently stuff some onion–tomato mixture into each aubergine. Pour the reserved tomato juice over the aubergines, sprinkle with flat-leaf parsley, cover tightly with a lid or foil, and bake for 35–40 minutes.

7   Remove from the oven, and cool slightly before garnishing with toasted pine nuts (if using) and serving.

INGREDIENTS

6 small aubergines

120ml (4fl oz) extra-virgin olive oil, plus extra to taste

3 large sweet onions, halved and thinly sliced

6 ripe plum tomatoes, peeled, julienne cut, and juice reserved

6 cloves garlic, thinly sliced

4 tbsp fresh flat-leaf parsley, finely chopped, plus more for garnish

30g (1oz) toasted pine nuts (optional)

Red Cabbage with Apples and Pecans

Lightly pickled red onions pair perfectly with just-cooked red cabbage and apple with a toasty pecan topping. The gorgeous red colours of this dish make it a perfect choice to brighten a festive dinner.

SERVES 8 PREP 15–20 MINS COOK 15 MINS

1 Heat the extra-virgin olive oil in a large non-stick frying pan or wide, large saucepan over a medium–high heat. Add the red onion and salt, and cook, stirring frequently, for 4–5 minutes or until the onion is limp.

2 Reduce the heat to medium and remove the pan from the hob for about 30 seconds.

3 Stir in the vinegar and mustard, and stir to and coat onions.

4 Return the pan to the hob and cook for 30–60 seconds to reduce slightly if needed.

5 Stir in the apple and red cabbage. If the mixture looks dry, add 1 tablespoon of water. Cover and cook for 5 minutes, stirring once or twice and adding more water as needed.

6 Uncover, stir, and continue to cook until the cabbage is crisp-tender.

7 Season with black pepper, and sprinkle with pecans. This dish can be served hot, warm, or cold.

INGREDIENTS

2 tbsp extra-virgin olive oil

1 large red onion, halved and thinly sliced

1 tsp sea salt

4 tbsp apple cider vinegar

1 tsp wholegrain Dijon mustard

1 large, crisp apple, such as Fuji, skin on, cored, and thinly sliced

1 small red cabbage, cored, quartered, and thinly sliced

1 or 2 tbsp water

½ tsp freshly ground black pepper

60g (2oz) pecans, toasted and chopped

To make *Toasted Nuts,* preheat the oven to 180°C (350°F/Gas 4). Spread pecans or your favourite nuts on a baking sheet lined with baking parchment and bake, stirring once or twice, for 6-7 minutes or until the nuts are fragrant and toasty. I like to roast a big batch and store them in a tightly sealed glass jar at room temperature until needed. They'll keep for weeks this way, and it saves time to have them toasted and ready to go to add quick crunch and nuttiness to a finished dish or baked item.

Stir-Fried Chinese Cress with Fermented Black Beans

UNDER 30

The bitterness of Chinese watercress is a perfect foil to the deeply umami flavour of fermented black beans (available from Oriental supermarkets) and the kick of garlic.

SERVES 4 **PREP** 5 MINS **COOK** 5 MINS

1 Heat a wok or large cast-iron frying pan over a medium heat until hot. Add the grapeseed oil, garlic, and ginger, and stir for 30 seconds.

2 Add the Chinese watercress and stir for 30 seconds.

3 Stir in the vegetable stock, fermented black beans, and crushed chillies. Stir for a further 1–2 minutes or until the beans are heated through and the watercress is tender, and serve immediately.

INGREDIENTS

2 tbsp grapeseed oil

8 cloves garlic, very thinly sliced

1 tbsp grated fresh ginger

4 bunches Chinese watercress, washed well, bottom 2.5cm (1in) of stem removed

4 tbsp vegetable stock

8 tbsp fermented black beans

½ tsp crushed chillies

For *Quick and Easy Stir-Fry* – and dinner on the table in under 15 minutes – serve this dish over cooked rice noodles.

Roasted Tomatoes

Small tomatoes become ever so sweet, with a concentrated tomato flavour, when roasted slowly with garlic, salt, and olive oil. Toss them with pasta, pile into a sandwich, stir into salads, use them as a base for savoury sauces, or just pop them straight in your mouth!

SERVES 4 **PREP** 20 MINS **COOK** 1 HOUR

1 Preheat the oven to 150°C (300°F/Gas 2). Arrange two racks in the lower third of the oven.

2 Divide the cherry tomatoes, cut side up, between 2 baking sheets. Insert 1 garlic slice into each half, drizzle with olive oil, and season lightly with salt and black pepper.

3 Bake for about 1 hour, stirring once or twice, or until the tomatoes are reduced and very soft. Serve warm or at room temperature. Leftovers will keep in the fridge for up to 3 days.

INGREDIENTS

900g (2lb) cherry tomatoes, halved

3 cloves garlic, sliced very thin

2 tbsp olive oil

1 tsp sea salt

½ tsp freshly ground black pepper

Cherry tomatoes

For Tomato Basil Pasta Salad, toss a batch of these tomatoes with 450g (1lb) of penne pasta, cooked according to packet instructions, drained, and rinsed with cold water. Stir in 25g (scant 1 oz) of torn fresh basil leaves and 60g (2oz) of pitted Niçoise olives, and serve.

Herbed Courgettes (T) (UNDER 30)

Tender slices of courgette are brushed with plant-based mayo and encrusted with panko breadcrumbs, fresh herbs, and olive oil for a lower-fat version of a fried favorite. Serve plain or with tomato sauce.

SERVES 4   PREP 10 MINS   COOK 20 MINS

1   Preheat the oven to 200°C (400°F/Gas 6). Line a baking sheet with baking parchment.

2   Trim each courgette, cut into 5mm (¼in) slices. Blot dry with kitchen paper and brush both sides of each courgette slice with mayonnaise.

3   In a small, shallow bowl, combine the panko breadcrumbs, herbs, extra-virgin olive oil, salt, black pepper, and lemon zest.

4   Dredge each courgette slice in the panko mixture, coating both sides, and lay the slices on the prepared baking sheet.

5   Bake for 20 minutes, carefully turning with a spatula halfway through cooking, and serve immediately.

INGREDIENTS

2 large courgettes

4 tbsp plant-based mayonnaise

250g (9oz) panko breadcrumbs

8 tbsp finely chopped fresh mixed herbs such as parsley, chives, chervil, and/or tarragon

120ml (4fl oz) extra-virgin olive oil

2 tsp sea salt

1 tsp freshly ground black pepper

2 tsp lemon zest

Sautéed Broccoli

Purple-sprouting and tenderstem broccoli are cruciferous vegetables that work well paired with garlic and olive oil. Try this dish as a side, within a sandwich, added to cooked beans, or served with pasta.

SERVES 4   PREP 5 MINS   COOK 10 MINS

1 Wash the broccoli and trim off the tough bottom end of each stem (about 1cm (½in).

2 In a medium pan over a high heat, bring enough water to cover the broccoli by 2.5cm (1in) to the boil. Add half the salt along with the broccoli, blanch for 1 minute, transfer to an iced bath to cool quickly, drain, and set aside.

3 Heat the extra-virgin olive oil and garlic in a medium frying pan over a medium heat. When the garlic begins to sizzle and turn a golden colour (but before it browns), add the broccoli, toss to combine, and cook, stirring frequently, for 5 minutes or until the broccoli is tender.

4 Season with the remaining salt and crushed chillies, and serve immediately.

INGREDIENTS

450g (1lb) purple-sprouting or tenderstem broccoli

1 tsp sea salt

2 tbsp extra-virgin olive oil

3 cloves garlic, thinly sliced

½ tsp crushed chillies

Southern-Style Braised Greens

Nutritious greens are slowly braised until tender in flavourful vegetable stock seasoned with olive oil, garlic, onions, and a little smoked sea salt. Add some beans and fresh bread and you have dinner.

SERVES 3–6   PREP 15 MINS   COOK 35 MINS

1 In a large pan over a high heat, combine the vegetable stock, extra-virgin olive oil, smoked sea salt, black pepper, and garlic. Bring to the boil.

2 Stir in the spring greens, mustard greens, and curly kale. Reduce the heat to medium, and cook, uncovered and stirring occasionally, until the greens are tender, about 35 minutes. Adjust the heat to maintain a gentle simmer.

3 Season the greens with apple cider vinegar, and serve with a little of the liquid that remains in the pan.

INGREDIENTS

960ml (1¾ pints) vegetable stock

4 tbsp extra-virgin olive oil

1 tsp smoked sea salt

½ tsp freshly ground black pepper

2 cloves garlic, crushed and finely chopped

1 large bunch spring greens, tough stems removed, cut into small pieces

1 large bunch mustard greens, tough stems removed, cut into small pieces

1 large bunch curly kale, tough stems removed, cut into small pieces

1 tbsp apple cider vinegar, or juice of ½ lemon (1 tbsp)

CRUCIFEROUS VEGETABLES

Cruciferous vegetables, such as broccoli, cauliflower, and cabbage, are loaded with vitamin A carotenoids, vitamin C, folic acid, and fibre. They're easily adaptable to fit a wide variety of dishes. **Benefits** Lower cancer risk; support liver function; improve skin health; aid eye health; boost immunity. **Uses** Choose firm and brightly coloured vegetables with moist ends, and eat raw in salads and wraps, or boil, steam, stir-fry, sauté, bake, or braise. **Recipes** Sesame Ginger Broccoli, Curried Cauliflower Coconut Soup, Mushroom and Cabbage Borscht, Red Cabbage with Apples and Pecans, Savory Stuffed Cabbage, *Insalata Rinforzo*, Minestrone.

Spinach and Rice Stuffed Tomatoes (T)

When juicy beef tomatoes are in season, buy the largest ones you can find and stuff them with cheesy rice, spinach, and pine nuts. Bake until tender and sweet for an irresistible taste of summer.

SERVES 6 **PREP 20 MINS** **COOK 60 MINS**

1 Preheat the oven to 200°C (400°F/Gas 6). Lightly grease a baking dish large enough to hold the tomatoes snugly.

2 In a small saucepan over a medium–high heat, bring the water to the boil. Add the Arborio rice and ½ teaspoon of salt, and cook for exactly 10 minutes. Remove from the heat, drain, and set aside.

3 Working over a colander set over a large bowl, core the beefsteak tomatoes and scoop out the insides, removing the seeds and pulp while leaving the outer flesh and skin intact. Press gently on the pulp to remove as much liquid as possible. Place the hollowed tomatoes in the dish, and set juice aside.

4 Heat the olive oil in a wide frying pan over a medium heat. Add the onion, season with ¼ teaspoon of the salt, and cook, stirring frequently, for about 5–7 minutes or until soft and beginning to colour.

5 Add the garlic and cook for 1 minute.

6 Increase the heat to high, add the spinach, and cook for about 3 minutes or until the spinach has wilted.

7 In a large bowl, combine the rice, spinach, mozzarella-style cheese, toasted pine nuts, nutritional yeast, flat-leaf parsley, basil, nutmeg, black pepper, and the remaining salt.

8 Spoon this rice mixture into the tomatoes, filling each to the top. Pour the tomato juice over and around the stuffed tomatoes, cover the dish tightly with foil, and bake for 25 minutes or until hot and bubbling.

9 Uncover and cook 5 more minutes. Drizzle with lemon juice, and serve hot or warm.

INGREDIENTS

660ml (1 pint 2fl oz) water

150g (5½oz) Arborio rice

1½ tsp sea salt

6 large beef tomatoes

3 tbsp olive oil

1 red onion, finely chopped

2 cloves garlic, thinly sliced

450g (1lb) spinach, washed in several changes of cold water, shaken dry in a colander, thick stems removed, thinly sliced

100g (3½oz) shredded plant-based mozzarella-style cheese, preferably almond based

60g (2oz) pine nuts, toasted

4 tbsp nutritional yeast

2 tbsp finely chopped fresh flat-leaf parsley leaves

2 tbsp torn or sliced fresh basil leaves

¼ tsp freshly ground nutmeg

¼ tsp freshly ground black pepper

Juice of 1 lemon (2 tbsp)

Fried Green Tomatoes (UNDER 30)

Unripe green tomatoes are dredged in cornmeal and quickly fried for a delicious classic born of the desire not to waste food. Make these in autumn, before the first frost, with the last tomatoes on the vine – or cheat and sneak some in early summer before they've had a chance to ripen!

SERVES 4–5   PREP 5 MINS   COOK 10 MINS

1 Core each beef tomato, trim and discard 3mm ($^1/_8$in) from the top and bottom, and cut into 5 even slices. Set aside.

2 In a medium bowl, whisk together the soya milk and lemon juice. Set aside to curdle for a few minutes.

3 Place cornmeal on a rimmed plate or shallow bowl.

4 Heat 1cm (½in) of grapeseed oil in a large frying pan over a medium–high heat until it's shimmering.

5 Working with just enough tomato slices to fit comfortably in the pan, dip each tomato slice in the soya milk mixture and then dredge in cornmeal. Add to the pan, fry for about 2 minutes, adjusting the heat as necessary to prevent burning. Turn carefully with a spatula, and fry the other side for a further 2 minutes. Transfer to a plate lined with several thicknesses of kitchen paper, season with a little salt and black pepper, and keep warm. Continue until all the tomato slices have been fried, replacing the oil if the cornmeal begins to burn. Serve hot.

INGREDIENTS

4 large, green beef tomatoes
120ml (4fl oz) unsweetened soya milk
Juice of ½ lemon (1 tbsp)
200g (7oz) fine cornmeal
Grapeseed oil, for frying
½ tsp sea salt
½ tsp freshly ground black pepper

Sea salt

For a *Fried Green Tomato Sandwich*, pile fried tomato slices into a crusty roll spread with a little plant-based mayo, hot pepper sauce, and crispy lettuce.

Stuffed Artichokes (T)

This Italian American classic is a fantastic starter, but it also makes a wonderful supper accompanied by a cup of soup and a simple salad. Artichokes are easier to prepare than you might think, and they are simply delicious when stuffed with a tasty breadcrumb mixture bursting with the briny tang of capers, olives, and plenty of garlic.

SERVES 4 PREP 25 MINS COOK 50 MINS

1 Preheat the oven to 190°C (375°F/Gas 5). Lightly grease a baking dish large enough to hold the artichokes.

2 Clean and prep the artichokes, see below.

3 Heat the extra-virgin olive oil in a small frying pan over a medium heat. Add the olives, capers, and garlic, and cook, stirring frequently, for 3 minutes or until the garlic just begins to colour. Remove from the heat.

4 In a medium bowl, combine breadcrumbs, Italian herb seasoning, garlic salt, flat-leaf parsley, lemon zest, black pepper, and olive oil mixture.

5 Pat the artichokes dry. Spread apart the leaves of 1 artichoke, and spoon one-quarter of the breadcrumb mixture between the leaves and into the centre of the artichoke. Repeat with the remaining artichokes, nestling them snugly in the baking dish after stuffing.

6 Pour 2.5cm (1in) of boiling water around the artichokes, taking care not to pour water directly over them (this will result in a soggy filling). Lightly grease a piece of foil and cover the pan tightly.

7 Bake for 45 minutes, uncover, and bake for a further 5 minutes. Serve hot or at room temperature.

INGREDIENTS

4 large globe artichokes

120ml (4fl oz) extra-virgin olive oil

30g (1oz) green Spanish (Manzanilla) olives, finely chopped

1 tbsp salted capers, rinsed, drained, and finely chopped

6 cloves garlic, minced

175g (6oz) breadcrumbs

2 tbsp Italian herb seasoning

1 tsp garlic salt

4 tbsp finely chopped fresh flat-leaf parsley

1 tsp grated lemon zest

½ tsp freshly ground black pepper

Boiling water

To prepare artichokes for cooking, cut off the bottom part of the stem and the top 5mm (¼in) of leaves, and snap off the first few layers of tough, dark green outer leaves. With a sharp pair of kitchen scissors, cut the sharp edges off the top of each remaining leaf. Spread out the artichoke leaves from the centre, and use a sharp grapefruit spoon to scrape out the spiny, purple "choke" from the centre, leaving the heart intact. Rub the artichokes with a cut lemon as you work, and place each cleaned artichoke into a bath of cold water with a few tablespoons lemon juice to keep them from turning brown.

Almond and Breadcrumb Stuffed Piquillo Peppers (T)

Tangy piquillo peppers are stuffed with a savoury almond and breadcrumb filling. Present them at your next party on a platter and watch how quickly they disappear!

SERVES 7 PREP 10 MINS COOK 30 MINS

1 Preheat the oven to 180°C (350°F/Gas 4).

2 Heat 1 tablespoon of the extra-virgin olive oil in a small saucepan over a medium–high heat. Add the garlic, shallot, and crushed chillies, and cook for 30 seconds. Stir in the flat-leaf parsley and remove from the heat.

3 In a small bowl, combine the breadcrumbs, almonds, capers, and garlic mixture. Stir in 1 tablespoon of the extra-virgin olive oil.

4 Drizzle a medium baking dish with half of the remaining extra-virgin olive oil. Gently fill each piquillo pepper with about 1 tablespoon of the stuffing, and place the filled peppers in the baking dish. Drizzle the stuffed peppers with the remaining extra-virgin olive oil and bake for 20 minutes. Serve hot, warm, or at room temperature.

INGREDIENTS

3 tbsp extra-virgin olive oil

2 cloves garlic, finely chopped

1 small shallot, finely chopped

½ tsp crushed chillies

2 tbsp finely chopped fresh flat-leaf parsley

60g (2oz) fresh breadcrumbs

75g (2½oz) Marcona almonds, finely chopped

1 tbsp salted capers, rinsed, drained, and finely chopped

400g (14oz) can whole piquillo peppers, drained

Piquillo peppers are small, pointed, slightly spicy peppers from Spain. If you don't have a well-stocked Spanish grocery nearby, you can find them online and in some large grocery stores. If you absolutely can't get them, you could use some jarred Peppadew peppers instead.

Vegetables

Vegetables offer a fresh, and delicious way to get protein, fibre, vitamins, and minerals into your body. Eating a rainbow of colourful vegetables each, and every day provides a great supply of disease-fighting antioxidants, and micronutrients. Raw, and cooked vegetables form the bulk of a healthy plant-based diet, so choose a wide variety every day to reap the greatest nutritional benefits.

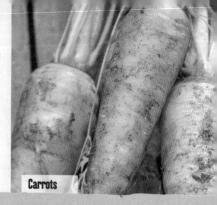

Carrots

	ARTICHOKES	ASPARAGUS	AVOCADOS	BROCCOLI	SPROUTING BROCCOLI	BRUSSEL SPROUTS	CARROTS	CAULIFLOW
USES	Scoop out choke, trim ends of leaves, rub with lemon, and steam, stuff, or use prepared artichoke hearts in salads, dips, andcasseroles.	Steam, roast, grill, or blanch. Use in soups, salads, casseroles, and pasta dishes.	Halve, pit, and scoop out creamy flesh. Slice or cube for salads, stews, soups, or Mexican dishes. Spread on toast or bagels, or use in dips, salad dressings, and even desserts.	Blanch, steam, sauté, or serve raw. Use in soups, salads, casseroles, and pasta dishes.	Blanch or steam, then sauté with garlic, and olive oil.	Roast, steam, sauté, or serve raw.	Aromatic, use with celery, and onions to flavour soups, stews, or sauces. Roast, steam, or sauté.	Steam, blanc roast, or serv raw. Use in salads, soups casseroles, p dishes, currie and stews.
GOOD SOURCE OF ...	Protein, fibre, vitamins C, K, and B_3, magnesium, phosphorus, potassium, copper, folate, and manganese.	Protein, fibre, vitamins C, A, E, K, B_1, B_2, B_3, folate, phosphorus, potassium, copper, manganese, and selenium.	Healthy fats, protein, fibre, vitamins K, and C, and folate.	Protein, vitamins E, A, C, K, B_6, B_1, and B_2, pantothenic acid, calcium, iron, magnesium, phosphorus selenium, fibre, folate, potassium, and manganese.	Protein, fibre, vitamins A, C, E, K, B_6, B_1, B_2, and B_3, folate, calcium, iron, magnesium, phosphorus, potassium, zinc, and manganese.	Fibre, vitamins B_1, and B_2, iron, magnesium, phosphorus, copper, vitamins A, C, K and B_6, folate, potassium, and manganese.	Fibre, vitamins B_1, B_3, B_6, A, C, and K, folate, manganese, and potassium.	Protein, fibre vitamins B_1, I and B_3, magnesium, phosphorus, vitamins C, K and B_6, folate pantothenic acid, potassiu and mangan

Artichokes

Asparagus

Broccoli
Tomatoes
Potatoes

...EETCORN	GREENS	KALE	MUSHROOMS	PEPPERS	POTATOES	SPiNACH	SWEET POTATOES	TOMATOES
...am, blanch, ...roast. Use ...oups, ...ws, ...seroles, ...an dishes, ...shes, and ...ads.	Steam or blanch, andthen sauté. Use in soups, stews, and bean dishes.	Steam, blanch, sauté, or use raw. Use in soups, salads, casseroles, pasta dishes, and bean dishes.	Sauté, roast, bake, and stuff, or enjoy raw. Use in salads, sautéed dishes, soups, and stews. Coat in breadcrumbs, and fry for a meaty "cutlet".	Sauté or serve raw. Use as an aromatic flavour base for soups, stews, and sauces when combined with celery, and onions.	Steam, bake, or roast. Use in side dishes, casseroles, soups, and stews.	Steam, blanch, sauté, or serve raw. Use in soups, stews, salads, casseroles, and curries.	Bake, roast, steam, and mash. Use in soups, stews, casseroles, salads, and side dishes.	Serve raw, roasted, or sautéed or in sauces, soups, stews, salads, dressings, chillies, and casseroles.
...tein, fibre, ...n, and ...amin A.	Protein, fibre, vitamins B_1, B_2, and B_3, iron, magnesium, vitamins A, C, E, K, B_6, folate, calcium, phosphorus, potassium, copper, and manganese.	Protein, thiamin, riboflavin, folate, iron, magnesium, vitamins A, C, K, B_6, calcium, potassium, copper, and manganese.	Protein, fibre, vitamins C, D, B_6, folate, iron, zinc, manganese, thiamin, riboflavin, niacin, pantothenic acid, phosphorus, potassium, copper, and selenium.	Fibre, vitamins K, A, C, E, B_6, B_1, B_2, andB_3, potassium, manganese, and folate.	Protein, fibre, vitamins C, andB_6, potassium, and manganese.	Protein, fibre, vitamin B_3, zinc, vitamins A, C, E, K, B_6, B_1, and B_2, folate, calcium, iron, magnesium, phosphorus, potassium, copper, and manganese.	Protein, fibre, vitamins B_6, A, and C, potassium, and manganese.	Fibre, vitamins B_1, B_6, A, C, and K, folate, magnesium, phosphorus, copper, potassium, and manganese.

Mushrooms
Peppers

Roasted Sweetcorn with Poblano-Coriander Butter

Corn on the cob is rubbed with olive oil, salt, and pepper and then roasted in a hot oven until charred. When it's done, it's rolled in a wonderfully spicy, savoury butter.

SERVES 6   PREP 5 MINS   COOK 10 MINS

1   Preheat the oven to 220°C (425°F/Gas 7).

2   Place the poblano pepper directly over the flame on a gas hob or roast under the grill as it preheats before you cook the corn, turning to char on all sides. Transfer to a small bowl, cover with cling film, and set aside to steam the charred skin. After 5 minutes, remove the cling film. Core, deseed, and peel the poblano, and chop it very finely (or pulse in the small bowl of a food processor until it's nearly smooth). Set aside.

3   Brush the corn with extra-virgin olive oil, and sprinkle with salt and black pepper. Place the corn on a large baking sheet, and roast, turning once, for about 10 minutes or until tender and charred.

4   In a small bowl, stir the chopped poblano into the soft plant-based butter, and stir in the coriander and nutritional yeast.

5   Spread the hot corn with the spicy butter and serve.

INGREDIENTS

1 poblano pepper

6 ears fresh sweetcorn, shucked and trimmed

1 tbsp extra-virgin olive oil

½ tsp sea salt

½ tsp freshly ground black pepper

4 tbsp plant-based butter, softened

2 tbsp finely chopped fresh coriander

1 tbsp nutritional yeast

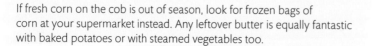

If fresh corn on the cob is out of season, look for frozen bags of corn at your supermarket instead. Any leftover butter is equally fantastic with baked potatoes or with steamed vegetables too.

Sautéed Mushroom Medley (T) (UNDER 30)

Sautéed mushrooms are so versatile – have them as a side dish, toss them with pasta, spread them on toasted French bread for crostini... the possibilities are endless. Dried porcini mushrooms lend an earthiness to this dish, but if you don't have them, just add an extra 115g (4oz) of shiitakes.

SERVES 6   PREP 15 MINS   COOK 15 MINS

1 In a small bowl, place the porcini mushrooms. Pour boiling water over them and set aside to soak for about 5 minutes or until softened. Lift the porcini from the soaking water, agitating gently to release any soil. Chop the mushrooms and set aside. Reserve the soaking water.

2 Heat extra-virgin olive oil in a large frying pan over a medium–high heat, . Add the shallots and garlic, and cook, stirring continuously, for 2 minutes. Adjust the heat as necessary to prevent burning.

3 Add the porcini, chestnut mushrooms, white button and shiitake mushrooms, along with the rosemary, and thyme, and cook, stirring occasionally, for 10 minutes or until the mushrooms begin to brown.

4 Season with salt and black pepper, increase the heat to high, and cook, stirring frequently, for 3–5 minutes or until the mushrooms are golden brown and small bits are sticking to the pan.

5 Strain the mushroom soaking liquid, leaving the last couple of teaspoons behind to eliminate any grit. Add the mushroom liquid and white wine all at once to deglaze the pan, stirring vigorously to scrape up any browned bits from the bottom of the pan, and cook until all the liquid is absorbed.

6 Remove from the heat, stir in flat-leaf parsley, and taste. Season with additional salt and pepper if desired, and serve immediately.

INGREDIENTS

15g (½oz) dried porcini mushrooms

120ml (4fl oz) boiling water

3 tbsp extra-virgin olive oil

2 shallots, finely chopped

3 cloves garlic, minced

225g (8oz) chestnut mushrooms, thinly sliced

225g (8oz) white button mushrooms, thinly sliced

115g (4oz) shiitake mushrooms, stemmed and thinly sliced

1 tsp chopped fresh rosemary or ½ tsp dried

1 tsp chopped fresh thyme or ½ tsp dried

1 tsp sea salt, or to taste

½ tsp freshly ground black pepper, or to taste

2 tbsp dry white wine

4 tbsp finely chopped fresh flat-leaf parsley

For Mushroom Puffs, roll out a sheet of puff pastry on a flour-dusted surface. Spread the cooled mushroom mixture evenly over the pastry, sprinkle with 8 tablespoons of Cashew Ricotta, and roll from the long end of the pastry to form a cylinder. Wrap in baking parchment and freeze until almost solid. To cook, remove the parchment and cut into 5mm (¼in) slices. Bake cut side down on a parchment-lined baking sheet at 200°C (400°F/Gas 6) for 10 minutes or until golden. Serve immediately.

Sesame Ginger Broccoli (UNDER 30)

Broccoli is quickly blanched to preserve its vibrancy and crunch and then flavoured with garlic and ginger for a simple, perfectly spiced plate of veggies.

SERVES 5–6   PREP 10 MINS   **COOK** 10 MINS

1   Wash the broccoli, and separate the florets into small pieces. Peel the broccoli stem and slice into 5mm (¼in) rounds.

2   Prepare an iced water bath for the broccoli.

3   Bring a medium pan of water to the boil over a high heat, and add salt. Blanch the broccoli and stems for 2 minutes. Using tongs, immediately remove the broccoli and plunge into the ice bath. Drain and set aside.

4   Heat the sesame oil in a large frying pan over a medium–high heat. Add the garlic and ginger, and stir for 1 minute.

5   Add the broccoli and cook for 2 minutes.

6   Sprinkle with gomasio, and serve immediately.

INGREDIENTS

1 large head broccoli

1 tsp sea salt

2 tbsp light sesame oil

2 cloves garlic, thinly sliced

1 tsp freshly grated ginger

1 tsp gomasio

Broccoli

Gomasio is a savoury Japanese condiment made from roasted, unhulled sesame seeds and salt. Some varieties also contain seaweed. It's considered a healthier alternative to salt and brings a pleasant, nutty flavour to a dish. Try passing it round at the table with noodle dishes, salads, or stir-fries.

Braised Brussels Sprouts with Chestnuts (UNDER 30)

This dish of golden Brussels sprouts with the sweet, warm flavour of roasted chestnuts is best served in winter, when sprouts and chestnuts are both in season. If you can't find fresh chestnuts, you can use jarred roasted, peeled chestnuts or ones that are in a vacuum pack instead.

SERVES 8   PREP 5 MINS   COOK 15 MINS

1   Preheat the oven to 200°C (400°F/Gas 6). Line a baking sheet with baking parchment.

2   In a large bowl, toss Brussels sprouts with extra-virgin olive oil, balsamic vinegar, ½ teaspoon of the salt, and black pepper. Spread the sprouts on the prepared baking sheet, cut side down, and roast for 10 minutes.

3   Heat the plant-based butter in a large frying pan over a medium–high heat. Stir in the sugar, remaining salt, and chestnuts. Cook, stirring, for 2 minutes.

4   Add the Brussels sprouts, and cook, stirring twice, for 2 minutes. Serve immediately.

INGREDIENTS

450g (1lb) fresh Brussels sprouts, trimmed and halved

1 tbsp extra-virgin olive oil

1 tbsp balsamic vinegar

1 tsp sea salt

½ tsp freshly ground black pepper

2 tbsp plant-based butter

1 tbsp sugar

140g (5oz) roasted, peeled chestnuts, roughly chopped (about 18 chestnuts)

Look for firm chestnuts with a dark, glossy shell. To roast chestnuts, preheat the oven to 200°C (400°F/Gas 6). Score each chestnut with an "X" and spread on a baking sheet. Roast for about 10 minutes or until the chestnuts split open. Let the chestnuts cool until you can comfortably pick them up and peel them. Store roasted chestnuts in the fridge in a tightly sealed glass jar for up to 2 weeks.

Stuffed Mushrooms

Aromatic vegetables, herbs, and mushroom stems are sautéed in plenty of olive oil, mixed with crunchy panko breadcrumbs, and baked in mushroom caps. Simple and simply delicious! Choose small mushrooms for this savoury dish – they also make little bites perfect for passing around at parties.

SERVES 6   PREP 10 MINS   COOK 35 MINS

1 Preheat the oven to 200°C (400°F/Gas 6). Brush a baking dish just large enough to hold the mushroom caps with 1 tablespoon of the olive oil.

2 Gently remove the stems from the button mushroom caps. Place the mushrooms in the prepared baking dish. Chop the mushroom stems finely.

3 Heat 2 tablespoons of the olive oil in a medium frying pan over a medium-high heat. Add the mushroom stems, red pepper, shallots, and garlic, and cook for about 5 minutes or until the mushrooms begin to brown.

4 Deglaze the pan with 1 tablespoon of the white wine. Add the panko breadcrumbs, flat-leaf parsley, thyme, oregano, salt, and black pepper, and remove from the heat.

5 Pour the remaining white wine into the baking dish around the mushrooms. Evenly distribute the filling into the mushroom caps, lightly spooning a little filling into each. Drizzle the remaining olive oil over the mushroom caps.

6 Bake for 20 minutes or until the mushrooms are tender and the filling is golden. Serve hot, warm, or at room temperature.

INGREDIENTS

5 tbsp extra-virgin olive oil

300g (10oz) white button mushrooms

¼ small red pepper, ribs and seeds removed, and finely chopped

2 small shallots, finely chopped

3 cloves garlic, finely chopped

4 tbsp dry white wine

60g (2oz) panko breadcrumbs

2 tbsp finely chopped fresh flat-leaf parsley

1 tsp dried thyme

½ tsp dried oregano

1 tsp sea salt

½ tsp freshly ground black pepper

For a *"Cheesy" Stuffed Mushrooms* starter, use 12 "stuffing-size" portobello mushrooms instead and spoon 1 tablespoon of Cashew Ricotta into the bottom of each mushroom cap before stuffing. Serve 3 or 4 mushrooms per person.

Minted Peas and Baby Potatoes

Sweet peas and tender new potatoes are tossed in a simple dressing of olive oil and fresh mint for a super-summery side dish. Seek out the tiniest potatoes you can for this recipe.

SERVES 6 PREP 10 MINS COOK 10 MINS

1 In a large pan with a tight-fitting lid, bring 2.5cm (1in) water to the boil over a medium heat. Place new potatoes in a steamer basket, set in the pan, and steam for about 10 minutes or until the potatoes are tender and easily pierced with a fork. Drain and cool slightly. If the potatoes are larger than 2.5cm (1in) in diameter, cut them in half.

2 Meanwhile, heat the extra-virgin olive oil in a large saucepan over a medium–high heat. Add the shallots and salt, and cook for about 5 minutes or until softened.

3 Stir in the peas and water, and cook for 2 minutes.

4 Add the reserved potatoes, increase the heat to high, and stir for 1 minute.

5 Remove from the heat. Add the mint, lemon juice, and black pepper. Serve.

INGREDIENTS

450g (1lb) very small new potatoes

2 tbsp extra-virgin olive oil

1 shallot, thinly sliced

1 tsp sea salt

300g (10oz) shelled fresh peas or frozen peas, thawed

2 tbsp water

2 tbsp finely chopped fresh mint

Juice of ½ lemon (1 tbsp)

½ tsp freshly ground black pepper

Peas

For *Herbed Peas and Potatoes,* replace the mint in the recipe above with chervil, parsley, chives, tarragon, or any combination of these herbs.

Sesame Asparagus (UNDER 30)

This recipe may contains only a few ingredients but it boasts huge flavour. Whether you grill or roast the asparagus, you'll love the counterpoint of sweet, tender spears with the warm savouriness of sesame.

SERVES 4 PREP 5 MINS COOK 35–40 MINS

1 Preheat the oven to 200°C (400°F/Gas 6), or preheat a grill for high heat. Line a baking tray with baking parchment.

2 Grasp an asparagus spear, and gently bend it to snap off the tough bottom of the spear. Trim remaining spears to this length, and peel the lower two-thirds of the asparagus stem. Transfer to the baking tray and toss with sesame oil, salt, and black pepper.

3 Roast for 8 minutes, or grill, turning once or twice, for about 5 minutes or until the asparagus is tender. (When you pick up a single spear with a pair of tongs and it droops slightly, it's done.) Serve hot, warm, or cold, sprinkled with the toasted sesame seeds.

INGREDIENTS

450g (1lb) slender asparagus spears

1 tbsp dark sesame oil

1 tsp sea salt

½ tsp freshly ground black pepper

1 tbsp toasted sesame seeds or gomasio

For *Asian Asparagus,* add 1 teaspoon of finely grated ginger and a drizzle of tamari. For *Lemon Garlic Asparagus,* replace the sesame oil with extra-virgin olive oil, add 1 clove of finely chopped garlic, and garnish with some grated lemon zest instead of the sesame seeds.

Latkes

Latkes are tender, crisp, freshly fried potato pancakes. They freeze wonderfully, so you can make a big batch and simply heat them up whenever you want a potato fix.

SERVES 4–5   PREP 15 MINS   COOK 10 MINS

1 Place the grated potatoes in a large, fine-mesh sieve, and use a handful of kitchen paper to press down on them, removing as much liquid as possible. Preheat the oven to 130°C (250°F/Gas ½).

2 In a large bowl, whisk the onion, egg replacer, warm water, flours, salt, and black pepper until completely smooth.

3 When the potatoes are dry, quickly stir them into the onion mixture.

4 Heat 4 tablespoons of grapeseed oil in a large, heavy frying pan over a medium–high heat. Scoop 4-tablespoon measures of the potato mixture into the pan, and press gently flat with a spatula. Fry for about 2–3 minutes or until golden brown, flip over, and fry the other side until golden.

5 Remove the *latkes* to a wire rack placed on a baking sheet and keep warm in the oven while you fry remaining batches, adding additional oil and adjusting heat as necessary. Serve hot, with apple sauce or plant-based soured cream.

INGREDIENTS

1.35kg (3lb) Maris Piper potatoes, peeled and grated

1 onion, very finely chopped (in food processor if possible)

2 tbsp egg replacer

3 tbsp warm water

2 tbsp plain flour

2 tbsp potato flour or cornflour

1 tsp sea salt

½ tsp freshly ground black pepper

4–8 tbsp grapeseed oil

Apple sauce or plant-based soured cream, to serve

Roasted Root Vegetable Medley

For this satisfying dish of root vegetables accented with fresh herbs and plenty of olive oil, I like to choose a mix of carrots, celeriac, potatoes, swede, turnips, and parsnips.

SERVES 6   PREP 20 MINS   COOK 35–40 MINS

1 Preheat the oven to 200°C (400°F/Gas 6).

2 Place the root vegetables in a 23 × 33cm (9 × 13in) glass baking dish, and drizzle the extra-virgin olive oil over evenly. Season with the rosemary, thyme, sage, salt, and black pepper, and toss with your hands to mix well.

3 Bake, uncovered and stirring once or twice, for 35–40 minutes or until the vegetables are tender and turning a dark golden brown at the edges. Serve hot or warm.

INGREDIENTS

750g (1lb 10oz) assorted root vegetables, peeled and cut into 2.5cm (1in) chunks

120ml (4fl oz) extra-virgin olive oil

1 tsp finely chopped fresh rosemary

1 tsp fresh thyme leaves

1 tsp fresh sage, finely chopped

1 tsp sea salt

½ tsp freshly ground black pepper

SWEET POTATOES

Sweet potatoes are known for their orange flesh, but they also come in white, yellow, purple, and pink varieties. **Benefits** High in vitamin C, beta-carotene, and antioxidants; regulate blood sugar; improve skin health; and boost immunity. **Uses** Peak season is late summer and autumn; choose firm, fat, unblemished tubers that feel heavy for their size, and eat baked with plant-based butter and cinnamon, mashed, roasted in salads and casseroles, or simmered in soups and stews. **Recipes** Southern Sweet Potatoes with Pecan Streusel, Winter Vegetable Pot Pie.

Southern Sweet Potatoes with Pecan Streusel (T)

Creamy sweet potatoes are spiced with a touch of cinnamon and adorned with a sweet and savoury pecan streusel topping in this moreish accompaniment. Double up the recipe for a family meal.

SERVES 8 PREP 10 MINS COOK 50 MINS

1 Preheat the oven to 180°C (350°F/Gas 4).

2 Lightly coat a 20 x 20cm (8 × 8in) baking dish with cooking spray.

3 In a large pan fitted with a steamer basket over a medium–high heat, bring 2.5cm (1in) water to the boil. Place the sweet potatoes in the basket, cover, and cook for 10 minutes or until the potatoes are tender. Cool slightly.

4 Place the sweet potatoes in a medium bowl and, using a potato masher, mash until smooth. Stir in 2 tablespoons of the plant-based butter, 2 tablespoons of the brown sugar, cinnamon, salt, and black pepper. Spread this sweet potato mixture evenly in the bottom of the baking dish.

5 Next, make the streusel topping. In a medium bowl, combine the plain flour, remaining brown sugar, walnuts, and cayenne.

6 Cut the remaining plant-based butter into small chunks, sprinkle over the flour mixture, and use your hands to rub the mixture until it begins to stick together. Sprinkle the streusel over the sweet potatoes, and bake for about 20 minutes or until golden. Serve immediately.

INGREDIENTS

900g (2lb.) sweet potatoes, peeled and cut into 5cm (2in) chunks

6 tbsp plant-based butter

6 tbsp brown sugar

½ tsp ground cinnamon

½ tsp sea salt

¼ tsp freshly ground black pepper

4 tbsp plain flour

4 tbsp chopped walnuts

Pinch cayenne

Mashing potatoes with a potato masher yields the best results. Try to avoid using your food processor or mixer because they can leave you with gluey potatoes. If you don't have a potato masher, just use a large fork or a pastry blender.

Casseroles and One-Pot Meals

You still can enjoy comfort food while eating a plant-based diet. Satisfy your craving for familiar flavours with a warm, hearty casserole, lasagne, or one-pot supper.

Winter Vegetable Pie (T)

Lots of herb-seasoned veggies in a creamy sauce make this vegetable pie a comfort food favourite.

SERVES 6 PREP 15 MINS COOK 45 MINS

1 Preheat the oven to 200°C (400°F/Gas 6).

2 Heat 2 tablespoons of the grapeseed oil in a small saucepan over a medium heat. Whisk in the flour until smooth, and cook, stirring constantly, for about 2 minutes or until the flour is lightly golden and smells toasty.

3 Whisk in 480ml (16fl oz) of the Golden Chicken-y Stock, and simmer for 5 minutes. Remove from heat, and set aside.

4 Heat the remaining grapeseed oil in a wide frying pan over a medium–high heat. Add the onion, celery, carrots, mushrooms, and garlic, and cook, stirring frequently, for about 10 minutes, adjusting the heat as necessary, or until the vegetables are softened and beginning to colour.

5 Stir in the remaining stock, potatoes, sweet potatoes, broad beans, bay leaf, thyme, salt, and black pepper. Cover and cook, stirring once or twice and adding a bit of water if it seems dry, for 10 minutes.

6 Remove the bay leaf, stir in the reserved sauce, and pour the vegetable mixture into a 23 × 33cm (9 × 13in) baking dish.

7 Roll out the puff pastry on a floured surface to fit the top of the baking dish with an overhang of 1cm (½in). Prick the pastry all over with a fork, transfer it to the top of the baking dish, and lay it gently over the vegetables. Tuck the overhanging edge down into the inside of the baking dish.

8 Bake for about 30 minutes or until the pastry is puffed and the filling is hot and bubbling. Serve immediately.

INGREDIENTS

4 tbsp grapeseed oil

3 tbsp plain flour

720ml (1 pint 4fl oz) *Golden Chicken-y Stock*

1 large onion, cut into small dice

4 large sticks celery, cut into small dice

3 carrots, cut into small dice

300g (10oz) chestnut mushrooms, quartered

3 cloves garlic, minced

4 large red-skinned potatoes, cut into small dice

1 sweet potato, cut into small dice

325g (11oz) frozen broad beans

1 bay leaf

1 tsp dried thyme

1 tsp sea salt, plus extra to taste

½ tsp freshly ground black pepper

1 sheet puff pastry, thawed

For *Chicken-Style Pie*, add 200–400g (7–14oz) shredded seitan. You also could add leafy greens, such as kale, to the vegetables when you sauté them or make your favourite stuffing mixture to replace the puff pastry topping altogether and bake as directed above.

Bisteeya (Moroccan Filo Pie) Ⓣ

Bisteeya, also known as *pastille,* is a dish of Berber origins often served at the beginning of a celebratory Moroccan meal. Layers of crisp filo pastry and lightly sweetened almonds enclose a savoury spiced filling of chickpeas and vegetables.

SERVES 6 PREP 55 MINS COOK 45 MINS

1 Preheat the oven to 200°C (400°F/Gas 6). Line a baking sheet with baking parchment.

2 Heat 2 tablespoons of the extra-virgin olive oiln a wide frying pan over a medium–high heat. Add the onions, garlic, ginger, and hot green chilli, and cook, stirring frequently, for 10 minutes.

3 Add ½ teaspoon of the cinnamon, the saffron threads, and Golden Chicken-y Stock, and bring to the boil. Stir in the chickpeas, potato, and preserved lemon peel. Reduce the heat to medium, and cook, stirring often, for about 10 minutes or until the vegetables are very tender and most of the liquid has evaporated.

4 Stir in the coriander, salt, and black pepper, and set aside to cool.

5 Spread the almonds on the prepared baking sheet, and toast in the oven for 6 minutes. Remove from the oven, and cool.

6 In a food processor fitted with the metal blade, pulse together the almonds, the remaining ½ teaspoon of cinnamon, and icing sugar until the mixture resembles fine breadcrumbs.

7 Brush a 23cm (9in) round cake tin with a little extra-virgin olive oil. Lay 1 sheet of filo in the tin, and sprinkle with one-fifth of the almond mixture. Brush a second sheet of filo with extra-virgin olive oil, and lay it oiled side up on top of the second sheet in a criss-cross direction. Sprinkle with one-quarter of the remaining almond mixture and continue to layer the remaining filo and almonds, placing the filo so the overhang of pastry is evenly spaced around the tin (first in a cross shape, then in an X shape, then a slightly offset X shape). Spoon the vegetable–chickpea mixture into the tin and spread evenly. Gather the overhanging filo to cover the top of the pie, and brush with a little more extra-virgin olive oil.

8 Place the tin on a baking sheet, and bake for about 35 minutes or until crisp and golden. Cool slightly, remove carefully from the tin, and dust with a little more icing sugar and cinnamon. Cut into wedges and serve.

INGREDIENTS

6 tbsp extra-virgin olive oil

2 large red onions, finely chopped

2 cloves garlic, finely chopped

1 tbsp grated fresh ginger

1 small hot green chilli, deseeded and finely chopped

1 tsp ground cinnamon, plus extra for dusting

½ tsp saffron threads, crushed

240ml (8fl oz) *Golden Chicken-y Stock*

2 (400g; 14oz) cans chickpeas, rinsed and drained

1 Maris Piper potato, peeled and finely chopped

1 preserved lemon, peel only, finely chopped

2 tbsp finely chopped fresh coriander

½ tsp sea salt

½ tsp freshly ground black pepper

150g (5½oz) blanched almonds

1 tbsp icing sugar, plus extra for dusting

6 (23 × 35.5cm; 9 × 14in) sheets filo pastry

Savoury Stuffed Cabbage

From their humble origins, cabbage rolls are incredibly flavourful Eastern European comfort food. Serve them with mashed potatoes and some rye bread for a real treat.

SERVES 4–6 PREP 15 MINS PLUS 1 HOUR FREEZING TIME COOK 40 MINS

1 Preheat the oven to 200°C (400°F/Gas 6). Lightly coat a 23 × 33cm (9 × 13in) glass baking dish with cooking spray.

2 Thaw the cabbage leaves at room temperature, and squeeze the excess moisture from each leaf. Set aside on a kitchen paper-lined surface.

3 Heat the extra-virgin olive oil in a large frying pan over a medium–high heat, Add the onion, salt, and black pepper, and stir for 2 minutes.

4 Add the mushrooms, and cook, stirring often, until they begin to colour. Remove from the heat, and stir in the dill, flat-leaf parsley, thyme, and rice.

5 In a small saucepan over a medium–high heat, combine the vegetable stock, tomato purée, sugar, allspice, and white wine. Bring to the boil, reduce the heat to medium, and cook, stirring to dissolve the purée and white wine, for about 10 minutes or until the sauce is reduced and slightly thickened. Keep warm while you fill the cabbage rolls.

6 Working with 1 cabbage leaf at a time, spoon a few tablespoons of filling in the centre and roll up like a burrito: tucking up the short ends first, then rolling each into a long cylinder. Place each finished cabbage roll in the prepared baking dish and repeat with remaining ingredients.

7 Pour the sauce over the cabbage rolls, cover the pan with heavy-duty foil, and bake for 30 minutes. Serve hot.

INGREDIENTS

12 large cabbage leaves, bottom 7.5cm (3in) of the stem removed, frozen for at least 1 hour

2 tbsp extra-virgin olive oil

1 small yellow onion, finely chopped

1 tsp sea salt

¼ tsp freshly ground black pepper

225g (8oz) chestnut mushrooms, finely chopped

1 tbsp finely chopped fresh dill

1 tbsp finely chopped fresh flat-leaf parsley

½ tsp dried thyme leaves

160g (5½oz) cooked brown rice

480ml (16fl oz) vegetable stock

4 tbsp tomato purée

2 tbsp sugar

½ tsp ground allspice

4 tbsp dry white wine

Cabbage leaves

Vegetable Enchiladas with Roasted Tomato Sauce (T)

A filling of tender vegetables is wrapped in tortillas and baked in a savoury sauce of roasted tomatoes. This dish has a mild chilli flavour and freezes beautifully.

SERVES 4 **PREP** 45 MINS **COOK** 1 HOUR, 40 MINS

1 Preheat the oven to 190°C (375°F/Gas 5). Lightly coat a 23 × 33cm (9 × 13in) baking dish with a little extra-virgin olive oil.

2 Cut the tomatoes in half, place in the baking dish, and toss with 2 tablespoons of the extra-virgin olive oil, red pepper strips, ½ teaspoon of the salt, and oregano. Roast for 1 hour, stirring occasionally, and cool slightly.

3 Purée the tomato mixture, vegetable stock, and chilli powder in batches in a blender or a food processor. Set aside.

4 Heat the remaining extra-virgin olive oil in a wide frying pan over a medium–high heat. Add the onion and poblano chillies, and cook, stirring occasionally, for 4–5 minutes, adjusting heat as necessary.

5 Add the garlic, and stir for 1 minute. Add the courgettes, and cook for about 4–5 minutes or until the vegetables are golden. Stir in the roasted corn, and cook another 1 or 2 minutes. Stir in the black beans, coriander, remaining salt, and 120ml (4fl oz) of the reserved sauce, and remove from the heat.

6 Spread 120ml (4fl oz) of the sauce on the bottom of the prepared dish. Spoon about one-twelfth of the filling into the centre of 1 tortilla, filling it generously, gently roll, and place in the dish. Repeat with the remaining tortillas and filling, fitting them snugly into the dish. Pour some of the remaining sauce over the top of the enchiladas, lightly covering them while leaving edges exposed, and sprinkle with the cheese (if using). Cover with foil, and bake for about 40 minutes or until hot and bubbling. Serve immediately.

For *Tortilla Soup,* stir 480ml (16fl oz) of sauce into 480ml (16fl oz) of vegetable stock. Heat and stir in 30g (1oz) of lightly crushed tortilla chips and 175g (6oz) of black beans. Serve topped with a spoonful of plant-based soured cream and diced avocado.

INGREDIENTS

550g (1¼lb) small tomatoes, such as Campari

4 tbsp extra-virgin olive oil

2 red peppers, ribs and seeds removed, and cut into 2.5cm (1in) strips

1 tsp sea salt

½ tsp dried oregano

480ml (16fl oz) vegetable stock

3 tbsp chilli powder

1 large onion, finely chopped

2 poblano chilli peppers, deseeded and finely chopped

2 cloves garlic, finely chopped

2 large courgettes, cut into 1cm (½in) dice

450g (1lb) roasted sweetcorn kernels, or regular frozen sweetcorn kernels

1 (400g; 14oz) can black beans, rinsed and drained

2 tbsp finely chopped fresh coriander

16 (15cm; 6in) tortillas

60g (2oz) shredded plant-based Cheddar–style cheese (optional)

Mushroom Lasagne

The meaty flavour of mushrooms blends perfectly with Cashew Ricotta and zesty Tomato Sauce. Using ready-to-use lasagne sheets makes this an easy weeknight dish.

SERVES 8 PREP 30 MINS COOK 50 MINS

1 Preheat the oven to 190°C (375°F/Gas 5). Lightly coat a 23 × 33cm (9 × 13in) baking dish with cooking spray.

2 Place the porcini mushrooms in a small bowl, pour boiling water on top, and soak for about 5 minutes or until softened. Lift the porcini from the soaking water, agitating gently to release any soil. Reserve the soaking liquid. Chop the mushrooms and set aside.

3 Heat the extra-virgin olive oil in a large frying pan over a medium–high heat. Add the garlic and cook, stirring continuously, for 1 minute.

4 Add the porcini mushrooms, mushrooms, rosemary, salt, oregano, and black pepper, and cook, stirring occasionally, for 10 minutes or until the mushrooms begin to brown.

5 Strain the mushroom-soaking liquid, leaving the last few teaspoons behind to eliminate any grit, and add to the mushrooms along with the red wine, stirring vigorously to deglaze the pan. Stir until the liquid has evaporated, and set the mushrooms aside.

6 Spread 240ml (8fl oz) of Tomato Sauce evenly over the bottom of the baking dish, lay 3 sheets of lasagne over the sauce, spoon half of the mushroom mixture and half of the Cashew Ricotta evenly over the lasagne sheets. Pour 180ml (6fl oz) of Tomato Sauce over the Cashew Ricotta, layer a further 3 lasagne sheets, add the remaining mushrooms and Cashew Ricotta, followed by another 180ml (6fl oz) of Tomato Sauce. Finish with another 3 sheets of lasagne and another 180ml (6fl oz) of Tomato Sauce. Cover the dish with foil, folding back a corner slightly to allow steam to escape. Reserve the remaining 120ml (4fl oz) of sauce for serving.

7 Bake for 50 minutes or until hot and bubbling. Remove from the oven and set aside to rest for 5–10 minutes before cutting. Reheat the remaining sauce to serve as an accompaniment at the table.

INGREDIENTS

15g (½oz) dried porcini mushrooms

120ml (4fl oz) boiling water

4 tbsp extra-virgin olive oil

3 cloves garlic, minced

225g (8oz) chestnut mushrooms, thinly sliced

115g (4oz) shiitake mushrooms, stemmed and thinly sliced

1 tsp chopped fresh rosemary or ½ tsp dried

1 tsp sea salt, or to taste

½ tsp dried oregano

½ tsp freshly ground black pepper, or to taste

4 tbsp dry red wine

960ml (1¾ pints) *Tomato Sauce*

9 ready-to-use lasagne sheets

480ml (16fl oz) *Cashew Ricotta*

Squash and Onion Bake (T)

Tender courgettes and yellow summer squash slices are bathed in a creamy béchamel sauce with plenty of sweet onions and then topped with breadcrumbs and baked until golden.

SERVES 4–6 PREP 15 MINS COOK 40 MINS

1 Preheat the oven to 180°C (350°F/Gas 4). Lightly grease a 20 x 20cm (8 × 8in) square baking dish.

2 Heat 2 tablespoons of the extra-virgin olive oil in a wide frying pan over a medium–high heat. Add the onions and cook, stirring, for 5 minutes or until softened.

3 Add the garlic and stir for 1 minute. Remove the onions and garlic from the pan and keep warm.

4 Add 1 tablespoon of the olive oil, courgettes, and yellow squash, and season with salt and black pepper. Increase the heat to high and cook, stirring every minute or so, for 5 minutes or until the vegetables begin to turn golden.

5 Sprinkle with the flour, reduce the heat to medium, and stir for 1 minute to combine well. Return the onion mixture to the pan.

6 Stir in the non-dairy milk, nutmeg, and rosemary. Bring to the boil, and cook for about 2 minutes or until thickened. Remove from the heat.

7 In a small bowl, combine the panko breadcrumbs, chives, thyme, and the remaining extra-virgin olive oil.

8 Pour the squash mixture into the baking dish, spread gently, and sprinkle evenly with the breadcrumb mixture. Bake, uncovered, for 30 minutes. Serve immediately.

INGREDIENTS

4 tbsp extra-virgin olive oil

2 large sweet onions, thinly sliced into rings

2 cloves garlic, finely chopped

2 courgettes, thinly sliced

2 yellow squash, thinly sliced

1 tsp sea salt

¼ tsp freshly ground black pepper

2 tbsp plain flour

360ml (12fl oz) non-dairy milk, such as rice or soya milk

¼ tsp ground nutmeg

½ tsp finely chopped fresh rosemary

115g (4oz) panko breadcrumbs

2 tbsp finely chopped fresh chives

1 tsp dried thyme

Rosemary

For a *"Cheesy" Vegetable Bake*, gently stir in 110g (3½oz) of your favourite shredded plant-based cheese into the vegetables and sauce before baking.

Aubergine and Roasted Tomato Polenta Lasagne

it takes some time to assemble this dish, but the savoury flavours of roasted aubergine, tomatoes, pesto, toasted pine nuts, and creamy polenta are well worth it. You won't miss the cheese or saturated fat of the classic meaty version in this flavour-packed dish.

SERVES 6 PREP 45 MINS PLUS COOLING TIME COOK 45 MINS

1 Line a 23 × 23cm (9 × 9in) baking dish with baking parchment and brush it with a little olive oil.

2 In a large saucepan over a high heat, bring the water to the boil. Stirring constantly, add the polenta in a thin stream. Add ½ teaspoon of the salt, reduce the heat to medium, and continue to stir until the polenta is fully cooked. (It will be creamy and smooth with no "bite" when you taste it.)

3 Pour the polenta into the prepared baking dish and allow to cool for a bit. Cover and refrigerate for at least 2 hours or overnight or until set.

4 Preheat the oven to 200°C (400°F/Gas 6).

5 Sprinkle the aubergine cubes with ½ teaspoon of the salt and place in a colander to drain for 30 minutes. Rinse and gently squeeze out any remaining water.

6 In a large baking tray, toss the aubergine cubes and cherry tomatoes with sliced garlic and 3 tablespoons of extra-virgin olive oil. Spread evenly, and roast, stirring once or twice, for 30 minutes. Remove from the oven, and reduce the temperature to 190°C (375°F/Gas 5).

7 When the polenta has set, carefully turn it out of the dish. Cut into thirds, and slice each third horizontally into 3 equal pieces so you have 9 polenta "lasagne sheets." Handle carefully using a spatula, but don't worry if they break – just fit them back together in the dish.

8 To assemble the lasagne, brush the baking dish with the remaining extra-virgin olive oil. Spread 120ml (4fl oz) of Tomato Sauce over the bottom of the dish and cover with 3 pieces of polenta. Top with half of the tomato–aubergine mixture and half of Summer Pesto, followed by another layer of polenta. Add another 120ml (4fl oz) of Tomato Sauce, the remaining aubergine–tomato mixture, and the remaining Summer Pesto. Top with the final layer of polenta and spread the remaining Tomato Sauce evenly over the top. Cover and bake for about 40 minutes or until hot and bubbling.

9 Just before serving, sprinkle basil and toasted pine nuts over the top of the lasagne. Serve hot.

INGREDIENTS

1.2 litres (2 pints) water

160g (5½oz) coarse polenta (not instant)

1½ tsp sea salt

1 large aubergine, cut into 2.5cm (1in) cubes

350g (12oz) cherry tomatoes, halved

3 cloves garlic, thinly sliced

4 tbsp extra-virgin olive oil

360ml (12fl oz) *Tomato Sauce*

240ml (8fl oz) *Summer Pesto*

6 large basil leaves, cut in thin ribbons

60g (2oz) pine nuts, toasted

Tamale Casserole Ⓣ

A tender crust of cornmeal and golden cornflour (masa harina) encloses a slightly spicy, savoury filling of veggies and pinto beans in this lighter version of a *tamale* casserole.

SERVES 6   PREP 10 MiNS   COOK 80 MiNS

1 Preheat the oven to 190°C (375°F/Gas 5). Lightly oil a 23 × 23cm (9 × 9in) baking dish.

2 Heat 3 tablespoons of the extra-virgin olive oil in a large frying pan over a medium–high heat. Add the onion, green pepper, and garlic, and cook for 3 minutes, adjusting the heat as needed to prevent burning.

3 Add the cumin, oregano, chipotle chilli, adobo sauce, and kale, and cook, stirring frequently, for 5 minutes.

4 Stir in the pinto beans, diced tomatoes with their juice, vegetable stock, and pimiento-stuffed green olives, and cook for 10 minutes or until all the vegetables are tender and the sauce has reduced slightly.

5 Meanwhile, in a large saucepan over a high heat, bring the water to the boil. Stir in the salt, and slowly whisk in the yellow cornmeal and masa harina. Reduce the heat to medium and cook, stirring frequently, for 15 minutes.

6 Stir in the sweetcorn and remaining extra-virgin olive oil.

7 Spoon half of the cornmeal mixture into the bottom of the prepared baking dish, and spread evenly. Top with the vegetables, followed by the remaining cornmeal mixture. Sprinkle the Cheddar-style cheese over the top, and bake for 40 minutes. Serve immediately.

INGREDIENTS

4 tbsp extra-virgin olive oil

1 large onion, finely chopped

1 green pepper, ribs and seeds removed, and finely chopped

3 cloves garlic, finely chopped

1 tsp ground cumin

½ tsp dried oregano

1 canned chipotle chilli in adobo (available online), finely chopped

2 tbsp adobo sauce (from the canned chilli)

1 bunch kale, tough stems removed, and roughly chopped

2 (400g; 14oz) cans pinto beans, rinsed and drained

1 (400g; 14oz) can diced tomatoes, with juice

240ml (8fl oz) vegetable stock

30g (1oz) pimiento-stuffed green olives, chopped

1.3 litres (2¼ pints) water

2½ tsp sea salt

115g (4oz) coarse yellow cornmeal

85g (3oz) masa harina (golden cornflour)

200g (7oz) fresh or frozen sweetcorn kernels

115g (4oz) shredded plant-based Cheddar-style cheese

Green pepper

Using a mixture of coarse cornmeal and masa harina gives this dish great *tamale* flavour, but you can use a total of 200g (7oz) cornmeal if you don't have masa harina. If you can source roasted corn in the freezer section, it adds fantastic flavour to this dish. An unbaked casserole can be frozen for up to 3 months and baked from frozen at 180°C (350°F/Gas 4).

Mixed Vegetable Cottage Pie Ⓣ

This rich, intensely flavoured comforting favourite is a real crowd pleaser. Substitute parsnips for swede in the topping if you like.

SERVES 4   PREP 30 MINS   COOK 1 HOUR

1   Heat the vegetable oil in a large saucepan over a medium–high heat. Add the onion and sauté, stirring, for 3 minutes or until lightly golden.

2   Add the mushrooms, carrots, turnips, peas, and pinto beans. Stir in the vegetable stock, soy sauce, vegan Worcestershire sauce, herbes de Provence, salt, and black pepper. Bring to the boil, reduce the heat to medium, cover, and simmer gently for 10 minutes or until the vegetables are tender.

3   In a small bowl, blend the flour with the water. Stir he mixture into the saucepan and cook, stirring constantly, for 2 minutes to thicken.

4   Meanwhile, cook the swede and potatoes in a large saucepan of salted, boiling water over a medium–high heat for 15 minutes or until tender. Drain and return the vegetables to the pan, reduce the heat to low, and cook to dry out slightly.

5   Add the plant-based butter, rice milk, a generous grating of nutmeg, and a generous grinding of black pepper, and mash. Beat well with a wooden spoon until smooth.

6   Preheat the oven to 190°C (375°F/Gas 5).

7   Spoon the vegetable and bean mixture into a 2-litre (3½-pint) ovenproof baking dish or 4 ramekins. Top with the swede mash and fluff with a fork. Sprinkle the Cheddar-style cheese (if using) over the top, and bake for about 40 minutes or until golden. Serve hot.

INGREDIENTS

1 tbsp vegetable oil

1 onion, finely chopped

115g (4oz) white mushrooms, sliced

2 carrots, grated

2 small turnips, grated

60g (2oz) shelled fresh or thawed frozen peas

2 (400g; 14oz) cans pinto beans, rinsed and drained

480ml (16fl oz) vegetable stock

1 tbsp soy sauce

1 tbsp vegan Worcestershire sauce

1 tsp herbes de Provence

½ tsp sea salt

¼ tsp freshly ground black pepper, plus more to taste

4 tbsp plain flour

4 tbsp water

1 small swede, cut into small chunks

450g (1lb) Maris Piper potatoes, peeled and cut into small chunks

2 tbsp plant-based butter

4 tbsp rice milk

Grated nutmeg

60g (2oz) plant-based Cheddar-style cheese, grated (optional)

Not all Worcestershire sauce is plant-based, so read the ingredients. Look for an organic brand made without anchovies, such as Annie's.

Cassoulet Ⓣ

This slow-cooked dish is perfect to pop in the oven on a cold winter's day. Fresh thyme, herbes de Provence, red wine, and aromatic vegetables slowly infuse the creamy beans with flavour. Serve steaming bowls of this delicious stew with a simple salad and plenty of crusty French bread.

SERVES 4 PREP 15 MINS COOK 3 HOURS, 45 MINS

1 Preheat the oven to 150°C (300°F/Gas 2).

2 Rinse the white beans, pick over, and drain.

3 Combine the beans and vegetable stock in a heavy earthenware or cast-iron dish with a lid. (Alternatively, you can use a heavy stainless-steel casserole with a lid.) Set aside.

4 Heat the extra-virgin olive oil in a medium frying pan over a medium–high heat. Add the leeks, celery, carrot, and shallot, and stir for 5 minutes.

5 Stir in the garlic, thyme, and herbes de Provence, and cook for 1 minute.

6 Stir in the tomato purée, followed by the red wine, salt, and black pepper. Combine thoroughly and remove from heat.

7 Pour the vegetable mixture over the beans, stir gently, and bake, covered, stirring once or twice, for 3½ hours or until the beans are tender. Remove the lid during the last hour of cooking.

8 Remove from the oven, stir in the flat-leaf parsley, and serve.

INGREDIENTS

360g (12oz) dried white beans, such as flageolet

960ml (1¾ pints) vegetable stock, preferably home-made

120ml (4fl oz) extra-virgin olive oil

2 leeks, cut into 3mm (¹/₈in) pieces

3 sticks celery, cut into 3mm (¹/₈in) pieces

1 carrot, halved and cut into 3mm (¹/₈in) slices

2 shallots, minced

2 cloves garlic, thinly sliced

1 tbsp fresh thyme leaves

1 tsp herbes de Provence

2 tbsp tomato purée

360ml (12fl oz) dry red wine

1 tsp sea salt

½ tsp freshly ground black pepper

8 tbsp finely chopped fresh flat-leaf parsley

For *Slow Cooker Cassoulet,* combine the beans and vegetable broth in a 4-litre (7-pint) slow cooker, and set the heat to low. Sauté the vegetables as directed, add to the slow cooker, cover, and cook for 8 hours or until the beans are tender.

Butternut Squash Tagine (T)

A *tagine* is both a Moroccan dish and the container it's cooked in. If you have a tagine, use it to cook and serve this fragrant, gently spiced, warming stew; if not, a big pan with a lid works just fine.

SERVES 4   PREP 20 MINS   COOK 25 MINS

1. Heat the extra-virgin olive oil in a tagine or a large pan with a lid over a medium-high heat. Add the butternut squash and onion, and cook, stirring, for 5 minutes.

2. Add the garlic, preserved lemon peel, tomato purée, cumin, coriander, cinnamon, and black pepper, and stir for 1 minute.

3. Stir in the salt, vegetable stock, chickpeas, and apricots. Cover, reduce the heat to low or medium–low, and cook at a brisk simmer, stirring occasionally, for 15–20 minutes or until the squash is tender but not mushy.

4. Add the green olives, garnish with coriander, and serve.

INGREDIENTS

2 tbsp extra-virgin olive oil

1 butternut squash, peeled and cut into 1cm (½in) cubes

1 large onion, halved and thinly sliced

2 cloves garlic, finely chopped

½ preserved lemon, peel only, finely chopped

1 tbsp tomato purée

1 tsp ground cumin

1 tsp ground coriander

½ tsp ground cinnamon

½ tsp freshly ground black pepper

1 tsp sea salt

480ml (16fl oz) vegetable stock

1 (400g; 14oz) can chickpeas, rinsed and drained

125g (4½oz) dried apricots, chopped

65g (2oz) pitted green olives

4 tbsp finely chopped fresh coriander

If you can't source preserved lemon at your supermarket or local grocers or deli, substitute by adding 1 tablespoon of freshly squeezed lemon juice along with the vegetable stock.

Seeds, Grains, and Pasta

When you want to feed a crowd, look no further. The pasta, risotto, paella, and quinoa dishes in this section are sure to please. Feeling adventurous? Make your own ravioli!

Crispy Quinoa Cakes (T)

Quinoa and lentils form a crispy exterior and tender interior in these savoury little bites. Feel free to mix up the spices – add curry and ginger for an Indian-inspired flavour or replace the coriander and cumin with basil and lemon zest for some Italian flair.

SERVES 6 PREP 25 MINS COOK 25 MINS

1 Preheat the oven to 200°C (400°F/Gas 6). Line a baking sheet with baking parchment.

2 In a small bowl, whisk together the flax meal and warm water. Set aside.

3 Heat 2 tablespoons of the extra-virgin olive oil in a medium frying pan over a medium–high heat. When the oil begins to shimmer, add the onion and cook, stirring frequently, for about 3 minutes or until the onion is translucent and just beginning to turn golden around edges.

4 Add the garlic, reduce the heat to medium, and stir for 30 seconds. Add the kale and cook, stirring occasionally, for about 5 minutes. Remove from the heat and set aside to cool slightly.

5 In a large bowl, combine the quinoa, lentils, pumpkin seeds, flat-leaf parsley, and coriander.

6 Whisk the tahini, lemon juice, and flour into the flax mixture until smooth, and add to the quinoa mixture. Stir in the salt, cumin, black pepper, and kale mixture, and combine well.

7 Using wet hands, divide the mixture into 12 even-sized balls, and flatten into 2.5cm (1in) cakes, spacing them evenly on the baking sheet. (If desired, you could use a cooking ring to form perfectly round cakes.)

8 Brush each cake lightly with the remaining extra-virgin olive oil, and bake for 20 minutes or until golden brown and crisp. Serve immediately.

INGREDIENTS

2 tbsp flax meal (ground flax seeds)

6 tbsp warm water

3 tbsp extra-virgin olive oil

¼ red onion, finely chopped

2 cloves garlic, finely chopped

1 bunch kale, stemmed and finely chopped

375g (13oz) cooked quinoa

300g (10oz) cooked brown or green lentils

4 tbsp roasted pumpkin seeds, roughly chopped

4 tbsp finely chopped fresh flat-leaf parsley

2 tbsp finely chopped fresh coriander

2 tbsp tahini

Juice of 1 lemon (2 tbsp)

2 tbsp plain flour

1 tsp sea salt

1 tsp ground cumin

½ tsp freshly ground black pepper

For *Gluten-Free Quinoa Cakes,* simply use gluten-free flour instead of plain flour. Serve these protein-packed patties on salad, in a pitta, add Guacamole or Romesco Sauce, or drizzle with lemon juice and tahini.

QUINOA

Quinoa's high protein and healthy fat content make it a nutritious and filling choice for main and side dishes. This ancient seed, often thought of as a grain, is also rich in calcium and iron. **Benefits** Is gluten free; good source of protein; promotes heart health; and contains antioxidants. **Uses** Quinoa has a springy texture and a grassy, slightly bitter flavour. Toast it in a dry pan, add water, and steam as you would rice. Available as wholegrain seeds, flour, or flakes, it goes well with apples, black beans, chilles, coriander, sweetcorn, grapes, nuts, oranges, squash, and sweet potatoes. **Recipes** Crispy Quinoa Cakes, Quinoa Vegetable Salad.

Quinoa Vegetable Salad (T)

Nutty quinoa teams up with edamame, kale, and crunchy jicama for a protein-packed powerhouse of a salad that's perfect for lunches, picnics, and potluck suppers.

SERVES 4 PREP 10 MINS COOK 25 MINS

1 Toast the quinoa in a dry, medium pan with a tight-fitting lid over a medium–high heat, stirring constantly, for 1 minute.

2 Pour in the water and add ½ teaspoon of the salt. Bring to the boil, reduce the heat to low, and cook, covered, for 15 minutes. Let it stand covered for 10 minutes, and then fluff up with a fork.

3 In a large bowl, toss the kale leaves with 1 tablespoon of the lemon juice, 1 tablespoon of the extra-virgin olive oil, and a pinch of salt. Using clean hands, massage the kale for 5 minutes or until softened and reduced. Stir in garlic, and set aside.

4 In a small bowl, whisk the remaining 1 tablespoon of lemon juice, remaining 2 tablespoons of oil, remaining ½ teaspoon of salt, along with the apple cider vinegar and tahini. Set aside.

5 Add the quinoa, jicama, edamame, red onion, almonds, cranberries, and reserved dressing to the kale, and toss. Serve warm or cold.

INGREDIENTS

190g (6¾oz) quinoa

360ml (12fl oz) water

1 tsp sea salt, plus a pinch extra

1 bunch kale, leaves only

Juice of 1 lemon (2 tbsp)

3 tbsp extra-virgin olive oil

1 clove garlic, finely chopped

2 tbsp apple cider vinegar

2 tbsp tahini

1 small jicama (or use turnip or yam), cut into 5mm (¼in) dice

150g (5½oz) frozen edamame, thawed

½ small red onion, very thinly sliced

45g (1½oz) sliced almonds, toasted

60g (2oz) dried cranberries

For *Gluten-Free Quinoa Vegetable Salad,* replace the edamame with 175g (6oz) of cooked broad beans.

Risotto Milanese (T)

Golden, saffron-scented rice is slowly stirred with stock to gradually release the rice's starch, resulting in a comforting, creamy-tasting, plant-based version of a beloved Italian classic.

SERVES 4–6 **PREP** 5 MINS **COOK** 35 MINS

1 Heat the extra-virgin olive oil in a large, wide saucepan over a medium heat. Add the shallots and salt, and cook, stirring frequently, for about 10 minutes or until the shallots are softened and just beginning to turn a light golden colour (without browning).

2 In a large saucepan over a medium–high heat, heat the Golden Chicken-y Stock. Reduce the heat to a simmer.

3 Place the saffron threads in a small bowl and ladle about 1 tablespoon of the stock over the saffron. Set aside to steep.

4 Increase the heat under the shallots to high, add the Arborio rice all at once, and cook, stirring constantly, for 2 minutes or until the rice smells nutty.

5 Add the white wine and saffron, reduce the heat to medium, and stir until most of the wine has been absorbed.

6 Add 480ml(16fl oz) of the simmering stock to the pan and reduce the heat to low or medium-low. (Adjust the heat as needed to keep the risotto at a gentle simmer as you cook it.) Cook, stirring constantly until the stock is almost completely absorbed and add another 240ml (8fl oz) of stock. Continue in this manner until the rice is tender but *al dente* (still a bit firm to the bite) and risotto is creamy.

7 Remove from the heat, stir in the nutritional yeast, plant-based butter, flat-leaf parsley, chives, and black pepper. Taste and add more salt if desired, and serve immediately.

INGREDIENTS

3 tbsp extra-virgin olive oil

4 small shallots, finely minced

1 tsp sea salt, plus extra to taste

1.9 litres (3½ pints) *Golden Chicken-y Stock* or home-made vegetable stock

¼ tsp saffron threads

375g (13oz) Arborio or carnaroli rice

240ml (8fl oz) dry white wine

2 tbsp nutritional yeast

1 tbsp plant-based butter

1 tbsp finely chopped fresh flat-leaf parsley

1 tbsp finely chopped fresh chives

½ tsp freshly ground black pepper

For *"Cheesy" Risotto*, stir in 8 tablespoons of Cashew Ricotta just before serving. For *Lemon Asparagus Risotto*, stir in the peas or thinly sliced asparagus with 1 teaspoon of lemon zest. For *Mushroom Risotto*, replace the stock with Mushroom Stock and stir in some Sautéed Mushroom Medley.

Moroccan Couscous Ⓣ

Try this easy-to-cook and wonderfully fluffy grain as a side dish with tempeh or tofu, or top it with a vegetable stew such as Butternut Squash Tagine.

SERVES 4 **PREP** 10 MINS **COOK** 30 MINS

1 Heat the extra-virgin olive oil in a medium saucepan over a medium heat. Add the onion and cook, stirring occasionally, for 10 minutes.

2 Stir in the cumin, turmeric, salt, cinnamon stick, and saffron threads, and cook for 30 seconds.

3 Add the Golden Chicken-y Stock, reduce the heat to low, and simmer for 10 minutes.

4 In a small bowl, place the apricots and raisins. Add 4 tablespoons of the hot stock, cover, and set aside.

5 Measure the remaining stock to be sure you have exactly 480ml (16fl oz). Return the stock to the pan and bring to the boil over a high heat. Remove from the heat, stir in the couscous, cover, and set aside for 10 minutes.

6 Drain the apricots and raisins. Remove the cinnamon stick from the couscous, and fluff the grains with a fork. Stir the fruit and pine nuts into the couscous, garnish with coriander, and serve immediately.

INGREDIENTS

2 tbsp extra-virgin olive oil

1 onion, halved and thinly sliced

½ tsp ground cumin

½ tsp ground turmeric

½ tsp sea salt

1 cinnamon stick

½ tsp saffron threads, lightly crushed

600ml (1 pint) *Golden Chicken-y Stock* or vegetable stock

60g (2oz) dried apricots, chopped

60g (2oz) raisins

165g (6oz) instant couscous

8 tbsp pine nuts, toasted

1 tbsp finely chopped fresh coriander

Dried apricots

Traditional Moroccan couscous is steamed over a pan of flavourful liquid and cooled and rubbed by hand several times, resulting in a fluffy grain that grows to several times its original size. You can avoid this time-consuming process by purchasing unseasoned instant couscous (the kind in boxes in supermarkets), which has already been steamed and dried.

Arancini (Risotto Balls)

These crunchy-on-the-outside, creamy-on-the-inside rice balls are the perfect choice to serve at a party when you want to indulge yourself and your guests. Or enjoy Risotto Milanese for supper one night, and have *arancini* on the side with a bowl of soup or a salad later in the week.

SERVES 6   PREP 45 MINS   COOK 10 MINS

1   Line two baking sheets with baking parchment.

2   Place the flour, water, and breadcrumbs in separate small, shallow bowls.

3   Scoop out portions (of about 120ml (4fl oz/about half a mug) of chilled Risotto Milanese. Using wet hands, form each portion into a ball, tucking 1 plant-based mozzarella cheese cube and a few peas into the centre. Place the balls on one of the baking sheets.

4   Working one at a time, quickly roll each ball in the flour, dip in water, and roll in the panko breadcrumbs, being sure to thoroughly coat each ball. Roll once more in the flour, shake off the excess, and set aside on the second baking sheet. When all balls are breaded, chill for 30 minutes or overnight.

5   Just before you're ready to serve, preheat the oven to 130°C (250°F/Gas ½).

6   Heat 7.5–10cm (3–4in) of grapeseed oil in a wide saucepan over a medium–high heat. Use a deep-frying thermometer to bring the oil to 190°C (375°F) and add balls, 3 or 4 at a time. Cook, turning frequently, for about 3 minutes or until golden brown all over. Transfer to a wire rack set over a baking tray to keep the balls crisp and keep warm in the oven as you fry subsequent batches. Serve hot with Tomato Sauce for dipping.

INGREDIENTS

125g (4½oz) plain flour

120ml (4fl oz) water

175g (6oz) panko breadcrumbs

½ batch *Risotto Milanese* or your favourite risotto, chilled overnight

10 (1cm; ½in) cubes plant-based mozzarella cheese

40g (1½oz) frozen peas

Grapeseed oil

Tomato Sauce

Declare one evening a week "leftover night" when all leftovers are eaten, or have fun creating something new out of your remnants from earlier meals. One of my favorite leftover meals was tacos made from beans and veggies I scooped out of soup. Stir leftovers into polenta, or mix with pasta and bake in a casserole. Leftover tofu, tempeh, or seitan make a great sandwich filling.

Farro Risotto
with Roasted Fennel and Mushrooms Ⓣ

Farro is an ancient grain. It's a type of wheat that yields a firm bite and a nutty flavour – the perfect foil for sweet, roasted fennel and meaty mushrooms.

SERVES 4 PREP 10 MINS COOK 35 MINS

1 Preheat the oven to 200°C (400°F/Gas 6). Line a baking tray with baking parchment.

2 In a medium saucepan over a high heat, combine the farro with 1 teaspoon of the salt and enough water to cover by 2.5cm (1in). Bring to a boil, reduce the heat to medium, and cook, stirring occasionally, for 20 minutes. (Adjust the heat as necessary to maintain a brisk simmer.) Drain and set aside.

3 Toss the mushrooms, fennel, and garlic with 2 tablespoons of the extra-virgin olive oil in the baking tray. Roast, stirring once or twice, for 20 minutes. Set aside.

4 In a small saucepan over a medium–high heat, bring the vegetable stock to a simmer.

5 Heat the remaining 2 tablespoons of extra-virgin olive oil in a large frying pan over a medium–high heat. Add the spring onions and stir for 1 minute.

6 Add the drained farro and white wine, stir until the wine is evaporated, and add 240ml (8fl oz) of stock. Cook, stirring, until the stock is absorbed.

7 Add the remaining stock along with the roasted vegetables, and stir until the stock is absorbed.

8 Stir in the reserved dark green parts of spring onions, season to taste with remaining salt, and serve.

INGREDIENTS

350g (12oz) farro

1½ tsp sea salt

300g (10oz) chestnut mushrooms, quartered

2 bulbs fennel, tops removed, cut into 1cm (½in) chunks

2 cloves garlic, finely chopped

4 tbsp extra-virgin olive oil

480ml (16fl oz) vegetable stock

1 bunch spring onions, white and light green parts separated from the dark green parts, thinly sliced

120ml (4fl oz) dry white wine

Grains

Grains, both ancient and common, are a great source of protein. In particular, breads made from sprouted grains are a fantastic way to add protein to your favourite veggie sandwiches. Some grains can stand in for meat, too, such as seitan, a meat substitute made from wheat gluten.

Couscous

	AMARANTH	BUCKWHEAT	BULGUR WHEAT	SWEETCORN	COUSCOUS	DURUM WHEAT	FARRO	FREEKEH
WHAT IT IS	A seed rather than a grain, it can be found in both cereal and flour forms. Has an earthy and nutty flavour, with a slightly chewy texture, just like bulgur or quinoa.	A para-cereal, most commonly found as a husked whole grain or flour. The husked whole grain, or kasha, is nutty and earthy tasting.	A nutty, neutral-flavour cereal wheat that's cracked and partially cooked. Available in coarse, medium, and fine (instant) grinds.	Sweet and starchy, fresh corn is chewy and dense with a high sugar content. Cornmeal or flour is sweet without being sugary and is creamy in texture.	Made from semolina, couscous is neutral-flavoured granules of durum wheat that have been husked and crushed.	The hardest type of wheat, durum has a higher protein content than many other kinds of wheat and is most often found milled in pasta and flour.	Dense, chewy, and nutty, farro comprises a group of whole grains (einhorn, emmer, and spelt).	Green wheat that's been dried, roasted and cracked, resulting in a smoky and n grain that lo like green b wheat with a chewy textu
USES	Use as a starchy base for stews; combine with fruit for porridge; or mix with pastry, batter, or dough.	Used in pancakes, breads, and noodles (such as soba).	Is great in salads. Use as you would use brown rice.	Eat fresh, either on or off the cob; mill into a coarse or fine meal or flour for baked goods and tortillas; as polenta; or as grits or *posole*.	Serve as a starchy side to tagines or grilled vegetables, or stir into cold salads.	Primarily used for making fresh pasta dough but occasionally also for risen breads.	Use interchangeably with barley. Try it in risottos, in any dish you'd use brown rice or barley, or in hot cereals and wholegrain breads.	Make in a ric cooker on th brown rice setting.
GLUTEN FREE	Yes	Yes	No	Yes	No	No	No	No
GOOD SOURCE OF ...	Excellent source of complete proteins, with a perfect amino acid balance.	Protein, fibre, antioxidants, B vitamins, magnesium, phosphorus, and potassium.	Protein, fibre, iron, and B vitamins.	Protein, fibre, and iron.	Protein and selenium.	Protein, magnesium, selenium, manganese, and phosphorus.	Protein, fibre, vitamin B_3, and zinc.	Very high protein and content. Manganese, folate, phosphorus magnesium, iron.

Amaranth

Corn

Freekeh

Oats

Rye flour

...ET	OATS	QUINOA	RICE	RYE FLOUR	SPELT	SPROUTED GRAIN	TEFF	TRITICALE
ncient with a ral flavour a hint eet ness that s like tiny ts.	Available rolled, steel cut, or as flour, oats have a neutral, slightly nutty flavour and a higher fibre content.	Another para-cereal, quinoa is actually a seed that's nutty, chewy, and filling.	Brown rice is nutty, starchy, and nutritious. Wild rice is nutty and chewy.	A cereal grain that can be found in its whole or cracked form or ground into a flour. Wholegrain rye has a deep, nutty, distinctive flavour with slightly sour notes.	Spelt, or dinkel wheat, is most commonly found ground into flour.	Sprouted grains are believed to have more easily assimilated nutrients and proteins than unsprouted grains. They're often nutty with a hint of bitterness.	Teff is a tiny seed, similar to quinoa, but much smaller. It has a neutral flavour profile, texture similar to millet, and cooks quickly.	A hybrid of wheat and rye.
k as a al or are as for	Cook as a breakfast cereal; use to provide body to veggie burgers and other meat substitutes; or grind into flour for breads, muffins, and other baked goods.	Cook as you would brown rice, or use as a hot cereal.	Enjoy in side dishes, salads, pilafs, and stuffings.	Use it in sourdough breads or breakfast cereals.	Use spelt flour in breads, pastry, and sweet baked goods.	Look for sprouted breads, cereals, and pastas.	Use in porridges and stews, as stuffing, or as a pilaf side dish.	Usually found in cereals or some breads.
Yes	Yes	Yes	Yes	No	No.	Varies; see type of grain	Yes	No
ein, fibre, sphorus, nesium, er, and ganese.	Protein, fibre, vitamin B$_1$, magnesium, phosphorus, and manganese.	Very high protein and fibre content. Iron, calcium, magnesium, potassium, and zinc.	Protein, fibre, selenium, manganese, magnesium, zinc, and B vitamins.	Protein, fibre, manganese, phosphorus, copper, pantothenic acid, and magnesium.	Protein, fibre, phosphorus, and manganese.	Sprouted grains are a good source of protein and fibre. They're nutritionally comparable to unsprouted grains.	Protein, fibre, iron, and calcium.	Protein, phosphorus, manganese, and iron.

Buckwheat

Millet

Creamy Pasta with Swiss Chard and Tomatoes (T) (UNDER 30)

This quick and tasty pasta dish couldn't be easier. Swiss chard is chock full of vitamins, and it's a good source of iron, too. The stems are edible, so don't throw them away!

SERVES 4–5   PREP 5 MINS   COOK 10 MINS

1   Cook the fettuccine in well-salted water according to the packet instructions.

2   Meanwhile, heat the extra-virgin olive oil in a large frying pan over a medium heat. Add the garlic and cook, stirring, for 30 seconds.

3   Add the Swiss chard and salt, and cook, stirring once or twice or until tender. Remove from the heat and cover to keep warm while pasta finishes cooking.

4   When the pasta is ready, reserve 120ml (4fl oz) cooking water, and drain the pasta. Add the pasta to the Swiss chard along with the tomatoes, soured cream, and crushed chillies. Toss well, adding a little reserved pasta water, if needed, and serve immediately.

INGREDIENTS

450g (1lb) fettuccine

4 tbsp extra-virgin olive oil

3 cloves garlic, thinly sliced

1 bunch Swiss chard, washed well and torn into small pieces

½ tsp sea salt

2 large tomatoes, cored, deseeded, and cut into 5mm (¼in) strips

8 tbsp plant-based soured cream

½ tsp crushed chillies

For super-fast meals, keep quick-cooking varieties of pasta to hand, such as angel hair or thin spaghetti, which cook in about 3–6 minutes.

Wholewheat Pasta *e Ceci* (Pasta with Chickpeas) (T) (UNDER 30)

In this easy dish, wholewheat pasta and chickpeas combine in a spicy tomato sauce that's just brothy enough to eat with a spoon. It's the perfect choice for a fast, filling, and nutritious supper.

SERVES 4   PREP 5 MINS   COOK 20 MINS

1 Bring a large pan of salted water to the boil over a medium–high heat, and cook the pasta according to the packet instructions until *al dente* (fully cooked but still firm to the bite). Drain (do not rinse), and set aside.

2 Meanwhile, heat the extra-virgin olive oil in a large saucepan over a medium–high heat. Add the onion and salt, and cook, stirring frequently, for about 5 minutes or until the onion is softened and translucent. (Adjust the heat as necessary.)

3 Stir in the garlic and crushed chillies, and stir for 30 seconds. Stir in the tomato purée, and add the plum tomatoes with their juice and filtered water. Bring to the boil, reduce the heat to medium, and cook for 5 minutes.

4 Stir in the chickpeas and cooked pasta, and cook for 2 minutes. Then, stir in the white wine and oregano, remove from the heat, and serve immediately.

INGREDIENTS

225g (8oz) tube-shaped wholewheat pasta, such as chocchiole, or medium conchiglie

3 tbsp extra-virgin olive oil

½ large sweet onion, minced

½ tsp sea salt

2 cloves garlic, minced

¼ tsp crushed chillies

1 tbsp tomato purée

2 (400g; 14oz) cans peeled plum tomatoes, with juice, lightly crushed by hand

120ml (4fl oz) filtered water or vegetable stock

1 (400g; 14oz) can chickpeas, rinsed and drained

4 tbsp dry white wine

¼ tsp dried oregano

Crispy, salty, *Toasted Breadcrumbs* are an easy way to enhance dishes such as this. In a food processor fitted with a metal blade, process 2 slices of wholemeal bread to coarse crumbs. In a medium non-stick frying pan over a medium heat, stir together the breadcrumbs with 1 tablespoon of extra-virgin olive oil, ½ teaspoon of sea salt, and ¼ teaspoon of freshly ground black pepper until the breadcrumbs are golden and evenly toasted. Toss with 1 tablespoon of finely chopped fresh flat-leaf parsley, and add to your dish just before serving. Store leftovers at room temperature in a tightly sealed glass jar for up to 7 days.

Swiss Chard Ravioli Ⓣ

Swiss chard and almonds make a creamy and delicious ravioli filling. This recipe uses wonton wrappers for a quick and easy ravioli, but you could make some Fresh Pasta Dough instead if you like.

SERVES 4–6   PREP 30 MINS PLUS SOAKING TIME   COOK 25 MINUTES

1   Soak the almonds in cold water for at least 4 hours or overnight.

2   Discard the soaking water, rinse the nuts well, and drain.

3   Heat the extra-virgin olive oil in a large frying pan over a medium–high heat. Add the garlic and stir for 30 seconds. Add the Swiss chard, with water still clinging to the leaves, and cook, stirring frequently, for about 10 minutes or until tender. Add water if the chard begins to dry out. Season with salt and black pepper, and cool slightly.

4   In a food processor fitted with a metal blade, process the almonds, Swiss chard, lemon juice, and nutritional yeast in pulses until smooth, adding water if necessary to bring the mixture together. Cool completely.

5   Place wonton wrappers, a few at a time, on a lightly floured surface. Spoon about 1½ teaspoons of filling into the centre of each wrapper, brush the edges of the wrappers with water, and pinch the edges to seal, pressing out the air as you go. (Alternatively, roll Fresh Pasta Dough using a pasta machine or a rolling pin until about 3mm (¹/₈in) thick. Use a 7.5cm (3in) round cutter to cut pasta circles and fill as directed.)

6   Bring a large pan of salted water to the boil over a medium–high heat. Gently drop the ravioli into the boiling water, and cook for 3–5 minutes or until tender. Serve with your favourite sauce.

INGREDIENTS

75g (2½oz) raw almonds

3 tbsp extra-virgin olive oil

4 cloves garlic, finely chopped

2 bunches Swiss chard, leaves only, roughly chopped

1 tbsp water

½ tsp sea salt

¼ tsp freshly ground black pepper

Juice of ½ lemon (1 tbsp)

1 tbsp nutritional yeast

1 tsp water

40 wonton wrappers, or 1 batch *Fresh Pasta Dough*

Swiss chard

Read the ingredients on your wonton wrappers, as many supermarket brands contain eggs. A trip to your local Asian market might be in order to find egg-free wrappers. And don't throw away the Swiss chard stems! Sauté them with garlic and olive oil, and enjoy.

One-Pan Pasta Primavera (UNDER 30)

This is a "throw everything in one pan" pasta dish. It's chock full of good-for-you veggies, and afterwards it's also great for whoever's on washing up duty!

SERVES 5   PREP 10 MINS   COOK 20 MINS

1 Heat the extra-virgin olive oil in an extra-large frying pan with a lid over a medium–high heat. Add the onion and sauté for 2 minutes.

2 Add the garlic, spaghetti, vegetable stock, tomatoes with their juice, broccoli, carrot, and salt. Bring to the boil, reduce the heat to medium–low, cover, and cook for 3 minutes.

3 Uncover, stir, and continue cooking, stirring constantly and adjusting the heat as necessary to maintain a brisk simmer, for about 8 minutes or until the stock is absorbed and the pasta is tender.

4 Stir in the baby spinach, peas, and black pepper, toss for 1 minute, and serve immediately.

INGREDIENTS

4 tbsp extra-virgin olive oil

1 onion, halved and thinly sliced

2 cloves garlic, thinly sliced

350g (12oz) thin spaghetti

1.1 litres (1¾ pints) vegetable stock or water

1 (400g; 14oz) can diced tomatoes, with juice

140g (5oz) fresh or frozen broccoli florets

1 carrot, peeled, halved, and thinly sliced

1 tsp sea salt

140g (5oz) baby spinach

70g (2½oz) fresh or frozen baby peas

½ tsp freshly ground black pepper

For *Tomato Basil One-Pan Pasta,* omit the broccoli, carrot, peas, and spinach, and add a handful of torn fresh basil leaves before serving.

Sesame Noodles (UNDER 30)

Tahini (sesame paste) and peanut butter combine with tamari sauce, ginger, and garlic in this quick version of a Chinese food classic.

SERVES 4   **PREP** 10 MINS   **COOK** 10 MINS

1 Bring a large pan of water to the boil over a medium–high heat. Add the salt and linguine, and cook according to the packet instructions until the pasta is tender. Drain, rinse the pasta under cold water, and set aside.

2 In a large bowl, whisk together the tahini, peanut butter, hot water, tamari, rice vinegar, ginger, toasted sesame oil, and chilli garlic sauce.

3 Add the cooked linguine, carrot, and cucumber to the sauce. Toss gently, garnish with gomasio and spring onions, and serve immediately.

INGREDIENTS

2 tsp sea salt

450g (1lb) thin linguine

4 tbsp tahini

4 tbsp creamy peanut butter

4 tbsp hot water

2 tbsp reduced-sodium tamari or soy sauce

2 tbsp rice vinegar

2 tbsp grated fresh ginger

1 tsp toasted sesame oil

1 tsp chilli garlic sauce or Thai chilli paste

1 carrot, in julienne sticks

1 cucumber, in julienne sticks

3 tbsp gomasio

4 tbsp thinly sliced spring onions, both light and dark green parts

For a complete *Sesame Noodle Dinner*, simply add some grilled tofu along with a few handfuls of tender Asian greens, such as mizuna or tatsoi, garnish with roasted peanuts, and serve.

Tofu, Tempeh, and Seitan

These versatile transition foods provide healthy, flavourful alternatives to meat. Seitan stars in cheesesteaks, kebabs, and satay. Sear or stir-fry tofu for a light and healthy protein source, or make some tasty tempeh dishes.

Tofu Summer Rolls

These refreshing tofu and veggie-filled wraps with a spicy peanut dipping sauce are a doddle to make. They keep nicely in the fridge overnight, so you can enjoy them again for lunch tomorrow.

SERVES 4 PREP 15 MINS PLUS 30 MINS SOAKING TIME COOK 3 MINS

1 Place the tofu on several layers of kitchen paper on a chopping board, top with a few more layers of kitchen paper, place a heavy plate on top of the tofu, and top with a heavy weight, such as a large can of tomatoes. Set the tofu aside to drain for 30 minutes. Blot dry with kitchen paper and cut the tofu into 5mm (¼in) strips.

2 Heat the sesame oil in a small non-stick frying pan over a medium–high heat. Add the tofu, and sear, turning once or twice, for about 2 minutes or until browned on all sides. Drain on kitchen paper.

3 Soak 1 rice paper wrapper in warm water for 30 seconds, remove from the water, and place on your work surface. Quickly line the wrapper with 1 lettuce leaf, 2 tablespoons of carrot, 2 tablespoons of cabbage, and one-quarter of the tofu, and sprinkle with 1 tablespoon of spring onions. Fold the short ends of rice paper inwards, roll the wrapper as if making a burrito, and press to seal the seam. Repeat with the remaining rice wrappers and filling. Refrigerate the rolls while you make the sauce, or overnight.

4 In a small pan over a medium–low heat, whisk together the peanut butter, hoisin sauce, lime juice, tamari, and sambal oelek until smooth. Pour into small bowls and serve hot or cold with the summer rolls.

INGREDIENTS

115g (4oz) firm or extra-firm tofu

1 tsp sesame oil

4 (20cm; 8-in) rice paper wrappers

4 large leaves soft green leaf lettuce

1 carrot, shredded

35g (1oz) shredded cabbage

4 or 5 spring onions, thinly sliced

125g (4½oz) smooth peanut butter

2 tbsp hoisin sauce

Juice of 2 limes (2 tbsp)

2 tsp reduced-sodium tamari

1 tsp sambal oelek (chilli garlic sauce)

For *Vegetable Summer Rolls*, substitute 2 ripe avocados, peeled, seeded, and cut into strips for the tofu and skip the sautéing. Other delicious fillings include cooked rice noodles, sautéed shiitake mushrooms, shredded red cabbage, or thin jicama strips.

Sesame Tofu Ⓣ

Tofu pieces are marinated in ginger, soy, sesame, and garlic and fried crisp with a sesame and breadcrumb crust. They're great with steamed greens and rice, on a salad, or in a sandwich.

SERVES 3   PREP 2½ HOURS   COOK 10 MINS

1   Cut the tofu horizontally into thirds, and cut each third into half. Place the tofu pieces on several layers of kitchen paper, top with more kitchen paper, set a heavy plate on top, and add a weight. Set aside to drain for 30 minutes.

2   In a large baking dish, whisk together the tamari, lemon juice, sesame oil, ginger, and garlic. Add the tofu and refrigerate for 2 hours, turning the pieces once or twice in that time.

3   In a small bowl, combine the panko breadcrumbs and sesame seeds.

4   Dredge each tofu piece in the breadcrumb mixture, dip in the marinade again, and coat in breadcrumbs a second time.

5   Heat the grapeseed oil in a large frying pan over a medium–high heat until it begins to shimmer. Add the tofu and fry, turning once and adjusting the heat as necessary, for about 3 minutes per side or until golden and crisp.

INGREDIENTS

450g (1lb) firm tofu

2 tbsp reduced-sodium tamari

Juice of 1 lemon (2 tbsp)

1 tbsp toasted sesame oil

1 tbsp grated fresh ginger

2 cloves garlic, finely chopped

60g (2oz) panko breadcrumbs

4 tbsp sesame seeds

4 tbsp grapeseed oil

For Sesame Seitan, just use seitan instead of tofu.

Grilled Tofu Caprese

Silken tofu is grilled with marinated aubergine and stacked with sweet tomatoes and fresh basil.

SERVES 4   PREP 30 MINS   COOK 10 MINS

1   Sprinkle the aubergine with ½ teaspoon of the salt, and set aside on kitchen paper for 5 minutes. Rinse and pat dry.

2   In a shallow bowl, whisk together 2 tablespoons of the extra-virgin olive oil, garlic, oregano, and 1 tablespoon of the balsamic vinegar. Add the aubergine and marinate for 15 minutes.

3   Heat a grill to high, or set a griddle pan over a high heat.

4   Brush the tofu with 1 tablespoon of the extra-virgin olive oil and sprinkle with a pinch of salt. Add to the grill or griddle pan and cook for about 2 minutes per side or until nicely marked. Brush the grill with 1 tablespoon of olive oil and grill the aubergine for about 3 minutes per side or until tender.

5   Stack 1 slice of aubergine, 1 slice of beefsteak tomato, 1 slice of tofu, and 1 basil leaf on each of 4 plates, and repeat. Drizzle with the remaining olive oil and balsamic vinegar, season with black pepper, and serve.

INGREDIENTS

1 small aubergine, skin on, trimmed and cut into 8 even slices

1 tsp sea salt

5 tbsp extra-virgin olive oil

2 cloves garlic, finely chopped

½ tsp dried oregano

3 tbsp balsamic vinegar

225g (8oz) firm or extra-firm tofu, cut into 8 slices

2 large beefsteak tomatoes, each cored and cut into 4 slices

16 large, fresh basil leaves

½ tsp freshly ground black pepper

ALLIUMS

The allium family includes fragrant bulbs and shoots such as onions, garlic, and leeks. **Benefits** Are anti-bacterial; are anti-inflammatory; lower cholesterol; and promote healthy gut bacteria. **Uses** Choose firm onions and garlic and straight leeks with some "give" to them. Enjoy onions raw in salads and sandwiches or cooked as a flavouring for a variety of dishes. Add garlic to dressings, sauces, marinades, soups, stews, and more. Eat leeks in soups, stews, and savory pies. **Recipes** Caramelized Onions, Summer Squash and Onion Bake, *Pissaladiere,* Potato Leek Soup, Herbed Mushroom and Leek Tart, Stir-Fried Chinese Cress with Fermented Black Beans.

Tofu and Veggie Stir-Fry Ⓣ ㉚

i love the clean, bright flavours of this crunchy, colourful stir-fry, which uses a ginger vinaigrette to lightly dress the seared tofu and fresh vegetables.

SERVES 4   PREP 15 MINS   COOK 10 MINS

1 In a small bowl, whisk together the soy sauce, sesame oil, rice vinegar, and ginger. Set aside.

2 Heat a large wok or cast-iron skillet over a medium heat. When hot, add 1 tablespoon of the grapeseed oil along with the garlic, and cook, stirring, for 30 seconds. Add the tofu and cook, stirring, for about 1 minute or until the tofu begins to colour slightly.

3 Push the tofu to the side of the wok, add the pak choi, and stir for 1 minute.

4 Push the pak choi to the side, increase the heat to medium–high, and add the remaining grapeseed oil. Add the broccoli, red pepper, onion, and shiitake mushrooms, and cook, stirring, for 2 minutes.

5 Add the mangetout and water, mix the tofu and vegetables, and continue to cook, stirring, for about 2 minutes or until the water is nearly evaporated and the vegetables are tender.

6 Add the reserved dressing, toss, and serve.

INGREDIENTS

1 tbsp soy sauce

1 tbsp toasted sesame oil

1 tbsp rice vinegar

1 tbsp finely chopped fresh ginger

2 tbsp grapeseed oil

2 cloves garlic, finely chopped

225g (8oz) firm or extra-firm tofu, cut in 1cm (½in) cubes

150g (5½oz) thinly sliced pak choi

70g (2oz) small broccoli florets

1 red pepper, diced in 1cm (½in) chunks

1 onion, diced

50g (1¾oz) sliced shiitake mushrooms

175g (6oz) fresh snow peas

4 tbsp water or vegetable stock

For *Tofu and Stir-Fried Veggie Dinner,* serve over hot, cooked brown rice or rice noodles. For added flavour, sprinkle with some cashews.

Hearty Seitan Roast (T)

A simple seitan loaf is browned and then baked in a savoury, sweet and sour sauce with aromatic vegetables for a perfect centrepiece dish for festive dinners.

SERVES 6   PREP 15 MINS   COOK 30 MINS

1 Preheat the oven to 190°C (375°F/Gas 5).

2 Heat 1 tablespoon of the olive oil in a large, preferably cast-iron, frying pan over a medium–high heat.

3 Season the Basic Seitan evenly with ½ teaspoon of the salt and ¼ teaspoon of the black pepper. Add the seitan to the pan and brown on all sides, turning every 1 or 2 minutes or until evenly browned.

4 In a small roasting tin, toss together the onion, carrots, parsnips, and garlic with the remaining olive oil, herbes de Provence, remaining salt and black pepper. Place the browned roast on top of the vegetables.

5 In a small saucepan over high heat, whisk together the vegetable stock, red wine, ketchup, tamari, and balsamic vinegar. Cook, stirring often, for about 10 minutes or until the mixture has thickened slightly and reduced to about 240ml (8fl oz) of liquid. Pour over the roast and vegetables.

6 Cover the roasting tin with foil and bake for 20 minutes. Uncover, and bake for a further 10 minutes.

7 Using a sharp, serrated knife, cut the roast into paper-thin slices; place on a serving dish; and spoon some of the vegetables and the sauce over the slices. Serve immediately.

INGREDIENTS

2 tbsp olive oil

½ batch *Basic Seitan*

1 tsp sea salt

½ tsp freshly ground black pepper

1 large onion, cut into 1in (½in) wedges

2 carrots, peeled and cut into 2.5cm (1in) chunks

2 medium parsnips, peeled and cut into 2.5cm (1in) chunks

2 cloves garlic, thinly sliced

1 tsp herbes de Provence

240ml (8fl oz) vegetable stock (preferably Basic Seitan cooking stock)

120ml (4fl oz) dry red wine

2 tbsp tomato ketchup

1 tbsp reduced-sodium tamari

1 tbsp balsamic vinegar

For Seitan Steak Sandwiches, heat 1 tablespoon of olive oil in a cast-iron frying pan over a medium-high heat. Add 45g (1½oz) onion and 75g (2½oz) button mushrooms, both sliced paper thin, season with sea salt and black pepper, and cook, stirring often, for 5 minutes or until veggies begin to brown. Add the seitan and brown evenly for 2–3 minutes. Scrape the onions, mushrooms, and seitan into a 15cm (6in) long pile, and cover with 2 slices of plant-based cheese. Slice open a 15cm (6in) sub roll, place it over the mixture in the pan, and heat for 1 minute. Use a spatula to scrape everything into the roll and serve.

Tempeh Milanese (T)

Tempeh is breaded, quickly fried, and served with a refreshing lemon rocket salad for a meatless take on the classic Italian chicken Milanese.

SERVES 4 **PREP** 10 MINS **COOK** 60 MINS

1   Preheat the oven to 180°C (350°F/Gas 4).

2   Cut the tempeh in half horizontally, and cut each piece into 4 equal-size pieces. Place these in a baking dish large enough to hold them in one layer.

3   In a small bowl, whisk together the water, 2 tablespoons of the lemon juice, tamari, 2 tablespoons of the extra-virgin olive oil, and garlic. Pour over the tempeh, cover the dish tightly with foil, and bake for 50 minutes. Remove the foil, drain, and cool the tempeh slightly.

4   Place the Italian-seasoned panko breadcrumbs in a shallow bowl.

5   Heat the grapeseed oil in a large frying pan over a medium–high heat until it begins to shimmer.

6   Coat the tempeh pieces in the panko breadcrumbs, add to the frying pan, and fry, turning once, for about 2 minutes per side or until golden and crisp. (Adjust the heat as necessary to prevent burning.)

7   In a large bowl, toss the rocket leaves with the remaining lemon juice and extra-virgin olive oil, and season with salt and black pepper.

8   Divide the salad between 4 serving plates and equally divide the tomatoes and olives on top. Top each salad with 2 tempeh pieces and serve immediately.

INGREDIENTS

225g (8oz) tempeh

120ml (4fl oz) water

Juice of 2 lemons (4 tbsp)

2 tbsp reduced-sodium tamari

4 tbsp extra-virgin olive oil

2 cloves garlic, finely chopped

115g (4oz) Italian-seasoned panko breadcrumbs (see below)

120ml (4fl oz) grapeseed oil

½ tsp sea salt

¼ tsp freshly ground black pepper

85g (3oz) baby rocket

300g (10oz) baby plum tomatoes, halved

½ red onion, very thinly sliced

4 tbsp pitted kalamata olives

Lemons

Can't find Italian-seasoned panko? To make your own, combine 120g (4oz) plain panko breadcrums with 1 teaspoon of dried oregano, ½ teaspoon of dried basil, and ½ teaspoon of garlic powder.

Seitan and Dumplings (T)

Simple, delicious, cornmeal and herb-spiked batter puffs up into pillowy dumplings that are nestled atop a stew of seitan chunks and tender veggies.

SERVES 6 **PREP** 25 MINS **COOK** 40 MINS

1 Heat 1 tablespoon of the grapeseed oil in an ovenproof casserole dish over a medium–high heat. Add the Basic Seitan chunks in batches and sauté, stirring gently, for 5 minutes or until browned. Set aside on a plate, and cover to keep warm while you cook the remaining seitan.

2 Add the remaining grapeseed oil to the pan, along with the onion, carrots, button mushrooms, celery, 1 teaspoon of the salt, and ½ teaspoon of the black pepper. Cook, stirring frequently and adjusting the heat as needed to prevent burning, for 5 minutes.

3 In a medium bowl, whisk together the soya milk with the apple cider vinegar. Set aside to curdle slightly.

4 In a large bowl, whisk together 185g (6½oz) cups of the flour, yellow cornmeal, baking powder, flat-leaf parsley, thyme, seasoning, and the remaining salt and black pepper. Pour in the soya milk mixture and stir just until combined – do not knead. Set aside for 10 minutes.

5 Add the remaining flour to the vegetables and stir for 1 minute. Add the vegetable stock, and stir vigorously to release any browned bits from the bottom of the pan.

6 Stir in the seitan and petit pois, and bring to the boil. Drop in heaped tablespoonfuls of the dumpling mixture, spacing evenly (you'll have about 10 dumplings, which will cover the surface of the stew). Cover, reduce the heat to low, and cook – *without opening the lid* – for 15 minutes. Uncover, remove from the heat, and serve.

INGREDIENTS

2 tbsp grapeseed oil

1 loaf *Basic Seitan*, pulled into small chunks before simmering, or 1 (450g; 1lb) packet of seitan pieces

1 large onion, halved and thinly sliced

2 large carrots, peeled and cut into 1cm (½in) rounds

225g (8oz) button mushrooms, quartered

2 large sticks celery, cut into 1cm (½in) slices

2 tsp sea salt

1 tsp freshly ground black pepper

360ml (12fl oz) soya or hemp milk

1 tsp apple cider vinegar

225g (8oz) plain flour

80g (3oz) coarse yellow cornmeal

2 tbsp baking powder

2 tbsp finely chopped fresh flat-leaf parsley

½ tsp dried thyme

½ tsp Bell's seasoning or poultry seasoning

1.2 litres (2 pints) vegetable stock

140g (5oz) fresh or frozen petit pois

For light and fluffy dumplings, don't knead the dough; just stir it to combine and then let it rest for 10 minutes so the baking powder can create an airy batter. And don't peek! The steam created inside the pan is what cooks the dumplings. Skip any of these steps, or cheat and peek, and you'll end up with soggy, gummy, and leaden dumplings rather than fluffy pillows of cornbread-y dumpling goodness.

Seitan Satay (T)

Skewers of marinated seitan are grilled or broiled and dipped in a tasty peanut-tamarind sauce. Make a platter of these for your next party for rave reviews!

SERVES 4   PREP 2½ HOURS   COOK 10 MINS

1   Place the Basic Seitan chunks in a baking dish large enough to hold them in a single layer.

2   In a small bowl, whisk together 4 tablespoons of the tamari, water, sesame oil, coconut oil, 1 tablespoon of the ginger, and garlic. Pour over the seitan, and stir well. Cover and refrigerate for 2 hours or overnight.

3   Soak 8 bamboo skewers in warm water for at least 30 minutes. Drain.

4   Preheat a grill and lightly brush the grill pan and grill with oil.

5   In a medium bowl, whisk the tamarind paste with the hot water to soften. Add the peanut butter, coconut milk, the remaining grated ginger, remaining tamari, and crushed chillies, and whisk well.

6   Thread the marinated seitan onto the skewers and cook, turning once or twice, for 5–7 minutes or until browned on all sides. Serve immediately with the tamarind-peanut sauce.

INGREDIENTS

1 loaf *Basic Seitan*, cut into 2.5cm (1in) chunks

8 bamboo skewers

6 tbsp reduced-sodium tamari

4 tbsp water

1 tbsp toasted sesame oil

1 tbsp melted coconut oil

3 tbsp grated fresh ginger

2 cloves garlic, finely chopped

2 tbsp tamarind paste

2 tbsp hot (not boiling) water

125g (4½oz) crunchy peanut butter

120ml (4fl oz) full-fat coconut milk, well shaken

1 tsp crushed chillies

Can't find tamarind paste? Use 2 tablespoons of brown sugar instead and don't bother using any hot water in the mix.

Meat Substitutes

You have many options for replacing meat in recipes. Try substituting natural, nutritious, whole foods, such as cooked lentils, for the meat in your favourite taco or chilli recipe. Make a burger patty out of beans or marinate a portobello mushroom and toss it on the grill for a fantastic burger. To add a bit more substance, add millet or quinoa to beans and legumes when making meatloaf or burgers.

As the meatless diet becomes more mainstream, your options increase. Your supermarket produce section is likely to be filled with meat-free offerings, including sausages of all kinds – chorizo, hot dogs, Italian-style sausages, and even Andouille are available at many shops. Deli slices for sandwiches, fake bacon, and meatless burgers of all kinds are also available fresh or frozen.

	TOFU	TEMPEH	SEITAN
WHAT IT IS	Made from soy; it has a neutral flavour and soft texture.	Cultured and fermented soy protein; it has a nutty flavour and a slightly chewy texture.	Made from wheat gluten; it has a meaty and chewy texture with a similar "bite" to chicken.
USES	Stir-fries, soups and stews, grilling, spring rolls, and marinated dishes.	Fake bacon, sandwiches, baked dishes, and marinated dishes.	Soups and stews, grilling, chicken and beef substitute, and sandwiches.
GOOD SOURCE OF ...	Protein, calcium, iron, and isoflavones.	Protein, calcium, iron, B vitamins (except B_{12}), isoflavones, antioxidants, and fibre.	Protein, essential amino acids, vitamin C, vitamin B_3, iron, and vitamin B_2.

Tofu

Maple-Glazed Tofu (T)

Enjoy this sweet and savoury grilled tofu with a side of Southern-Style Braised Greens and a side of brown rice; or make a sensational sandwich with crisp lettuce, tomato, and a smear of spicy mustard.

SERVES 4 PREP 20 MINS COOK 10 MINS

1 Place the tofu on several layers of kitchen paper, top with more kitchen paper, set a heavy plate on top, and add a weight. Set it aside to drain for 15 minutes.

2 Meanwhile, in a small saucepan over a medium–high heat, combine the balsamic vinegar, maple syrup, 1 tablespoon of the extra-virgin olive oil, and tamari. Bring to the boil and cook, stirring often, for about 10 minutes or until sauce has reduced to a sticky glaze.

3 Preheat a grill to high. Brush the grill with the remaining extra-virgin olive oil.

4 Pat the tofu dry with kitchen paper, brush with the glaze, and grill each side for 2 minutes, turning carefully and brushing with more glaze. Serve.

INGREDIENTS

450g (1lb) firm or extra-firm tofu, sliced into 8 slices

4 tbsp balsamic vinegar

3 tbsp maple syrup

2 tbsp extra-virgin olive oil

1 tbsp reduced-sodium tamari

Tempeh Bacon (T)

This tempeh bacon is crispy, salty, smoky, and just a little sweet. An overnight marinade is best, so if you can, make it the day before you want to use it.

SERVES 4–6 PREP 10 MINS PLUS MARINATING TIME COOK 5 MINS

1 Using a serrated knife, cut thin slices from the long end of the tempeh. You should be able to get 12 slices (or more) from 1 packet. Lay the slices in 1 layer in a large baking dish or tray.

2 In a small saucepan over high heat, whisk together the water, tamari, maple syrup, apple cider vinegar, brown sugar, smoked sea salt, sesame oil, smoked paprika, and black pepper. Bring to the boil, remove from the heat, and pour the marinade over the tempeh slices. Cover the baking dish and refrigerate for at least 3 hours and up to 3 days.

3 Heat the grapeseed oil in a large, heavy, preferably cast-iron, frying pan over a medium heat. Allow some marinade to drain from the tempeh slices, but do not dry them completely. Discard the remaining marinade. Add the tempeh slices to the pan a few at a time, and cook, turning every 2 minutes, until crispy and browned on both sides, watching carefully to prevent any burning. Serve immediately.

INGREDIENTS

225g (8oz) tempeh

4 tbsp water

3 tbsp reduced-sodium tamari

2 tbsp maple syrup

1 tbsp apple cider vinegar

1 tbsp brown sugar

2 tsp smoked sea salt

1 tsp toasted sesame oil

½ tsp smoked paprika

½ tsp coarsely ground black pepper

1 tbsp grapeseed oil

Seitan Gyros Ⓣ

Sliced seitan is marinated with traditional Greek flavours of lemon, extra-virgin olive oil, and garlic, grilled until nicely charred, and served on warm pitta with all the usual gyros fixings.

SERVES 6 PREP 30 MINS COOK 10 MINS

1 In a small bowl, whisk together the extra-virgin olive oil, lemon juice, flat-leaf parsley, salt, black pepper, and garlic.

2 Slice the Basic Seitan loaf very thinly and place the slices in a single layer in a large baking dish. Pour the marinade over the top and set aside at room temperature for 25 minutes.

3 Preheat a grill and brush the grill with a little olive oil.

4 Remove the seitan slices from the marinade, add to the grill, and grill for about 1 minute per side or until charred.

5 Quickly grill the pitta breads just to warm them. Evenly divide the seitan among the pitta, and top with romaine lettuce, plum tomatoes, and red onion. Drizzle each gyro with Tzatziki, sprinkle with sweet paprika, roll, and serve immediately.

INGREDIENTS

4 tbsp extra-virgin olive oil, plus more for grilling

Juice of 2 lemons (4 tbsp)

2 tbsp finely chopped fresh Italian flat-leaf parsley

1 tsp sea salt

½ tsp freshly ground black pepper

1 clove garlic, crushed and finely chopped

1 loaf *Basic Seitan*

6 pitta breads, preferably pocketless, of Middle Eastern flatbreads

140g (5oz) shredded romaine lettuce

3 plum tomatoes, cored and cut into small dice

½ small red onion, very thinly sliced

1 batch *Tzatziki*, or 240ml (8fl oz) plain, plant-based yogurt mixed with juice of ½ lemon (1 tbsp)

1 tsp sweet paprika

For Seitan Reubens, slice seitan and brush with a few tablespoons of soy sauce. Brown in a cast-iron pan with 1 tablespoon of oil for 2–3 minutes, and pile it on rye bread with 70g (2½oz) of sauerkraut and 25g (scant 1oz) plant-based Havarti or Cheddar-style cheese per sandwich. In a small bowl, stir together 2 tablespoons plant-based mayo, 1 tablespoon ketchup, and 1 tablespoon of sweet pickle. Drizzle 1 tablespoon of the dressing over each sandwich, top with another slice of rye bread, and toast the sandwiches in the cast-iron pan over a medium heat. Serve immediately with mustard on the side.

Breads, Pizzas, and Savoury Tarts

Bake your own bread, or prepare a satisfying, savoury tart.
Pizza — with home-made dough — is here, too. Enjoy!

Easy, Slow-Rise Oatmeal Bread

This bread is simple, foolproof, easy to double, and just plain good. i find it's easily adaptable to a working person's schedule; it can rise at room temperature, or for longer periods of time in the fridge, and it makes great sandwiches and toast. All bases are indeed covered.

MAKES 1 LOAF **PREP** 10 MINS PLUS RISING TIME **COOK** 45 MINS

1 In a food processor fitted with a metal blade or in a blender, grind the rolled oats into a coarse flour.

2 In a large bowl, combine the oat flour with 375g (13oz) of the flour, salt, granulated cane sugar, and yeast. Slowly stir in the warm water to form a rough dough. Sprinkle with an additional 1 or 2 tablespoons of the flour, and knead for 50 turns. The dough will be sticky but cohesive. Place it back in the bowl, cover with lightly oiled cling film, and let it rise at room temperature for 6–8 hours.

3 Grease or oil a 23cm (9in) loaf tin.

4 Knock back the dough, knead for 1–2 minutes with an additional sprinkling of flour. Shape the dough into an approximate loaf form, and fit it into the prepared loaf tin. Cover with cling film or a clean tea towel, and let it rise at room temperature for about 5 more hours or until doubled in size.

5 About 20 minutes before you want to bake your bread, preheat the oven to 200°C (400°F/Gas 6).

6 Using a sharp knife, slash the centre of the loaf. Brush the loaf with non-dairy milk and bake for 45 minutes or until the loaf is golden and sounds hollow when tapped on the bottom. Cool completely in the tin on a wire rack before slicing.

INGREDIENTS

60g (2oz) rolled oats

400g (14oz) plain flour

1 tsp sea salt

½ tsp granulated cane sugar

½ tsp active dry yeast

360ml (12fl oz) very warm (43°C; 110°F) water

1 tsp non-dairy milk

For Rosemary Raisin Walnut Bread, steep 1 sprig rosemary in 360ml (12fl oz) of hot water. Let the water cool to warm, strain, and proceed with the recipe as above, using rosemary water to mix the dough. During the first kneading, work in 85g (2oz) of raisins and 60g (2oz) of toasted, chopped walnuts.

Pizza Dough

There's nothing quite like the fresh-from-the-oven flavour and aroma of home-made pizza. You can top this versatile dough with anything from olive oil and fresh herbs for a simple focaccia, to tomato sauce and your favourite sautéed veggies for a pizza supreme.

SERVES 8 **PREP** 15 MINS, PLUS 2 HOURS RISING TIME **COOK** 25 MINS

1 To "prove" the yeast, sprinkle it over the warm water and set aside for 10 minutes or until foamy. Then, whisk in extra-virgin olive oil.

2 In a large bowl, combine the flour and salt. Slowly pour the yeast mixture into the flour mixture and use a rubber spatula to gently combine. When the dough comes together in a sticky mass, use your hands to knead the dough against the side of the bowl for about 3 minutes, gently pressing it to ensure all the flour is incorporated.

3 Cover the bowl with cling film and set aside in a warm place, such as your oven with the light turned on, to rise for 1–1½ hours or until doubled in size.

4 Preheat the oven to 230°C (450°F/Gas 8), and lightly grease a 28 × 43cm (11 × 17in) baking sheet.

5 Using a spatula, turn out the dough onto the baking sheet. Using floured hands, gently stretch and press the dough into the baking sheet until it reaches all the corners. Cover the dough with oiled cling film and let it rise for another 30 minutes.

6 Gently add toppings to the crust and bake for 25 minutes or until the bottom of the crust is a golden brown.

INGREDIENTS

2½ tsp active dry yeast

400ml (14fl oz) very warm (43°C; 110°F) water

3 tbsp extra-virgin olive oil

500g (1lb 2oz) plain flour

1 tbsp sea salt

For *Simple Focaccia*, drizzle the dough with extra-virgin olive oil, and top with 1 tablespoon of chopped fresh rosemary and 4 tablespoons of pitted, chopped olives.

Herbed Mushroom and Leek Tart (T)

Here, we top ready-made puff pastry with some tender, sweet leeks and sautéed mushrooms in this beautiful free-form rectangular tart. Serve it with a salad for a light meal or cut it into cute little squares for a party-worthy pre-dinner nibble.

SERVES 4 **PREP** 15 MINS **COOK** 30 MINS

1 Preheat the oven to 200°C (400°F/Gas 6). Line a baking sheet with baking parchment.

2 Heat 2 tablespoons of the extra-virgin olive oil in a large frying pan over a medium heat. Add the leeks and cook, stirring 2 or 3 times, for 10 minutes.

3 Stir the nutritional yeast into the leeks, transfer to a small bowl, and set aside.

4 Wipe the frying pan clean and set over a medium–high heat. Pour in 4 tablespoons of the olive oil. When hot, add the mushrooms and garlic, and cook, stirring frequently, for 10 minutes, adding more of the remaining olive oil if necessary.

5 Stir in the salt, black pepper, thyme, chives, and flat-leaf parsley. Remove from the heat and set aside to cool slightly.

6 On a floured surface, roll out the puff pastry to a rectangle about 36 × 25cm (14 × 10in). Cut in half across and transfer both halves to the prepared baking sheet. Fold the outer 1cm (½in) of pastry inwards, forming a border, and press to seal tightly. Prick the single layer of pastry inside the border all over with a fork.

7 Spread the leek mixture evenly over the pastry, and add the mushroom mixture. Bake for 20 minutes or until the pastry is puffed and golden. Slice and serve immediately.

INGREDIENTS

8 tbsp extra-virgin olive oil

1 bunch leeks, sliced

1 tbsp nutritional yeast

175g (6oz) chestnut mushrooms, thinly sliced

175g (6oz) shiitake mushrooms, stemmed and thinly sliced

2 cloves garlic, finely chopped

½ tsp sea salt

½ tsp freshly ground black pepper

1 tbsp chopped fresh thyme

1 tbsp minced fresh chives

1 tbsp finely chopped fresh flat-leaf parsley

1 sheet puff pastry

Leeks

To make this in a tart tin, line a 25cm (10in) loose-bottomed tart tin with half of the Pie Pastry recipe, folding the edges inwards. Fill the pastry with the leek mixture, followed by the mushroom mixture. Bake for about 40 minutes or until the pastry is golden.

Pissaladière (Provencal Onion Tart)

Tender dough is piled high with sweet caramelized onions, briny capers, and olives in this Provençal treat. *Pissaladière* can be served hot or at room temperature, so if you're whipping this up for a party or a picnic, it's good to know you can prepare it in advance.

SERVES 8 PREP 90 MINS COOK 30 MINS

1   Heat the extra-virgin olive oil in a very large, wide frying pan with a lid over a medium–high heat. Add the onions all at once, and cook, stirring, for 5 minutes. Cover, reduce the heat to low, and cook, stirring occasionally, for 20 minutes.

2   Uncover and cook, stirring 2 or 3 times, for 20–30 minutes or until onions have caramelized into a soft, golden mass. Stir in the thyme, remove from heat, and set aside to cool slightly.

3   Preheat the oven to 220°C (425°F/Gas 7). Lightly oil a baking sheet.

4   Roll out the Pizza Dough to fit the baking sheet, gently pressing it into the corners. Cover with oiled cling film and let it stand at room temperature for 20 minutes.

5   Remove the cling film, spoon the onions evenly over the dough, scatter the capers and Niçoise olives evenly over the onions, and bake for about 30 minutes or until the crust is golden. Serve hot or at room temperature.

INGREDIENTS

2 tbsp extra-virgin olive oil

1.8kg (4lb) onions, halved and thinly sliced

2 tsp fresh thyme leaves, picked

1 batch *Pizza Dough*

2 tbsp salted capers, rinsed and drained

30 Niçoise olives, pitted

Desserts

Eating a plant-based diet doesn't mean going without dessert!
Whether you're in the mood for a cookie, a pie, or a simple
fruit dessert, you'll find plenty here to love.

Pumpkin Pudding Pie

Creamy pumpkin pudding, spiced with a little cinnamon and ginger, fills a sweet and salty gingernut biscuit crust for a perfect pud. Tapioca pearls might be a new texture for some, but they're a fantastic way to thicken an eggless custard.

SERVES 10   PREP 10 MINS PLUS COOLING TIME   COOK 30 MINS

1 Preheat the oven to 180°C (350°F/Gas 4).

2 In a food processor fitted with a metal blade, process the gingernut biscuits, butter, and 1 teaspoon of the salt until the mixture resembles coarse crumbs. Press this mixture into a deep 25cm (10in) pie dish, place the dish on a baking sheet, and bake for 20 minutes. Remove from the oven, and set aside to cool.

3 Meanwhile, in a medium saucepan, whisk together the instant tapioca, cinnamon, ginger, brown sugar, and remaining salt. Place the pan on the hob, set the heat to low, and slowly whisk in the coconut milk coffee creamer, half of the non-dairy milk, maple syrup, and vanilla extract. Increase the heat to medium and bring to the boil.

4 In a small bowl, whisk together the cornflour and remaining non-dairy milk. Whisk this mixture into the tapioca mixture and continue whisking slowly for about 3 minutes or until the mixture has thickened.

5 Whisk in the pumpkin purée, remove from the heat, and cool for 10 minutes.

6 Pour the pumpkin pudding into the baked biscuit crust, spreading with a spatula to smooth the top. Cool for 10 minutes, cover with cling film (or invert a large glass bowl over the top), and refrigerate overnight. Store any leftover pie in the fridge for up to 2 days.

INGREDIENTS

300g (10oz) gingernut biscuits

4 tbsp melted plant-based butter or coconut oil

2 tsp sea salt

4 tbsp instant tapioca, such as Minute Tapioca

1 tsp ground cinnamon

½ tsp ground ginger

125g (4½oz) brown sugar

240ml (8fl oz) coconut milk creamer

240ml (8fl oz) non-dairy milk

1 tbsp maple syrup

1 tsp vanilla extract

4 tbsp cornflour

1 (425g; 15-oz) can pumpkin purée

For *Perfect Pumpkin Pudding*, omit the biscuit crust and spoon the pudding mixture into dessert dishes, then cover, and chill. Garnish with crushed ginger or digestive biscuits or plant-based whipped cream.

Apple Crumble Pie (T)

The nutty streusel crumble on this pie crowns a filling of tender, sweet, cinnamon-kissed apples. Rather than gummy flour and cornflour thickeners, instant tapioca is used to thicken the filling and let the pure fruit flavours shine through.

SERVES 8   PREP 25 MINS   COOK 60 MINS

1   Preheat the oven to 180°C (350°F/Gas 4).

2   In a food processor fitted with a metal blade, pulse together wholemeal flour, walnuts, brown sugar, and ½ teaspoon of the cinnamon to combine. Add the plant-based butter and pulse until the mixture resembles coarse crumbs. Set this streusel topping aside.

3   Roll the Pie Pastry for the bottom crust into a 33cm (13in) circle and transfer to a deep 25cm (10in) pie dish. You'll have a 2.5cm (1in) overhang; fold up the overhanging dough, pinch into a rim, and use your fingers to crimp the crust. Refrigerate the pastry case while you make the filling.

4   In a large bowl, whisk together the remaining cinnamon, granulated sugar, and instant tapioca. Add the sliced apples and lemon juice, and toss well to combine. Pour the apple mixture into the prepared pastry case.

5   Using your hands, pick up small handfuls of the streusel topping, press into large crumbs, and break into smaller crumbs as you sprinkle it over the apple filling. Continue, covering the top of the pie evenly, until all the streusel has been used.

6   Put the pie dish on a baking sheet and bake in the lower third of the oven for about 1 hour or until the streusel topping is golden and the filling is bubbling. Check the pie once or twice during baking, and place a piece of foil over the top if the streusel becomes too brown.

7   Cool the pie at room temperature for 3 hours before slicing.

INGREDIENTS

120g (4oz) wholemeal flour

100g (3½oz) walnuts

85g (3oz) brown sugar

2½ tsp ground cinnamon

4 tbsp chilled plant-based butter, cut into small cubes

½ batch *Pie Pastry*, or prepared pastry case

170g (6oz) granulated sugar

1 tbsp instant tapioca, such as Minute Tapioca

7 apples, such as Granny Smith, peeled, cored, and thinly sliced (about 900g (2lb)

Juice of 1 lemon (2 tbsp)

Granny Smith apples

I love to bake apple pies with a mixture of apples – a majority of crisp baking apples along with one or two "sauce" apples that break down around the slices for a perfect consistency. My favourite sauce apple is Golden Delicious; Empire and good old Granny Smith are excellent for baking. Ask your local farmer which varieties are best in your local area, and have fun mixing it up.

Prairie Berry Pie Ⓣ

This pie, baked in a cast-iron frying pan (imagine you're cooking over an open fire on the American Prairies), is bursting with fresh berry flavour; the superior heat conductivity of cast iron produces a golden, tender pastry bottom. Make it with a combination of berries or just a single variety. Try blueberries, raspberries, blackberries, strawberries, or even local, seasonal varieties like loganberries.

SERVES 8 PREP 15 MINS COOK 70 MINS

1 Preheat the oven to 220°C (425°F/Gas 7).

2 In a large bowl, whisk together the light brown sugar, instant tapioca, cornflour, and salt. Fold in the mixed berries and set aside.

3 Roll the Pie Pastry for the bottom layer into a 33cm (13in) circle and transfer to a 25cm (10in) cast-iron frying pan; you'll have a 2.5cm (1in) overhang.

4 Pour the berry mixture into the pastry case and spread it out evenly.

5 Roll the pastry for the pie top into a 30cm (12in) circle and carefully lay this over the top of the pie. Trim the edges to fit snugly around the inside of the rim of the pan.

6 Fold the edges of the bottom pastry over the top one and pinch to seal securely. Refrigerate the pie for 10 minutes.

7 Crimp the edges of the chilled pie using the tines of a fork or your fingers. Cut a hole in centre of the pie using a small decorative cutter or a sharp paring knife, and cut a few evenly spaced 5cm (2in) slits around the pie to allow steam to escape during baking.

8 Brush the top of the pie with non-dairy milk and sprinkle it with the sugar.

9 Bake on a baking sheet for 30 minutes, reduce heat to 190°C (375°F/Gas 5), and bake for a further 40 minutes. If the top crust appears to be browning too quickly, cover loosely with after 30 minutes and then remove the foil for the last 10 minutes of baking time.

10 Cool the pie completely at room temperature before slicing – at least 4 hours – to allow the filling to set.

Crimping pie pastry doesn't just make for a pretty pie; it also secures the top and bottom crusts to ensure the filling won't leak. For a simple, decorative crimp, press one finger into the edge of the crust, and pinch the dough around that finger using your thumb and forefinger. Repeat all around the pie. Chilling the dough makes this process easier.

INGREDIENTS

175g (6oz) light brown sugar

5 tbsp instant tapioca, such as Minute Tapioca

1 tbsp cornflour

½ tsp sea salt

1kg (2¼lb) fresh mixed berries or frozen berries

1 batch *Pie Pastry*, or prepared pastry case

1 tsp non-dairy milk

1 tsp demerara sugar

Blueberry Peach Cobbler (T)

This delightful dish is a fabulous way to showcase summer's finest fruits. The fruit filling mixes with the biscuit topping for a gloriously messy dessert.

SERVES 8 PREP 15 MINS COOK 40 MINS

1 Preheat the oven to 180°C (350°F/Gas 4).

2 Place the plant-based butter in a 3-litre (5¼-pint) cast-iron casserole dish. Place the dish in the oven until it has melted.

3 In a large bowl, whisk together the cornflour with 60g (2oz) of the sugar. Next, add the peaches, blueberries, cinnamon, and lemon juice, and gently toss with the sugar mixture to combine.

4 In a medium bowl, whisk together the remaining sugar, flour, baking powder, and sea salt. Stir in the coconut milk creamer until the mixture forms a rough dough or batter.

5 Remove the dish from the oven, add the peach and blueberry mixture, and spread to cover the bottom of the dish. Drop spoonfuls of the batter evenly over the fruit, and bake on a baking sheet in the lower third of the oven for about 45 minutes. Serve warm.

INGREDIENTS

4 tbsp plant-based butter

2 tbsp cornflour

225g (8oz) sugar

450g (1lb) fresh peaches, unpeeled, pitted, and sliced

600g (1lb 5oz) fresh blueberries

½ tsp ground cinnamon

Juice of ½ lemon (1 tbsp)

125g (4½oz) plain flour

2 tsp baking powder

¼ tsp sea salt

240ml (8fl oz) coconut milk creamer

Nutty Berry Streusel Bars (T)

A gorgeous layer of jam peeks out from the coconut-laced streusel that tops these easy-to-make, deliciously crumbly bars. These treats come together in minutes in your food processor.

MAKES 25 PREP 10 MINS COOK 30 MINS

1 Preheat the oven to 190°C (375°F/Gas 5). Line a 23cm (9in) square baking tin with baking parchment or foil, letting the edges generously overhang. Spray lightly with cooking spray.

2 In a food processor fitted with a metal blade, pulse the ground almonds, rolled oats, walnuts, flour, and salt to a coarse meal. Add the brown sugar along with the melted coconut oil and plant-based butter, and process for about 30 seconds. Reserve a mugful of the oat mixture, and press the rest firmly into the bottom of the prepared tin. Bake for 10 minutes.

3 Using your fingers, mix the coconut into the reserved oat mixture. Set aside.

4 Dot the baked crust with spoonfuls of your choice of jam and spread to cover the crust. Crumble the reserved topping over the jam, and bake for a further 20 minutes. Cool completely before cutting into bars.

INGREDIENTS

115g (4oz) ground almonds

100g (3½oz) rolled oats

100g (3½oz) walnuts

60g (2oz) plain flour, or a gluten-free flour blend

½ tsp fine sea salt

85g (3oz) brown sugar

120ml (4fl oz) melted coconut oil

2 tbsp plant-based butter

20g (¾oz) desiccated coconut

325g (11oz) blueberry or raspberry jam

BERRIES

Blueberries, strawberries, raspberries, blackberries, cranberries, and others are packed with fibre and nutrients. They're delicious eaten raw, baked into desserts, or cooked in sauces. **Benefits** Are antibacterial; are antioxidants; promote eye health; improve memory; boost urinary tract health; help with digestion; and have anticancer properties. **Uses** Buy during their peak — spring and summer for most berries and winter for cranberries. Eat fresh as a snack, dessert, or side dish; bake in pies and cakes; or stew as a sauce. **Recipes** Strawberry Muffins, Prairie Berry Pie, Blueberry Peach Cobbler, Nutty Berry Streusel Bars, and Winter Fruit Compôte.

Banana Chocolate-Chip Oat Cookies (T) (UNDER 30)

Chewy, coconutty, and studded with chocolate chips, these cookies are a crowd pleaser and cake sale favourite. Banana is a great plant-based egg substitute when baking and adds a sweet, mild banana flavour.

MAKES 16 **PREP** 15 MINS **COOK** 12–14 MINS

1 Preheat the oven to 180°C (350°F/Gas 4). Line 2 baking sheets with baking parchment.

2 In a medium bowl, mash the banana with the sugars, grapeseed oil, and vanilla extract until smooth.

3 Stir the flour, rolled oats, bicarbonate of soda, cinnamon, salt, dark chocolate chips, and coconut into the banana mixture, using your hands to ensure the mixture is well combined. It will be very thick.

4 Scoop 3.75cm (1½in) balls of dough onto the baking sheets, spacing them about 6cm (2½in) apart. Using wet hands, gently pat down the cookies into 5cm (2in) rounds. Some chocolate chips might separate from the mixture, if they do just pat them back into the cookies.

5 Bake for 12–14 minutes or until cookies are golden. Cool for 3 minutes on baking sheets, and then transfer to a wire rack to cool completely. Cookies will keep in an airtight container for up to 5 days (if they last that long!).

INGREDIENTS

1 medium very ripe banana, peeled

75g (2½oz) granulated sugar

60g (2oz) brown sugar

80ml (2½fl oz) grapeseed oil

1 tsp vanilla extract

125g (4½oz) plain flour

170g (6oz) rolled oats

½ tsp bicarbonate of soda

½ tsp ground cinnamon

¼ tsp sea salt

85g (3oz) dark chocolate chips

4 tbsp unsweetened dried coconut

For *Nutty Banana-Coco-Oat Cookies*, replace the coconut with 40g (1½oz) of finely chopped toasted walnuts or pecans – or use both.

Cherry Cheesecake Squares

Sometimes, plant-based food isn't just about being healthy – it's about *dessert*. This dish is messy, delicious, and definitely an indulgence to be enjoyed once in a while.

MAKES 16 PREP 15 MINS COOK 35 MINS

1 Preheat the oven to 180°C (350°F/Gas 4). Line the bottom of a 23cm (9in) square baking tin with foil, leaving plenty of overhang on each side. Tuck the overhang under the edges of the tin and spray the foil with cooking spray.

2 In a food processor fitted with a metal blade, pulse the chocolate sandwich cookies to fine crumbs. Pulse in the plant-based butter, transfer the crumb mixture to the prepared baking tin, and press into the bottom of the tin, packing tightly using your hands or the bottom of a glass.

3 In a large bowl, and using an electric mixer fitted with a paddle attachment on medium–high speed, whip the soya cream cheese and vanilla soya yogurt until smooth.

4 Beat in the icing sugar, vanilla extract, and salt.

5 Pour the cream cheese mixture over the biscuit crumb base, and bake for 35 minutes or until set.

6 Spoon the cherry pie filling evenly over the warm cheese filling, and allow to cool completely. Once cooled, refrigerate for at least 6 hours or overnight before slicing into 16 equal squares.

INGREDIENTS

20 chocolate sandwich biscuits, such as Bourbons

2 tbsp plant-based butter, melted

450g (1lb) soya cream cheese, softened

170g (6oz) vanilla soya yogurt

5 tbsp icing sugar

1 tsp vanilla extract

Pinch sea salt

600g (21oz) canned cherry pie filling

For *Strawberry Cheesecake Squares,* replace the chocolate biscuits with about 14 digestive biscuits and use 600ml (1 pint) of strawberry jam in place of the cherry pie filling.

Triple-Ginger Treacle Cookies (T) (UNDER 30)

Fill your biscuit tin with these chewy, spicy, treacle and ginger treats, but be warned – they won't last long!

MAKES 24 **PREP** 15 MINS **COOK** 12 TO 14 MINS

1 Preheat the oven to 180°C (350°F/Gas 4). Line two baking sheets with baking parchment.

2 In a small bowl, whisk the sugar and cinnamon, and set aside.

3 In a medium bowl, whisk together the flour, ground ginger, bicarbonate of soda, baking powder, and salt.

4 In another medium bowl, mix together the sucanat, grapeseed oil, treacle, non-dairy milk, and grated ginger until well combined.

5 Stir the wet ingredients into dry. When nearly mixed, stir in the crystallized ginger pieces. Refrigerate the dough for 15 minutes.

6 Scoop up heaped tablespoonfulls of cooking dough, roll each ball in the cinnamon–sugar mixture, and arrange 5cm (2in) apart on the baking sheets. Bake for 12–14 minutes or until golden.

7 Cool the cookies on the baking sheets for 2 minutes before transferring to wire racks to cool completely. Store cookies in an airtight container at room temperature for up to 5 days.

INGREDIENTS

4 tbsp demerara sugar

1 tsp ground cinnamon

250g (9oz) wholemeal flour

2 tbsp ground ginger

½ tsp bicarbonate of soda

½ tsp baking powder

½ tsp sea salt

225g (8oz) sucanat (whole unrefined cane sugar)

120ml (4fl oz) grapeseed oil

4 tbsp treacle

4 tbsp non-dairy milk, such as rice or coconut

1 tbsp grated fresh ginger

4 tbsp finely diced crystallized ginger

Root ginger

Pineapple Cornmeal Upside-Down Cake (T)

In this fun and fabulous retro classic, caramelized pineapple slices are topped with a tender cornmeal batter and then turned upside down after baking.

SERVES 8 PREP 15 MINS COOK 45–50 MINS

1 Preheat the oven to 180°C (350°F/Gas 4). Grease a 23cm (9in) round, foil-lined springform cake tin.

2 In a small bowl, whisk together the coconut milk creamer and apple cider vinegar. Set aside to curdle slightly.

3 In another small bowl, whisk together the flour, yellow cornmeal, baking powder, and salt.

4 In a large bowl, whisk together 4 tablespoons of the grapeseed oil, banana, granulated sugar, and vanilla extract until smooth.

5 In a small saucepan over a medium–high heat, heat the remaining grapeseed oil, pineapple juice, and brown sugar. Bring to the boil, stirring constantly, and cook for 1 minute. Pour the caramel into the prepared springform tin and arrange the pineapple half-rings over the bottom of the tin in a decorative fashion.

6 Whisk the soya milk mixture into the wet ingredients, and quickly fold in the flour mixture just until incorporated, taking care not to overmix. Pour the mixture into the tin over the pineapple and smooth with a spatula or a spoon dipped into water.

7 Bake for 45–50 minutes or until a skewer inserted into the centre of the cake comes out clean and the cake springs back when pressed lightly.

8 Run a sharp knife around the edge of the cake and cool completely. Unclip the sides of the tin, carefully flip the cake onto a platter and gently remove the bottom of the springform tin, running a thin knife between the pineapple and bottom of the tin if necessary.

INGREDIENTS

80ml (2½fl oz) coconut milk creamer or soya milk

1 tsp apple cider vinegar

125g (4½oz) plain flour

4 tbsp fine yellow cornmeal

2 tsp baking powder

½ tsp sea salt

5 tbsp grapeseed oil

1 small ripe banana, peeled and mashed

115g (4oz) granulated sugar

1 tsp vanilla extract

1 tbsp pineapple juice (reserved from a can or fresh pineapple)

2 tbsp brown sugar

1 (425g; 15oz) can organic pineapple rings in juice, cut in half, or 1 small fresh pineapple, peeled, cored, and cut into half-rings

This moist, tender cake is easiest to get out of the tin when it's made in a springform tin. If you like, you can place a few maraschino cherries decoratively between the pineapple slices for more retro recipe fun.

Fudgy Oaty Thumbprints (T)

Little cocoa and cinnamon-kissed oaty cookies get a fibre boost from walnuts and cacao nibs. They're baked and then sandwiched with a fudgy chocolate ganache filling.

MAKES 24   PREP 15 MINS   COOK 12–14 MINS

1. Preheat the oven to 180°C (350°F/Gas 4). Line 2 baking sheets with baking parchment.

2. Place the flax meal in a small bowl.

3. In a small saucepan over a medium heat, heat the non-dairy milk just until it bubbles around edges. Pour the warm milk over the flax meal, stir, and set aside for 10 minutes.

4. In a food processor fitted with a metal blade, pulse the rolled oats to a coarse meal. Transfer the oats to a large bowl, and mix in the flour, cocoa powder, baking powder, cinnamon, and salt.

5. In a medium bowl, whisk together the melted coconut oil, brown sugar, and flax mixture vigorously until smooth. Stir into the dry ingredients, mixing with a large spatula or wooden spoon to combine. When the flour is nearly incorporated, add the walnuts and cacao, and mix quickly but thoroughly.

6. Place heaped tablespoon-sized balls of dough on the baking sheets about 6cm (2½in) apart. Pat the cookies gently to flatten slightly and bake for 12 minutes.

7. Remove from the oven and cool on the baking sheets for 1 minute. Using the handle of a wooden spoon, make an indentation in each cookie. (Be gentle – the cookies are crumbly.) Let them cool for another minute, and use your thumb to increase the size of the indentation. Transfer the cookies to a wire rack to cool completely.

8. Meanwhile, place the chocolate chips in a small, heatproof bowl, and put the coconut milk creamer in a small saucepan over a medium–high heat. Heat until hot and just beginning to bubble around the edges. (Do not boil.) Pour the creamer over the chocolate chips and let it stand for 5 minutes. Whisk until smooth, whisk in the maple syrup, and let the ganache stand for a further 5 minutes to firm slightly.

9. Fill the indentation in each cookie with the ganache. (I use a teaspoon-size cookie scoop to make this neat and easy.) Cool completely to allow the ganache to set up before serving. Cookies will keep, refrigerated, for 3 days.

For *Fruity Oaty Thumbprints*, just bake as above, cool, and fill the indentations with a fruity jam instead of the chocolate ganache.

INGREDIENTS

2 tbsp flax meal (ground flaxseeds)

120ml (4fl oz) non-dairy milk, such as almond

85g (3oz) rolled oats

125g (4½oz) plain flour

1 tbsp unsweetened cocoa powder

2 tsp baking powder

½ tsp ground cinnamon

½ tsp sea salt

120ml (4fl oz) melted coconut oil

85g (3oz) brown sugar, lightly packed

60g (2oz) walnuts, finely chopped

1 tbsp raw cacao nibs

85g (3oz) finely chopped dark chocolate or chocolate chips

4 tbsp plant-based creamer

1 tsp maple syrup

Walnuts

Pumpkin Gingerbread Cupcakes with Cinnamon Frosting Ⓣ

Spicy pumpkin cupcakes are accented with plenty of ginger and toasted pecans and topped with a creamy, fluffy frosting.

MAKES 18   PREP 20 MINS   COOK 25–35 MINS

1   Preheat the oven to 180°C (350°F/Gas 4). Line two 12-hole muffin tins with 18 paper cases, or grease with baking spray.

2   In a small bowl, whisk together 120ml (4fl oz) of coconut milk creamer and apple cider vinegar. Set aside to curdle slightly.

3   In a large bowl, whisk together the flour, 1 teaspoon of the cinnamon, ginger, bicarbonate of soda, baking powder, salt, nutmeg, and cloves.

4   In a medium bowl, whisk together the pumpkin, dark brown sugar, grapeseed oil, and 1 teaspoon of the vanilla extract until well combined. Whisk in the creamer mixture and stir the wet ingredients into the flour mixture, mixing well by hand just until smooth. Reserve 2 tablespoons of pecans for garnishing and quickly fold the rest into the batter.

5   Scoop the mixture into the prepared tins, filling each halfway and smoothing it gently with the back of a wet teaspoon. Bake for 25 minutes or until the cupcakes spring back when gently pressed. (To make a 23cm (9in) square cake, grease the tin and bake at 180°C (350°F/Gas 4) for 35–40 minutes or until the cake springs back when lightly pressed in the centre.) Cool completely before icing with the frosting.

6   Meanwhile, in a large bowl and using an electric mixer on a medium–high speed, beat the plant-based butter and soya cream cheese until well combined with no lumps. Sift in the icing sugar and remaining 1 teaspoon of cinnamon, a large spoonful at a time, beating well between each addition. Beat in the remaining creamer and vanilla extract. Refrigerate the frosting for about 30 minutes to firm slightly.

7   Generously ice each cupcake and garnish with reserved pecans. (For a cake, ice or simply sprinkle with icing sugar and pecans and cut into 5cm (2in) squares.) Serve immediately or refrigerate for up to 2 days.

Have fun icing your cupcakes! Fit a piping bag with a plain, large round nozzle, and swirl a big cloud of fluffy icing onto each cupcake. For a perfect pipe, gently press the piping bag to move the icing to the nozzle and remove any air bubbles. Holding the bag at a slight angle, squeeze gently from the top as you swirl the icing from the outer edge in.

INGREDIENTS

150ml (5fl oz) coconut milk creamer

½ tsp apple cider vinegar

190g (7oz) plain flour

2 tsp ground cinnamon

1 tsp ground ginger

¾ tsp bicarbonate of soda

½ tsp baking powder

½ tsp sea salt

¼ tsp ground nutmeg

Pinch ground cloves

1 (425g; 15oz) can pumpkin

175g (6oz) dark brown sugar

80ml (3fl oz) grapeseed oil

2 tsp vanilla extract

55g (2oz) pecans, toasted and finely chopped

4 tbsp plant-based butter, cut into chunks

4 tbsp soya cream cheese

350g (12oz) icing sugar

Parsnip Cupcakes with Soured Cream Icing (T)

These cupcakes are like carrot cakes in miniature, but way more interesting. They're tasty as well as pretty to look at when topped with a lightly sweetened soured cream icing, but they're equally wonderful without the icing and with a simple dusting of icing sugar.

MAKES 12 PREP 15 MINS COOK 22–25 MINS

1 Preheat the oven to 180°C (350°F/Gas 4). Line a 12-hole muffin tin with paper cases.

2 In a small saucepan over a medium heat, heat the non-dairy milk just until it begins to bubble around the edges.

3 Place the flax meal in a small bowl, pour the warm milk over the top, stir, and set aside for 10 minutes.

4 In a large bowl, whisk together the flour, baking powder, salt, cinnamon, and cardamom.

5 Whisk in the flax mixture, brown sugar, grapeseed oil, and vanilla extract until smooth. Stir into the dry ingredients until just combined.

6 Fold in the parsnips and raisins.

7 Fill each muffin case just over half full with mixture. Bake for 22–25 minutes until the centre of each cupcake springs back and a tester (such as a toothpick or skewer) comes out clean. Cool the cupcakes in the tin for 5 minutes and then remove to a wire rack to cool completely.

8 Meanwhile, in a medium bowl and using an electric mixer on a medium speed, cream the plant-based butter and icing sugar until smooth. Quickly beat in the plant-based soured cream just until smooth.

9 Spread a little icing on each cooled cupcake or dip the cupcakes into the icing for a more rustic look. Serve immediately. Uniced cupcakes will keep in the fridge for up to 2 days.

INGREDIENTS

6 tbsp non-dairy milk, such as soya or rice

2 tbsp flax meal (ground flaxseeds)

125g (4½oz) plain flour

1½ tsp baking powder

½ tsp sea salt

½ tsp ground cinnamon

½ tsp ground cardamom

125g (4½oz) brown sugar

160ml (5fl oz) grapeseed oil

1 tsp vanilla extract

2 parsnips, peeled and grated

4 tbsp raisins

4 tbsp plant-based butter

100g (3½oz) icing sugar, sifted twice

120ml (4fl oz) plant-based soured cream

Cardamom tastes best when it's freshly ground, so I stock a small jar of whole cardamom pods rather than ground, which would go stale before I could use it all. To use whole pods in this recipe, lightly crush 5 or 6 pods with a mortar and pestle, remove the seeds from the outer shell, discard shells, and crush the seeds with a tiny pinch of salt to yield ½ teaspoon of ground cardamom.

Baking Substitutions

Baking without eggs and butter is easier than you might think, and one look at the dessert recipes in this part shows you won't be missing out on anything when following a plant-based diet. Here are some helpful substitution hints for baking without eggs and dairy products.

Plant-based butter

REPLACE ...	EGGS			EGG WHITES	BUTTER			
WiTH ...	Flax	Banana	Apple sauce	Agar flakes	Plant-based butter	Non-hydrogenated shortening	Coconut oil	Grapeseed o olive oil
AMOUNT	1 egg = 1 tablespoon flax meal and 3 tablespoons warm water	1 egg = 1 medium, ripe mashed banana	1 egg = 4 tablespoons apple sauce	1 egg white = 1 tablespoon agar flakes plus 1 tablespoon water	Use same amount as butter.	115g (4oz) butter = 8 tablespoons shortening plus 1 tablespoon water	225g (8oz) butter = 240ml (8fl oz) coconut oil plus 1 tablespoon water	225g (8oz) bu = 6 tablespoo oil
USES	Whisk together flax meal and warm water, and let it stand 15 minutes before using.	Use in chewy recipes, such as cookies.	Use in quick breads and cakes for lower-fat baking.	Whisk together agar flakes and water, refrigerate for 5 minutes, and use immediately.	Use the same as butter. Do not attempt to brown in a recipe that calls for browned butter.	Use sparingly. Provides structure to recipes where butter is creamed with sugar as well as frosting recipes.	Coconut oil is soft-solid and scoopable at room temperature and firm-solid when chilled. Use solid to cream with sugar in recipes that call for butter or melted in recipes that call for oil.	Use in cake, cookie, and quick bread recipes. Add wet ingredier

Flax seeds

Bananas

Almond milk

Coconut

K			BUTTERMILK	HALF-AND-HALF OR LIGHT CREAM	EVAPORATED MILK	DOUBLE CREAM	HONEY	SUGAR PROCESSED WITH BONE CHAR
a, hemp, oconut beverage	Rice milk	Almond milk	Plant-based milk plus apple cider vinegar or lemon juice	Coconut milk coffee creamer	Canned coconut milk	Cream from canned coconut milk	Agave nectar, maple syrup, or vegan honey substitute	Beet sugar, unprocessed sugar
same me as for y milk.	240ml (8fl oz) milk = 180ml (6fl oz) plus 1 tablespoon rice milk	The same volume as for dairy milk.	240ml (8fl oz) buttermilk = 240ml (8fl oz) soya, hemp, or coconut milk beverage plus 2 teaspoons apple cider vinegar or lemon juice	The same volume.	The same volume.	The same volume.	The same volume.	The same volume.
stitute at a atio in any pe.	Rice milk is thinner than other plant-based milks, so reduce the quantity by 1 tablespoon.	Use when a nutty flavour is desired.	Whisk together and let it stand for 10 minutes to curdle and thicken.	Substitute in any recipe.	Shake the can well at room temperature to combine before measuring.	Refrigerate coconut milk until well chilled. Remove thick, solid "cream" at the top of the can, and use as a substitute for cream.	Substitute in any recipe.	Look for sugar labeled "vegan" or "unbleached" to avoid sugar processed with bone char, an animal product.

Oils

Maple syrup

Green Apple Sorbet

Fresh apple juice and a simple syrup of sugar and water are all you need to make this refreshing sorbet. Ascorbic acid (vitamin C) keeps the apple juice from turning an unappetizing shade of brown. Find it in the preserving section of your supermarket or ask for it at a pharmacy.

SERVES 8–12   PREP 10 MINS   COOK 5 MINS

1   In an electric juicer, juice Granny Smith apples. Stir in the ascorbic acid and measure out exactly 1.4 litres (2½ pints) of juice.

2   In a small saucepan over a medium heat, combine the sugar and water. Cook, stirring, for 8 minutes or until the sugar has completely dissolved.

3   Stir the sugar mixture into the apple juice and mix well.

4   Add vodka (if using) to slow the formation of crystals during freezing, which results in a smoother sorbet. Chill for at least 2 hours.

5   Freeze the sorbet in an ice-cream maker according to the manufacturer's instructions. Serve immediately for soft sorbet, or pack into a 1-litre (1¾-pint) container and freeze completely. The sorbet will keep in the freezer for 1 month.

INGREDIENTS

7 large Granny Smith apples

½ tsp ascorbic acid

150g (5½oz) sugar

80ml (3fl oz) water

1 tbsp vodka (optional)

For Apple Cider Sorbet, simmer 1.4 litres (2½ pints) of unpasteurized apple cider with a cinnamon stick and 150g (5½oz) sugar. Remove cinnamon stick and stir in the vodka (if using). Chill for at least 2 hours, and freeze in an ice-cream maker. For Melon Sorbet, make the sugar syrup as directed. Purée 675g (1½lb) of chopped honeydew, cantaloupe, or watermelon, and combine with the sugar syrup and 1 tablespoon of lemon juice. Chill and freeze as directed. For Strawberry Sorbet, purée 650g (1lb 7oz) fresh strawberries, press through a mesh strainer to remove seeds, and proceed as for the Melon Sorbet.

Chunky Apple Sauce

A mix of tart and sweet apples, plus the apple cider, cinnamon, and just a hint of sugar, makes a refreshing apple sauce that's a perfect accompaniment to meals at any time of the day.

SERVES 3–4 PREP 10 MINS COOK 45 MINS

1   In a medium saucepan over a high heat, bring the apples, apple cider, granulated cane sugar, and cinnamon stick to the boil.

2   Reduce the heat to medium–low, and cook, stirring occasionally, for 45 minutes or until the apples are easily broken down into a rough sauce when stirred.

3   Cool slightly, and remove the cinnamon stick. Serve warm or refrigerate for 2 hours to chill completely. Apple sauce will keep in a tightly sealed jar in the fridge for up to 1 week.

INGREDIENTS

3 large, tart apples, such as Granny Smith, peeled, cored, and chopped

3 large, sweet apples, such as Golden Delicious, peeled, cored, and chopped

360ml (12fl oz) apple cider

4 tbsp granulated sugar

1 cinnamon stick

Cinnamon sticks

For Smooth Apple Sauce, core the apples but do not peel. Cook as above, cool completely, and put through a food mill to purée and remove the skins.

Winter Fruit Compôte

Fresh, seasonal apples and pears combine with dried fruits for a sweet, nourishing, fibre-rich treat. Try this compôte with plant-based ice cream or cake for dessert, or spoon onto porridge, granola, or yogurt for breakfast. For a festive treat, serve it in place of cranberry sauce with savoury dishes.

SERVES 7   PREP 10 MINS   COOK 25 MINS PLUS RESTING/COOLING TIME

1   In a large saucepan with a tight-fitting lid over a high heat, combine the apple cider, dark rum, vanilla pod, cinnamon stick, lemon peel, and granulated sugar. Bring to the boil, stirring frequently to dissolve the sugar.

2   Stir in the apple and pear, reduce the heat to low, and cook, covered, for 10 minutes.

3   Uncover and stir in the dried apricots, figs, raisins, cranberries, and cherries. Cover and cook for 15 minutes or until the fruit is soft.

4   Set aside to cool for 1 hour to allow flavours to blend and then remove the vanilla pod and cinnamon stick.

5   Refrigerate in an airtight container for about 2 hours or until chilled, and serve. This compôte will keep in the fridge in an airtight container for 1 week.

INGREDIENTS

240ml (8fl oz) apple cider

2 tbsp dark rum

1 vanilla pod, split lengthwise

1 cinnamon stick

2 (5cm; 2in) strips lemon peel, thinly sliced

115g (4oz) granulated cane sugar

1 tart apple, such as Granny Smith, peeled, cored, and chopped

1 ripe pear, peeled, cored, and chopped

80g (3oz) dried apricots, roughly chopped

75g (2½oz) dried figs, roughly chopped

85g (3oz) raisins

60g (2oz) dried cranberries

80g (3oz) dried tart cherries

Pears

You can easily personalise this recipe based on your tastes and the fruit you have to hand. Dried prunes, apples, pears, and candied ginger are all lovely additions or substitutions. When oranges are in season, replace the lemon peel with orange peel, the chopped apple with fresh orange segments, and the apple cider with freshly squeezed orange juice. Vary the spices with star anise or cardamom, or use port or brandy instead of the rum.

Cranberry Poached Pears

Sweet pears are cooked in pear nectar with dried cranberries and spices for a naturally sweetened, light, and refreshing autumn or winter dessert with a gorgeous, rosy glow. Choose pears on the firm side of ripe for the best results.

SERVES 6 PREP 15 MINS COOK 35 MINS

1 In a saucepan just large enough to hold the pears, stir together the pear nectar, cranberry juice, and cranberries.

2 Using a double thickness of muslin, wrap the cinnamon stick, cardamom pods, and star anise. Pull the muslin up into a pouch and tie with kitchen string. Add to the saucepan and set over a medium–high heat.

3 Peel the pears, leaving the stems intact, and cut a small slice off the bottoms to allow the pears to stand upright. Immediately place the pears into the pear nectar mixture. When the mixture comes to the boil, cover, reduce the heat to low, and cook at a gentle simmer for 30 minutes or until the pears are easily pierced with a fork.

4 Transfer the pears to a serving dish. Remove and discard the spice bag.

5 Increase the heat under the saucepan to high, and cook the sauce, stirring frequently, until it's reduced by half (about 240ml (8fl oz) of liquid). Pour the sauce over the pears and cool completely.

6 Serve the pears at room temperature or refrigerate and serve chilled. Place 1 pear on each plate, and spoon a few tablespoons of sauce and cranberries over the top. The pears will keep, covered, in the fridge for up to 7 days.

INGREDIENTS

480ml (16fl oz) pear nectar or juice

4 tbsp cranberry juice

120g (4oz) dried cranberries

1 cinnamon stick

2 cardamom pods, cracked with a heavy knife

1 star anise

6 medium pears

Williams and Comice pears are excellent choices for poaching because they hold their shape when cooked. For a diminutive pudding, use 12 mini dessert pears instead.

Index

A

alliums, 207
  Caramelized Onions, 26
  Herbed Mushroom and Leek Tart, 225
  Pissaladière (Provençal Onion Tart), 227
  Stir-Fried Chinese Cress with Fermented
    Black Beans, 134
  Summer Squash and Onion Bake, 171
almonds, 40, 58
  Almond and Breadcrumb Stuffed Piquillo
    Peppers, 144
  Bisteeya (Moroccan Filo Pie), 166
apples
  Apple Cider Sorbet, 248
  Apple Crumble Pie, 231
  Chunky Apple Sauce, 249
  Green Apple Sorbet, 248
  Red Cabbage with Apples and Pecans, 132
  Smooth Apple Sauce, 249
  Winter Fruit Compôte, 249
Arancini (Risotto Balls), 188
artichokes, 143, 146
asparagus, 146
  Asian Asparagus, 157
  Lemon Asparagus Risotto, 186
  Lemon Garlic Asparagus, 157
  Sesame Asparagus, 157
aubergines, 36
  Aubergine and Roasted Tomato Polenta
    Lasagne, 173
  Aubergine Parm Subs, 68
  Giambotta (Italian Summer Vegetable
    Stew), 104
  Grilled Tofu Caprese, 206
  Imam Bayildi (Turkish Stuffed Aubergine),
    131
  Crispy Aubergine Subs, 68
Smoky Baba Ghanoush, 36
avocados, 63, 146
  Breakfast Burritos, 54
  Guacamole, 49
  Posole, 112

B

baking substitutions, 246–247
Banana Chocolate-Chip Oat Cookies, 236
Bánh Mì Portobello Burgers, 66
Basic Seitan, 21
beans/legumes, 11, 14, 19, 94–95, 110
  Bisteeya (Moroccan Filo Pie), 166
  Hearty Chilli, 109
  Hummus, 34
  Lentil and Vegetable Dhal, 106
  Minestrone, 103
  Pan Bagnat, 73
  Roasted Tomato and White Bean Salad,
    120
  Smoky White Bean and Tomato Soup, 86
  Stir-Fried Chinese Cress with Fermented
    Black Beans, 134
  Warm Lentil, Barley, and Sweet Potato
    Salad, 125
  White Bean and Red Pepper Salad, 120
  Wholewheat Pasta *e Ceci* (Pasta with
    Chickpeas), 196
Béchamel Sauce, 44
berries, 235

Blueberry Muffins, 56
Blueberry Peach Cobbler, 234
Cranberry Poached Pears, 251
Nutty Berry Streusel Bars, 234
Prairie Berry Pie, 231
Strawberry Cheesecake Squares, 238
Strawberry Muffins, 56
Strawberry Sorbet, 248
Bisteeya (Moroccan Filo Pie), 166
Black-Eyed Pea Stew, 110
black-eyed peas, 95
blanching, 17
Blueberry Muffins, 56
Blueberry Peach Cobbler, 234
Braised Brussels Sprouts with Chestnuts, 152
Brazil nuts, 40
breads
  Croutons, 91
  Easy Slow-Rise Oatmeal Bread, 222
  Italian-Seasoned Panko, 212
  Naan, 106
  Pizza Dough, 224
  Rosemary Raisin Walnut Bread, 222
  Simple Focaccia, 224
  Toasted Breadcrumbs, 196
breakfasts
  Blueberry Muffins, 56
  Breakfast Burritos, 54
  Breakfast Sausage Patties, 62
  Breakfast Scramble, 54
  "Cheesy" Breakfast Quiche, 60
  Coconutty Granola, 53
  Mushroom, Spinach, and Shallot Quiche,
    60
  Nutty Granola, 53
  Spicy Sausage Patties, 62
  Strawberry Muffins, 56
  Tempeh Bacon, 217
  Wholewheat Banana Pecan Pancakes, 55
broccoli, 146
  Sesame Ginger Broccoli, 151
  Sautéed Broccoli, 138
Brussels sprouts, 146
  Braised Brussels Sprouts with Chestnuts,
    152
butter substitutions, 246
Butternut Squash Tagine, 178

C

cabbage
  Mushroom and Cabbage Borscht, 90
  Red Cabbage with Apples and Pecans, 132
  Savoury Stuffed Cabbage, 167
Caramelized Onions, 26
carrots, 146
Cashew Ricotta, 39
cashews, 40, 58
Cassoulet, 176
cauliflower, 146
  Curried Cauliflower Coconut Soup, 85
  Insalata Rinforzo (Neapolitan Christmas
    Salad), 122
  Lentil and Vegetable Dhal, 106
Celeriac Remoulade, 116
"Cheesy" Breakfast Quiche, 60
"Cheesy" Risotto, 186
"Cheesy" Stuffed Mushrooms, 154
"Cheesy" Vegetable Bake, 171

Cherry Cheesecake Squares, 238
chestnuts, 40, 152
chia seeds, 40
Chicken-Style Pot Pie, 165
chickpeas, 95
  Bisteeya (Moroccan Filo Pie), 166
  Hummus, 34
  Pan Bagnat, 73
  Quick and Easy Hummus, 34
  Wholewheat Pasta *e Ceci* (Pasta with
    Chickpeas), 196
Chocolate Nut Milk, 29
Chunky Apple Sauce, 249
Classic Vegetable Soup, 87
Coconutty Granola, 53
cookies, *See* desserts
cooking techniques, 16–20
corn, 147, 192
  Creamy Corn Chowder, 93
  Gluten-Free Corn Chowder, 93
  Roasted Corn with Poblano-Coriander
    Butter, 148
courgettes
  "Cheesy" Vegetable Bake, 171
  Giambotta (Italian Summer Vegetable
    Stew), 104
  Herbed Courgettes, 136
Summer Squash and Onion Bake, 171
couscous, 192
  Moroccan Couscous, 187
Cranberry Poached Pears, 251
Creamy Corn Chowder, 93
Creamy Pasta with Swiss Chard and
  Tomatoes, 194
Crispy Quinoa Cakes, 182
Croutons, 91
Curried Cauliflower Coconut Soup, 85

D

dairy substitutes, 58–59
desserts
  Apple Cider Sorbet, 248
  Apple Crumble Pie, 231
  Banana Chocolate-Chip Oatmeal Cookies,
    236
  Blueberry Peach Cobbler, 234
  Cherry Cheesecake Squares, 238
  Chunky Apple Sauce, 249
  Cranberry Poached Pears, 251
  Fruity Oaty Thumbprints, 242
  Fudgy Oaty Thumbprints, 242
  Green Apple Sorbet, 248
  Melon Sorbet, 248
  Nutty Banana-Coco-Oat Cookies, 236
  Nutty Berry Streusel Bars, 234
  Orange Compôte, 250
  Parsnip Cupcakes with Soured Cream
    Icing, 245
  Perfect Pumpkin Pudding, 230
  Pie Pastry, 29
  Pineapple Cornmeal Upside-Down Cake,
    240
  Prairie Berry Pie, 233
  Pumpkin Gingerbread Cupcakes with
    Cinnamon Frosting, 243
  Pumpkin Pudding Pie, 230
  Smooth Apple Sauce, 249
  Strawberry Cheesecake Squares, 238

Strawberry Sorbet, 248
Triple-Ginger Treacle Cookies, 239
Winter Fruit Compôte, 250
Dinner Salad, 116
dips/sauces/spreads
Béchamel Sauce, 44
Cashew Ricotta, 39
Extra Garlicky Tzatziki, 37
Guacamole, 49
Hummus, 34
Mushroom Gravy, 45
Pico de Gallo, 49
Pimento Cheese, 39
Quick and Easy Hummus, 34
Romesco Sauce, 47
Smoky Baba Ghanoush, 36
Summer Pesto, 47
Tomato Sauce, 44
Truffled Mushroom Pâté, 42
Tzatziki, 37
Vinaigrette, 45
dried beans, 19

E

Easy Slow-Rise Oatmeal Bread, 222
egg substitutes, 246
Extra Garlicky Tzatziki, 37

F

Falafel Burgers, 72
Farro Risotto with Roasted Fennel and
Mushrooms, 190
flaxseeds, 40
Fresh Mint Tzatziki, 37
Fresh Pasta Dough, 30
Fried Green Tomato Sandwiches, 142
Fried Green Tomatoes, 142
fruit, 11, 14
Apple Cider Sorbet, 248
Apple Crumble Pie, 231
Banana Chocolate-Chip Oatmeal Cookies,
236
Blueberry Peach Cobbler, 234
Cherry Cheesecake Squares, 238
Chunky Apple Sauce, 249
Cranberry Poached Pears, 251
Fruity Oatmeal Thumbprints, 242
Green Apple Sorbet, 248
Melon Sorbet, 248
Nutty Banana-Coco-Oat Cookies, 236
Nutty Berry Streusel Bars, 234
Orange Compôte, 250
Perfect Pumpkin Pudding, 230
Pineapple Cornmeal Upside-Down Cake,
240
Prairie Berry Pie, 231
Pumpkin Gingerbread Cupcakes with
Cinnamon Frosting, 243
Pumpkin Pudding Pie, 230
Smooth Apple Sauce, 249
Strawberry Cheesecake Squares, 238
Strawberry Sorbet, 248
Winter Fruit Compôte, 250
Fruity Oatmeal Thumbprints, 242
Fudgy Oatmeal Thumbprints, 242

G

Giambotta (Italian Summer Vegetable Stew),
104
ginger, 99
Ginger Kale Soup, 80
Lentil and Vegetable Dhal, 106
Pumpkin Gingerbread Cupcakes with
Cinnamon Frosting, 243

Sesame Ginger Broccoli, 151
Triple-Ginger Treacle Cookies, 239
Gluten-Free Corn Chowder, 93
Gluten-Free Falafel, 72
Gluten-Free Quinoa Cakes, 182
Gluten-Free Quinoa Vegetable Salad, 184
Golden Chicken-y Stock, 28
grains, 11, 14, 147, 192–193
Grandma's Chicken-y Noodle Soup, 79
Green Apple Sorbet, 248
Green Curry Dinner, 107
Green Curry Vegetable Stew, 107
greens, 17, 117, 147
Creamy Pasta with Swiss Chard and
Tomatoes, 194
Ginger Kale Soup, 80
Southern-Style Braised Greens, 138
Spinach and Rice–Stuffed Tomatoes, 141
Swiss Chard Ravioli, 197
Wilted Spinach Salad, 116
Grilled Cheese Sandwiches, 39
Grilled Tofu Caprese, 206
Guacamole, 49
Gumbo, 102

H

hazelnuts, 40
Hearty Chicken-y and Rice Soup, 79
Hearty Chilli, 109
Hearty Seitan Roast, 210
Herbed Courgettes, 136
Herbed Mushroom and Leek Tart, 225
Herbed Peas and Potatoes, 155
Herbed Tabbouleh, 126
herbs, 15
Hominy Stew, 112
Hummus, 34

I–J

Imam Bayildi (Turkish Stuffed Aubergine), 131
Insalata Rinforzo (Neapolitan Christmas
Salad), 122
Italian Aubergine Cutlet Subs, 68
Italian Summer Vegetable Stew, 104
Italian-Seasoned Panko, 212

Japanese horseradish, 66
Jerusalem Artichoke Soup, 111

K

kale, 147
Ginger Kale Soup, 80
Quinoa Vegetable Salad, 184
kidney beans, 95
Kombu Stock, 28
Korean Barbecue Sliders, 74

L

larder, stocking, 14–15
Latkes, 158
Lemon Asparagus Risotto, 186
Lemon Garlic Asparagus, 157
lentils, 19, 95
Lentil and Vegetable Dhal, 106
Warm Lentil, Barley, and Sweet Potato
Salad, 125

M

Macadamia nuts, 41
Maple-Glazed Tofu, 217
meal plans, 22–23
meat substitutes, 11, 15, 20
Basic Seitan, 21

Breakfast Scramble, 54
Chicken-Style Pot Pie, 165
Grilled Tofu Caprese, 206
Hearty Chicken-y and Rice Soup, 79
Hearty Seitan Roast, 210
Korean Barbecue Sliders, 74
Maple-Glazed Tofu, 217
Miso Udon Bowl, 98
Quick Miso Soup, 98
Seitan and Dumplings, 213
Seitan Sandwiches, 210
Seitan Gyros, 219
Seitan Reubens, 219
Seitan Satay, 214
Sesame Tofu, 206
Tempeh Bacon, 217
Tempeh Milanese, 212
Tofu and Stir-Fried Veggie Dinner, 208
Tofu and Veggie Stir-Fry, 208
Tofu Summer Rolls, 204
Meaty Mushroom Stew, 101
Melon Sorbet, 248
milk substitutions, 247
Minestrone, 103
Minted Peas and Baby Potatoes, 155
Miso Udon Bowl, 98
Mixed Vegetable Cottage Pie, 175
Moroccan Couscous, 187
Moroccan Filo Pie, 166
Muffuletta, 70
mushrooms, 82, 147
Bánh Mì Portobello Burgers, 66
"Cheesy" Stuffed Mushrooms, 154
Farro Risotto with Roasted Fennel and
Mushrooms, 190
Gumbo, 102
Hearty Chilli, 109
Herbed Mushroom and Leek Tart, 225
Meaty Mushroom Stew, 101
Miso Udon Bowl, 98
Mushroom and Cabbage Borscht, 90
Mushroom Barley Soup, 83
Mushroom Gravy, 45
Mushroom Lasagne, 170
Mushroom Puffs, 150
Mushroom Risotto, 186
Mushroom, Spinach, and Shallot Quiche,
60
Mushroom Stock, 28
Oyster Mushroom Po'boys, 69
Sautéed Mushroom Medley, 150
Stuffed Mushrooms, 154
Truffled Mushroom Pâté, 42
Wilted Spinach Salad, 116

N

Naan, 106
Neapolitan Christmas Salad, 122
Nut Milk, 29
nuts/seeds, 11, 15, 40–41
almonds
cheese, 58
milk, 58
cashews, 39–40, 58
chestnuts, 40, 152
chia seeds, 40
flax seeds, 40
hazelnuts, 40
Macadamia nuts, 41
milk, 29, 59
nuts/seeds continued
peanuts, 95
pecans, 41
pine nuts, 41

pistachios, 41
pumpkin seeds, 41
quinoa, 183, 193
sesame seeds, 41
sunflower seeds, 41
toasted, 132
walnuts, 41
Nutty Banana-Coco-Oat Cookies, 236
Nutty Berry Streusel Bars, 234
Nutty Chocolate Granola, 53
Nutty Granola, 53

O
oats, 193
milk, 59
oils, 15, 46
One-Pan Pasta Primavera, 199
onions
Caramelized Onions, 26
"Cheesy" Vegetable Bake, 171
Herbed Tabbouleh, 126
Imam Bayildi (Turkish Stuffed Aubergine), 131
Pissaladière (Provençal Onion Tart), 227
Summer Squash and Onion Bake, 171
Orange Compôte, 250
Oyster Mushroom Po'boys, 69

P
Pan Bagnat, 73
Parsnip Cupcakes with Soured Cream Icing, 245
pasta, 18
Classic Vegetable Soup, 87
Creamy Pasta with Swiss Chard and Tomatoes, 194
Fresh Pasta Dough, 30
Grandma's Chicken-y Noodle Soup, 79
Minestrone with Pasta, 103
Miso Udon Bowl, 98
Mushroom Lasagne, 170
One-Pan Pasta Primavera, 199
Pasta with Chickpeas, 196
Sesame Noodle Dinner, 200
Sesame Noodles, 200
Swiss Chard Ravioli, 197
Tomato Basil One-Pan Pasta, 199
Tomato Basil Pasta Salad, 135
Wholewheat Pasta *e Ceci* (Pasta with Chickpeas), 196
peanuts, 95
pears
Cranberry Poached Pears, 251
Winter Fruit Compôte, 250
peas, 16, 94–95
pecans, 41
Nutty Banana-Coco-Oat Cookies, 236
Red Cabbage with Apples and Pecans, 132
Southern Sweet Potatoes with Pecan Streusel, 160
peppers, 147
Almond and Breadcrumb Stuffed Piquillo Peppers, 144
Giambotta (Italian Summer Vegetable Stew), 104
Hearty Chilli, 109
Roasted Corn with Poblano-Coriander Butter, 148
White Bean and Red Pepper Salad, 120
Perfect Pumpkin Pudding, 230
Picnic Potato Salad, 121
Pico de Gallo, 49
Pie Pastry, 29

pies, 233. *See also* desserts
Pimento Cheese, 39
pine nuts, 41
Pineapple Cornmeal Upside-Down Cake, 240
Pissaladière (Provençal Onion Tart), 227
pistachio nuts, 41
Pizza Dough, 224
plant-based diet
benefits, 10
transitioning strategies, 12–13
polenta
Aubergine and Roasted Tomato Polenta Lasagne, 194
Vegetable Stew with Polenta, 104
Posole, 112
potatoes, 160
Giambotta (Italian Summer Vegetable Stew), 104
Herbed Peas and Potatoes, 155
Latkes, 158
Minestrone, 103
Minted Peas and Baby Potatoes, 155
Picnic Potato Salad, 121
sweet. *See* sweet potatoes
Warm Potato Salad with Grainy Mustard Vinaigrette, 124
Warm Lentil, Barley, and Sweet Potato Salad, 125
Warm Potato Salad Supper, 124
Prairie Berry Pie, 231
Provençal Onion Tart, 227
pumpkin
Pumpkin Gingerbread Cupcakes with Cinnamon Frosting, 243
Pumpkin Pudding Pie, 230
seeds, 41

Q
Quick and Easy Hummus, 34
Quick and Easy Stir-Fry, 134
Quick Miso Soup, 98
quinoa, 183, 193
Crispy Quinoa Cakes, 182
Quinoa Vegetable Salad, 184

R
Red Cabbage with Apples and Pecans, 132
rice, 18, 193
Arancini (Risotto Balls), 188
"Cheesy" Risotto, 186
Hearty Chicken-y and Rice Soup, 79
Lemon Asparagus Risotto, 186
milk, 59
Mushroom Risotto, 186
Quick and Easy Stir-Fry, 134
Risotto Milanese, 186
Spinach and Rice-Stuffed Tomatoes, 141
Tomato Rice Soup, 88
Risotto Balls (*Arancini*), 188
Risotto Milanese, 186
Roasted Beetroot Salad, 119
Roasted Corn with Poblano-Coriander Butter, 148
Roasted Root Vegetable Medley, 158
Roasted Tomato and White Bean Salad, 120
Roasted Tomatoes, 135
roasting, vegetables, 16
Romesco Sauce, 47
Rosemary Raisin Walnut Bread, 222

S
salads
Celeriac Remoulade, 116
Dinner Salad, 116
Gluten-Free Quinoa Vegetable Salad, 184
Herbed Tabbouleh, 126
Insalata Rinforzo (Neapolitan Christmas Salad), 122
Picnic Potato Salad, 121
Quinoa Vegetable Salad, 184
Roasted Beetroot Salad, 119
Roasted Tomato and White Bean Salad, 120
Tomato Basil Pasta Salad, 135
Warm Potato Salad with Grainy Mustard Vinaigrette, 124
Warm Lentil, Barley, and Sweet Potato Salad, 125
Warm Potato Salad Supper, 124
White Bean and Red Pepper Salad, 120
Wilted Spinach Salad, 116
sandwiches
Bánh Mì Portobello Burgers, 66
Aubergine Parm Subs, 68
Falafel Burgers, 72
Fried Green Tomato Sandwich, 142
Grilled Cheese Sandwiches, 39
Crispy Aubergine Subs, 68
Korean Barbecue Sliders, 74
Muffuletta, 70
Oyster Mushroom Po'boys, 69
Pan Bagnat, 73
Seitan Sandwiches, 210
Seitan Gyros, 219
Seitan Reubens, 219
Tofu Summer Rolls, 204
Vegetable Summer Rolls, 204
sauces. *See* dips/sauces/spreads
Sautéed Broccoli, 138
Sautéed Mushroom Medley, 150
sautéing vegetables, 17
Savoury Stuffed Cabbage, 167
seasonings, 15
seeds. *See* nuts/seeds
seitan, 20, 216
Basic Seitan, 21
Chicken-Style Pot Pie, 165
Hearty Chicken-y and Rice Soup, 79
Hearty Seitan Roast, 210
Seitan and Dumplings, 213
Seitan Sandwiches, 210
Seitan Gyros, 219
Seitan Reubens, 219
Seitan Satay, 214
Sesame Asparagus, 157
Sesame Ginger Broccoli, 151
Sesame Noodle Dinner, 200
Sesame Noodles, 200
sesame seeds, 41
Sesame Tofu, 206
Simple Focaccia, 224
Simple Vegetable Stock, 28
Slow Cooker Cassoulet, 176
Smoky Baba Ghanoush, 36
Smoky White Bean and Tomato Soup, 86
Smooth Apple Sauce, 249
soups/stews
Black-Eyed Pea Stew, 110
Butternut Squash Tagine, 178
Cassoulet, 176
Classic Vegetable Soup, 87
Creamy Corn Chowder, 93
Curried Cauliflower Coconut Soup, 85

Giambotta (Italian Summer Vegetable
Stew), 104
Ginger Kale Soup, 80
Gluten-Free Corn Chowder, 93
Grandma's Chicken-y Noodle Soup, 79
Green Curry Vegetable Stew, 107
Gumbo, 102
Hearty Chicken-y and Rice Soup, 79
Hearty Chilli, 109
Jerusalem Artichoke Soup, 111
Lentil and Vegetable Dhal, 106
Meaty Mushroom Stew, 101
Minestrone, 103
Minestrone with Pasta, 103
Miso Udon Bowl, 98
Mushroom and Cabbage Borscht, 90
Mushroom Barley Soup, 83
Posole (Hominy Stew), 112
Quick Miso Soup, 98
Smoky White Bean and Tomato Soup,
86
Split-Pea Soup, 91
Tom Yum Soup, 96
Tomato Rice Soup, 88
Tortilla Soup, 168
Vegetable Stew with Polenta, 104
Southern-Style Braised Greens, 138
Southern Sweet Potatoes with Pecan
Streusel, 160
soya
milk, 59
products, 15
soya beans, 95
spices, 15
Spicy Sausage Patties, 62
spinach, 147
Lentil and Vegetable Dhal, 106
Mushroom, Spinach, and Shallot Quiche,
60
Spinach and Rice–Stuffed Tomatoes,
141
Wilted Spinach Salad, 116
Split-Pea Soup, 91
spreads. *See* dips/sauces/spreads
sprouted grains, 193
squash
Butternut Squash Tagine, 178
"Cheesy" Vegetable Bake, 171
Summer Squash and Onion Bake, 171
steaming vegetables, 16
stock, 28
Strawberry Cheesecake Squares, 238
Strawberry Muffins, 56
Strawberry Sorbet, 248
Stuffed Artichokes, 143
Stuffed Mushrooms, 154
substitutions
baking, 246–247
butter, 246
buttermilk, 247
double cream, 247
evaporated milk, 247
honey, 247
milk, 247
single cream, 247
sugar processed with bone char, 247
Summer Pesto, 47
Summer Squash and Onion Bake, 171
sunflower seeds, 41
sweet potatoes, 147, 159
Southern Sweet Potatoes with Pecan
Streusel, 160
Warm Lentil, Barley, and Sweet Potato
Salad, 135

Winter Vegetable Pot Pie, 165
Swiss chard
Creamy Pasta with Swiss Chard and
Tomatoes, 194
Swiss Chard Ravioli, 197

T–U
tabbouleh, 126
Tamale Casserole, 174
tempeh, 20, 216
Korean Barbecue Sliders, 74
Tempeh Bacon, 217
Tempeh Milanese, 212
Toasted Breadcrumbs, 196
Toasted Nuts, 132
tofu, 20, 216
Breakfast Scramble, 54
Grilled Tofu Caprese, 206
Maple-Glazed Tofu, 217
Miso Udon Bowl, 98
Quick Miso Soup, 98
Sesame Tofu, 206
Tofu and Stir-Fried Veggie Dinner, 208
Tofu and Veggie Stir-Fry, 208
Tofu Summer Rolls, 204
Tom Yum Soup, 96
Tomato Basil One-Pan Pasta, 199
Tomato Basil Pasta Salad, 135
Tomato Rice Soup, 87
Tomato Sauce, 44
tomatoes, 147
Creamy Pasta with Swiss Chard and
Tomatoes, 194
Fried Green Tomato Sandwich, 142
Fried Green Tomatoes, 142
Giambotta (Italian Summer Vegetable
Stew), 104
Grilled Tofu Caprese, 206
Hearty Chilli, 109
Herbed Tabbouleh, 126
Imam Bayildi (Turkish Stuffed Aubergine),
131
Roasted Tomato and White Bean Salad,
120
Roasted Tomatoes, 135
Smoky White Bean and Tomato Soup, 86
Spinach and Rice–Stuffed Tomatoes, 141
Tomato Basil One-Pan Pasta, 199
Tomato Basil Pasta Salad, 135
Tomato Rice Soup, 87
Tomato Sauce, 44
Tortilla Soup, 168
transitioning strategies, 12–13
Triple-Ginger Treacle Cookies, 239
Truffled Mushroom Pâté, 42
Turkish Stuffed Aubergine, 131
Tzatziki Sauce, 37

unrefined oils, 46

V
Vegetable Enchiladas with Roasted Tomato
Sauce, 168
Vegetable Stew with Polenta, 104
Vegetable Summer Rolls, 204
vegetables, 11, 14, 17, 146–147
Almond and Breadcrumb Stuffed Piquillo
Peppers, 144
Asian Asparagus, 157
Braised Brussels Sprouts with Chestnuts,
152
Caramelized Onions, 26
"Cheesy" Stuffed Mushrooms, 154
cruciferous, 139

Curried Cauliflower Coconut Soup, 85
Fried Green Tomatoes, 142
Herbed Courgettes, 136
Herbed Peas and Potatoes, 155
Imam Bayildi (Turkish Stuffed Aubergine),
131
Insalata Rinforzo (Neapolitan Christmas
Salad), 122
Latkes, 158
Lemon Garlic Asparagus, 157
Minestrone, 103
Minted Peas and Baby Potatoes, 155
Mushroom and Cabbage Borscht, 90
Mushroom Puffs, 150
Red Cabbage with Apples and Pecans, 132
Roasted Corn with Poblano-Coriander
Butter, 148
Roasted Root Vegetable Medley, 158
Roasted Tomatoes, 135
Sautéed Broccoli, 138
Sautéed Mushroom Medley, 150
Savoury Stuffed Cabbage, 167
Sesame Asparagus, 157
Sesame Ginger Broccoli, 151
Simple Vegetable Stock, 28
Southern Sweet Potatoes with Pecan
Streusel, 160
Southern-Style Braised Greens, 138
Spinach and Rice–Stuffed Tomatoes, 141
Stir-Fried Chinese Cress with Fermented
Black Beans, 134
Stuffed Artichokes, 143
Stuffed Mushrooms, 154
Vinaigrette, 45
vinegars, 15

W–X–Y–Z
walnuts, 41
Nutty Banana-Coco-Oat Cookies, 236
Roasted Beetroot Salad, 119
Rosemary Raisin Walnut Bread, 222
Wilted Spinach Salad, 116
Warm Potato Salad with Grainy Mustard
Vinaigrette, 124
Warm Lentil, Barley, and Sweet Potato Salad,
125
Warm Potato Salad Supper, 124
White Bean and Red Pepper Salad, 120
whole grains, 11, 14. *See also* grains
Wholewheat Banana Pecan Pancakes, 55
Wholewheat Pasta *e Ceci* (Pasta with
Chickpeas), 196
Wilted Spinach Salad, 116
Winter Fruit Compôte, 249
Winter Vegetable Pot Pie, 165

About the Author

Trish Sebben-Krupka is a chef, culinary educator, cookbook author, and freelance editor. She is the owner of Local Girl Makes Food, a personal chef and culinary education business catering to clients interested in vegan, vegetarian, and eco-friendly diets. She is the author of *The Complete Idiot's Guide® Greens Cookbook* and *Idiot's Guides®: Canning and Preserving* and contributor to *The Best of Vegan Cooking*. Trish took her Master Food Preserver training through the Cornell Cooperative Extension and is passionate about home food preservation, sustainable eating, bread baking, and vegetable cuisine. She lives in New Jersey with her husband, Jim, and an assortment of former junkyard cats. Visit her online at trishkrupka.com.

Acknowledgements

Many thanks are due to those who helped make this book possible: very special thanks to the wonderful editorial team at DK, especially Acquisitions Editor Lori Cates Hand and Development Editor Christy Wagner. Thanks also are due to my agent, Marilyn Allen, of the Allen O'Shea Literary Agency, and to Carolyn Doyle, for her careful testing of each recipe in this book. My endless thanks to Nigel Wright for the art direction and design of this beautiful book, and for spending a week with us directing the photo shoots. Thanks to photographer Kevin Bertolacci for the gorgeous photos, and for being such a kind, wonderful soul, and to Food Stylist Laura Kinsey-Dolph for making each dish look perfect and being an absolute joy to cook with. A million thanks to my amazing friends who helped me in the kitchen during the shoots, especially Tamara Cook, Joe Malone, Katlin Andersen (and Baby Jack), and Gina Hyams. Thanks as well to my "volunteer taste-testers", especially my niece, Rebecca Doherty, my siblings Kristin and Rob, and my clients, Alex and Jay, whose feedback was essential to making these recipes perfect for the omnivore's palate. A special debt of gratitude goes to my husband, Jim, whose love and unwavering support know no bounds. This book is for you.

Photo Credits